I am searching for words to descri
this book is, and I can't find them.
suasively. Both the portions on the Bible and the "real world" sections
are superb. He has opened up a new way for me to read Scripture,
which was a real "paradigm shift" for me. God is the great giver! If
this book receives the readership it deserves, then the church should
look very different as a result.
—**William Edgar**, Professor of Apologetics, Westminster
    Theological Seminary

Jim Petty's book is exactly what you would expect from him—gospel
centered, full of practical wisdom, and missional. When conviction
comes—and it does—it is followed by encouragement. When he
takes us through biblical history and then church history, his insights
are on point and convincing. And when he concludes his study, you
will love Jesus more and care more about continuing his mission
on earth. I wish every aspiring pastor I've ever taught and every
member of my congregation would read it and read it again until
gospel giving becomes the norm in their hearts and in the practice
of their lives.
—**Michael W. Honeycutt**, Senior Pastor, Westminster
    Presbyterian Church, Rock Hill, South Carolina

This book has the potential to wake up the "sleeping giant" of the
Western church. We have been entrusted with financial resources
that could change the world through our generosity. But sadly we
fulfill only a small fraction of our potential. Jim Petty presents a
thoughtful, inspiring, and compelling vision of how we can use
our resources to love and bless others and to fulfill the Lord's purposes in the world. With faith and joy (and without legalism), he
describes how individuals and churches can be transformed to "excel
in giving."
—**Ron Lutz**, Former Pastor, New Life Presbyterian Church,
    Dresher, Pennsylvania

This is a special book. I'm familiar with much writing on generosity, but I've never seen anything like this book, which surveys the entire Bible on generosity as well as church history down to our current day. I hope that every Christian reads this book and is inspired.

—**Paul E. Miller**, Executive Director, seeJesus; Author, *A Praying Life* and *J-Curve*

A sea change in our thinking about money is in order. Being financially generous for the cause of the kingdom is not something that anyone drifts into. A person must make a conscious resolution to act as if his money is not his but the Lord's. In *Act of Grace*, Jim Petty makes the case, from Scripture and history, for why we should make that resolution.

—**Andrée Seu Peterson**, Senior Writer, *WORLD* Magazine

Look around and you will soon see that the church is in desperate need of money sanity. That sanity will only ever be found in the pages of God's Word. This is why I am so enthusiastic about this book by Jim Petty. I know of no other book that digs more deeply into what Scripture has to say about money than this book. Petty plumbs the depths of the Old and New Testaments to give us a rich and expansive gospel understanding of money. I can't think of anyone who would not benefit from the wealth of money wisdom that Petty offers. I know I will go back to this book again and again to root myself again and again in the money sanity that comes only from God's Word.

—**Paul David Tripp**, Author, *Redeeming Money: How God Reveals and Reorients Our Hearts*

Our relationship with money is complicated, as we all know, and so we all need clear guidance. Jim's book provides that clear, wise guidance. It includes the revealing story of money and giving throughout Scripture, a history of giving in the Christian church, and next steps we can take in our own giving. You will find it compelling and hopeful.

—**Ed Welch**, Counselor and Faculty Member, Christian Counseling and Educational Foundation

Act of
GRACE

Act of
GRACE

THE POWER OF GENEROSITY
TO CHANGE YOUR LIFE,
THE CHURCH,
AND THE WORLD

JAMES C. PETTY

PUBLISHING
P.O. BOX 817 • PHILLIPSBURG • NEW JERSEY 08865-0817

Was this book helpful to you? Consider writing a
review online. The author appreciates your feedback!

Or write to P&R at editorial@prpbooks.com
with your comments. We'd love to hear from you.

Printed in the United States of America

Library of Congress Cataloging-in-Publication Data

Names: Petty, James C., 1944- author.
Title: Act of grace : the power of generosity to change your life, the
  church, and the world / James C. Petty.
Description: Phillipsburg : P&R Publishing, 2019. | Includes bibliographical references.
Identifiers: LCCN 2019014620| ISBN 9781629956053 (pbk.) | ISBN 9781629956060
  (epub) | ISBN 9781629956077 (mobi)
Subjects: LCSH: Wealth--Religious aspects--Christianity. | Money--Religious
  aspects--Christianity. | Generosity--Religious aspects--Christianity. |
  Wealth--United States.
Classification: LCC BR115.W4 P49 2019 | DDC 241/.68--dc23
LC record available at https://lccn.loc.gov/2019014620

In memory of my father and mother,
James Chalmers Petty Sr. and Katherine Johnston Petty

See that you excel in this act of grace.
(2 Cor. 8:7)

Contents

Preface

This book is written for Christians about the topic of giving. It focuses on the question of why God gives us money and on the surprising implications of the answer for the economic lives of Christians. The book addresses what we are called to do with the wealth that God grants us.

I believe that God has a controlling purpose for us regarding the use of our money. Understanding this purpose can provide us with two things. First, it provides light that will guide our spending, savings, investment, and contribution decisions. Second, it offers a vision that will motivate and unleash godly generosity in us, his disciples.

In Part 1 of this book, we will explore God's purpose for money by surveying how major biblical characters viewed the purpose of their wealth. The survey begins with the Old Testament saints, then moves to God's Son in the Gospels, and finally concludes with the apostolic teaching received from the risen, ruling Christ.

Part 2 explores the real-world implications of that God-ordained purpose for money as it was worked out in the early church, the medieval church, and the modern evangelical era. After that, we will look at the potential to be realized in the twenty-first century and its substantial impacts for world evangelization, church edification, and relief and development for the poor. I hope to demonstrate that the primary obstacle to the substantial completion of God's purposes on earth is *not* a lack of funding—even in view of the poverty of almost 200 million Christians and the need to evangelize 5 billion people.

This book is not the first to explore the topic of giving in the United States. Christian Smith, John and Sylvia Ronsvalle, Mark Noll, Robert Wuthnow, and others have done splendid work studying why Christians don't give more. They have generously offered their

9

tools of sociological and historical analysis for our cause, and for that we should be very grateful. They bring their gifts to bear on this topic not just because of professional interest but because of their faith in Christ and their desire to see the church address a glaring deficit in its health and mission. Many of the dynamics that they document are also described in Scripture. The fruitful overlap of their findings and biblical principles helps us to see why there is a problem and how we can change.

I am deeply grateful to God for those he placed in my life who pointed me to him, the fountain of all generosity and giving. Both of my grandmothers, Katherine Akers Johnston and Ruth Roberts Petty, modeled a deep love for God's Word and were the primary means through which the gospel was brought to our family. My mother, Katherine, embodied an activism of love for the lost and troubled—a demonstration to me of the real existence of selfless love in the face of her son's native skepticism.

I am also thankful for the faculty and students at Westminster Theological Seminary, who patiently challenged my blindly proud assumptions about the foundations of human knowledge. I am particularly grateful in this regard for Bill Edgar, Dick Keyes, Edmund Clowney, John Frame, and Cornelius Van Til. You were the means that God used to change me from skeptic to kingdom activist.

I must also mention John Bettler and my former colleagues at the Christian Counseling and Educational Foundation. They not only gave me the opportunity for a twenty-year ministry in stewardship but actually taught me how to repent and live out the life that I now professed as husband and father and then as pastoral counselor and fledging author. I also give thanks for the challenging examples of Bob and Katherine Arthur, Rex Anderson Jr., and Milton Velez, who lit the way for me to see kingdom generosity as a way of life for all of Christ's disciples.

Finally, I want to acknowledge the critical role of my two primary editors. My wife, Marsha, has spent hundreds of hours correcting, copyediting, and advising me on the initial texts of all my books and pamphlets. Without her, my works would have imploded on the launch pad. Second, I am also deeply thankful to God for providing Sue Lutz, an especially hearty soul, who edited and shaped my books from visionary ramblings into well-written prose that could be useful to the church. On the last day, these insightful women will be revealed as great ones in the kingdom.

Introduction

*He who supplies seed to the sower and bread for food will
supply and multiply your seed for sowing and increase
the harvest of your righteousness. You will be enriched in
every way to be generous in every way, which through us
will produce thanksgiving to God. (2 Cor. 9:10–11)*

Consider this scenario: The phone rings in the pastor's office. On the
other end is an excited church treasurer.

Treasurer: Hi, Pastor. The offerings last month blew the doors off
our budget again. We received three times the amount we budgeted
for the month. This is the sixth month in a row, and we are choking
on money. If we put $600,000 in money market accounts, it looks
like hoarding! If we invest it in the stock market, it could make the
problem worse. What should I do with it?

Pastor Bill: Yes, I know. The revival that started six months ago
is really creating some good problems—enormous enthusiasm and
excess giving. It seems like God wants us to underwrite some serious
mission efforts. Have you asked the missions committee if they can
use the funds?

Treasurer: Yes, that's the first thing I did. They said that they could
use only enough funds to support two new missionaries next year
at $50,000 each. But administratively, even that is a stretch. The
committee isn't equipped to vet and manage any more missionaries
or major mission projects—certainly not the ten new missionaries
that this money would support. We have a hard time keeping up

with our current missionaries. Our church would have to become a mini–mission agency to pull that off.

I also spoke to the deacons, and they said that they have already met every known need in the church from their monthly diaconal offerings. They now have $400,000 in the deacons' fund account. They have considered sending it overseas, but they don't have the time or expertise to check out where to send it so that it gets to the right people. They need a consultant to help them, but they don't know who to ask. The seminary said that it doesn't train folks to manage large sums for relief and development. And the denomination is swamped with similar requests from other congregations that are caught up in the revival.

Pastor Bill: Have you thought about starting an endowment for the church? We could squirrel away millions in that kind of fund.

Treasurer: The finance committee discussed that, but it would end up compounding the problem. Salary and building expenses would eventually be covered by the endowment, and then we would have no expenses! We would have to give away almost everything that came in through the weekly offerings.

We were wondering if the revival would die down soon. As lame as it sounds, that would actually help! This is only a medium-sized church, and we aren't equipped to manage this kind of money. Our church is not a relief and development agency, much less a mission organization.

Even if the revival continues, perhaps, Pastor, you should ask the congregation to stop giving so much. Didn't Moses have to do that with the gifts for the tabernacle?

Pastor Bill: I did a quick calculation based on the average household income in our zip code. Our average household is now giving about 10 percent of its income. Before the revival, it was 4 percent, which was all we needed to run the church and missions program. Frankly, we never needed much for the deacons, because the economy has been strong out here in the suburbs.

So how can I tell folks not to tithe—to go back to 4 percent? Ten percent was the guideline in the Old Testament. And when Moses raised money for the tabernacle, he wasn't asking people to tithe their income. He asked them to give out of their net worth. Imagine if we asked folks to do that. The average net worth in our zip code is $400,000 per household!

Anyway, I have already preached that 10 percent was a guideline for giving. How can I go back and say that 4 percent is actually all we need? I found out early in my ministry that if I preached about tithing, only 25 percent would actually tithe. We needed those 25 percent to underwrite the ministry of the church—but I never expected *everyone* to tithe!

Treasurer: I just hope that the local paper doesn't publish a story that we are sitting on $1 million with a prospect of receiving $2 million more in the next six months. We'd be seen as hoarding in the face of overwhelming need around the world. It's too bad that we retired our building debt. Maybe we could build something—but we don't really need a major addition.

Pastor Bill: What about church planting? Could we send it to home missions?

Treasurer: I called the denomination, and they are swamped with money—enough for a thousand new church plants—but they have only a hundred candidates from our seminary.

Maybe running the kingdom of God was more expensive in the Old Testament, and so God commanded 10 percent. Perhaps in our affluent communities we just don't need that much? But that doesn't make much sense; they didn't have to do world evangelization and international mercy ministry. So, Pastor Bill, what did they do with all that money in the Old Testament?

Pastor Bill: That problem "solved" itself because Old Testament people did not tithe very well. Only certain ones tithed, and that kept things at manageable levels. From the time of Deuteronomy 15 all the way through Malachi, they were evidently okay with having lots of poor Jewish people. Nobody with money had figured out how to help them. It's not that different today.

Treasurer: So what are we going to do?

Pastor Bill: I wonder if God is trying to tell us something. Maybe our vision and planning for the church need a major change—particularly in our outreach. We might need to budget 65 to 70 percent for mission and mercy and keep 30 to 35 percent to run the church. It will mean that our congregation might look more like a mission and mercy agency with a church attached.

Treasurer: Well, if we go in that direction, I will probably have to resign as treasurer. Managing so much money would require a full-time business manager.

Pastor Bill: And I wonder whether I can lead a church with such a wide-ranging mercy and mission ministry—I was not trained for this at seminary. I would also hate for us to be accused of believing in the social gospel. Maybe we both need a dose of this revival.

The Reality of Giving among Christians Today

This fictional scenario is, of course, far from the reality we experience today. Most of us who are committed Christians like to think that we possess a strong desire to see the good news proclaimed to the nations, the church edified, and the poor relieved to become self-sufficient. But there never seems to be enough money to accomplish all this, so we just move on with our lives and next year's church budget. We struggle to keep from cutting mission support in bad financial years. We wish we could pay better salaries, but we can't. We need more staff but can't afford them. We know many missionaries and relief workers who can't raise enough support to get to their assigned fields.

There is a simple but profound reason for this: low giving. Professing Christians in the United States give only 2.5 percent of their $2.5 trillion income to churches and charitable causes. Only 9 percent tithe.[1] This is not much higher than non-Christians, who give between 1 and 2 percent of their income. Within the group of US Christians, "evangelicals" give about 3 to 4 percent of their household income.[2] Only 27.5 percent of evangelicals tithe, according to Christian Smith—or 12 percent, according to Barna Group.[3] Only the very poor and the rich break this pattern, in general giving more than 5 percent of their income to charitable causes.[4]

The rate of giving by all Christians has not varied much since 1921, beginning then at about 3.5 percent and ending in 2000 at 2.5 percent, even though disposable wealth (adjusted for inflation) has increased sixfold since then.[5] This decline in giving is seen particularly in middle-class families. They give at the lowest percentage of any group and yet comprise most of the membership of congregations.

As giving to churches (and therefore missions) has receded, parachurch agencies have tried to fill the ministry void. But few are positioned to fulfill their lofty goals. Christian missions and parachurch organizations struggle even more than churches do to secure dependable and adequate resources.

Typically, churches have learned to restrict their vision and mission goals to a single-digit expansion of their previous year's budget. Churches tend to receive just enough funding for the building and staff that are needed for baseline internal spiritual services (such as worship, teaching, fellowship, youth, and so on). People give to pay that "bill" and are loath to give more. There is usually not much left for new initiatives. Churches that give 20 percent to missions and

1. See Christian Smith and Michael O. Emerson with Patricia Snell, *Passing the Plate: Why American Christians Don't Give Away More Money* (New York: Oxford University Press, 2008), 38.

2. See Smith and Emerson, 46.

3. See "Tithing Down 62% in the Past Year," Barna, May 19, 2003, https://www.barna.com/research/tithing-down-62-in-the-past-year/.

4. See Smith and Emerson, *Passing the Plate*, 47.

5. See Smith and Emerson, 49.

outreach can claim some bragging rights and often vigorously promote that fact to potential members.

Yet most of the needs and opportunities for kingdom growth lie outside the doors of our churches. Consider the following fields that are "white unto harvest."

Prisoners

Active chaplains to the 1.6 million state and federal prisoners in the United States estimate that two-thirds see themselves as Christians, with the largest portion of them Protestant.[6] There are virtually no atheists. These inmates may be our greatest mission and discipling opportunity, yet most of us do not know a prisoner.

Immigrants

Each year, many thousands of immigrant and foreign students flock to the United States. Yet, according to International Students, Inc., 75 percent of them are never invited to an American home.[7] Many of these students are eager to learn about the US—including about the beliefs and faith of Christians. We are currently missing a major missions opportunity.

Inner-City Children

In most inner-city communities, more boys are initiated into gangs than go to college. Chicago alone has between 70,000 and 150,000 gang members—and that higher number is roughly the same as the number of high school students in the city.[8] Yet only 24 percent of

6. See "Religion in Prisons: A 50-State Survey of Prison Chaplains," Pew Research Center, March 22, 2012, https://www.pewforum.org/2012/03/22/prison-chaplains -exec/.

7. See "Get Involved," International Students, Inc., accessed August 8, 2019, https://www.isionline.org/GetInvolved.aspx.

8. "According to the Chicago Crime Commission, a 2012 Chicago Police Department gang audit found there are more than 600 gang factions in the city, with a minimum combined membership of 70,000." "By the Numbers: Chicago-Area Gangs," CBS News, May 21, 2013, https://www.cbsnews.com/news/by-the -numbers-chicago-area-gangs/.

ninth graders end up going to a four-year college.[9] In contrast, typical urban Christian schools see 95 percent of their inner-city youth enroll in college. In Philadelphia, parents of 40,000 inner-city children applied for 1,000 partial scholarships to private (mostly Christian and Catholic) schools, but for the 39,000 students who were not chosen, neither the schools nor their families had the funds to enable them to attend.[10] If funds were provided, this dynamic could substantially heal our inner cities and disciple a generation to Christ.

Unreached People Groups

Worldwide, 1,600 languages need a written language and a translation of the core of the Bible into that language. According to best estimates from the Joshua Project, there are still 7,096 unreached people groups (over 41 percent of the world's population), or about 3.19 billion people. The Joshua Project suggests that the church will need to field more than 67,000 more missionaries in order to complete the task of reaching these groups. We have a lot of work to do in world evangelization.[11]

Children around the World

An estimated $50 from 100 million Christians could stop medically preventable deaths of children under five around the world.[12]

The Poor in the Developing World

Using the World Bank's $1.25/day income benchmark, 1.3 billion people live in a destructive cycle of poverty.[13] The *Mission Handbook*

9. See "Enrollment in College from Philadelphia High Schools," *Philadelphia Public School Notebook*, May 26, 2011, https://thenotebook.org/articles/2011/05/26/enrollment-in-college-from-philadelphia-high-schools/.

10. This was reported to the author by the Children Scholarship Fund of Philadelphia in 2000.

11. See "Lists: All Continents," Joshua Project, accessed July 12, 2019, https://joshuaproject.net/global/continents.

12. See "The State of Church Giving in America: An Interview with John and Sylvia Ronsvalle," *The Enrichment Journal*, Assemblies of God, accessed April 25, 2019, http://enrichmentjournal.ag.org/201501/201501_072_Church_Giving.cfm.

13. See Ruth Alexander, "Dollar Benchmark: The Rise of the $1-a-Day Statistic,"

counts 211 million of these as Christians.[14] Unfortunately, most of us do not know who they are. The missing tithe from US evangelicals equals significantly more than $100 billion and would allow for a wise investment in relief and development for each of these 211 million fellow Christians *each year*.[15]

Since the 1960s there has been a resurgence in evangelical concern for the poor, and single-digit billions are now being given. But this only begins to address the needs and opportunities that lie before us today.

We dream about what could be done if church members gave 10 percent of their income—but we rarely speak about it. Most of our churches don't even have a plan for how they would deploy that much money.

Parachurch agencies do a better of job of raising expectations and casting vision. Mission agencies and relief and development organizations broadcast what they hope to do with more funds. God's people have responded in very positive ways, propelling forward organizations like The Salvation Army, World Vision, Compassion International, Bread for the World, and Samaritan's Purse. These agencies have helped to offset the decline in funds that churches receive for outreach. Yet even these agencies' dreams of really fulfilling their mission are still only that. This is because parachurch missions do not have direct access to the ideal fundraising venue: local tithing congregations. So, despite their growth, their mission goes only partially fulfilled.

Stewardship: Good but Too Undefined

Evangelical leaders have been aware of this low level of giving (compared to the Old Testament guideline) for sixty years. Many in

BBC News, March 9, 2012, https://www.bbc.com/news/magazine-17312819.

14. See Linda J. Weber, ed., *Mission Handbook: U.S. and Canadian Protestant Ministries Overseas*, 21st ed. (Wheaton, IL: Evangelism and Mission Information Service of the Billy Graham Center, 2010), 23.

15. This would allow for a $500 microloan—an investment in education or development assistance—for each poor Christian in the world, each year.

ministry thought that the answer was strong teaching on stewardship. The consensus beliefs about money that were reflected in our teaching for sixty years might be summarized as follows:

- *I am not the originator of my money or wealth.* It is God's gift to me, even though my labor may be the means through which it was given.
- *I am not the ultimate owner of my money and possessions.* I am rather a trustee (or steward) of them for God's kingdom purposes.
- In acknowledgment of that, *I should give generously of that money to God's work.*
- *Any money that I give to promote God's purposes is an investment in eternity.* Its value will be realized in the age to come.[16]

For sixty years, that message has gone out from evangelical pulpits, colleges, and seminaries; it has been shared in Christian financial seminars and many fine books. But presenting these great truths has not brought about the breakthrough that's been needed. As noted earlier, since the depths of the Depression, members' giving has decreased from 3.3 percent of their income to 2.6 percent, even though disposable income has increased 100 percent in inflation-adjusted dollars. Rising expectations for affluence and standard of living seem to have swallowed up this new wealth and kept it from being available as a contribution to God's work.

The Bright Spot

But, as always, God is at work and there is a bright spot—the group that George Barna calls the evangelical "revolutionaries."[17] Among Christian leaders and stewardship professionals, there is a

16. See Randy Alcorn, *The Law of Rewards: Giving What You Can't Keep to Gain What You Can't Lose* (Carol Stream, IL: Tyndale, 2003), 21.

17. See "A Faith Revolution Is Redefining 'Church,' According to New Study," Barna, November 30, 1999, https://www.barna.com/research/a-faith-revolution-is-redefining-church-according-to-new-study/.

rough consensus that 20 percent of Christian donors give 80 percent of the funds to our churches and missions. One survey shows that 5 percent of Christians give 59 percent of the church's income.[18]

This minority are the "revolutionary" folks who contribute 10 percent or more of their income each year to charitable and mission causes. Seven out of ten of them actively serve their communities. They literally keep our churches, missions, and agencies going. They have singlehandedly funded most of the outreach, mission, and ministry of God's kingdom in the United States.

Many of us who have been a part of the Christian community know these revolutionaries. They are in our small groups, our extended families, our church leadership, our mission boards. But these individuals will not identify themselves and are not asked to give testimony about their giving, since that is rarely done in our churches. You have to stumble into finding out about them or get to know them over many years.

I was blessed to grow up in a family in which God did a remarkable work of grace on both my father's and my mother's sides. Here are three stories from my father's extended family that illustrate the reality of God's giving radicals.

"Buck"

"Hey, Buck," my father said as he stopped his older brother, David, in the parking lot of their small hardwood turnings company. "Can I give you a check for some cash?" With an approving grin, Uncle David pulled out his wallet and gave my father a crisp $100 bill in exchange for a check. As a twelve-year-old who was looking out from our 1956 Ford station wagon, I was fascinated at my first sighting of a real $100 bill. Back in the fifties, that was serious money.

As my father got in the car and drove off, I asked why Uncle David had so much money in his wallet. He explained that David ("Buck" to him) always hid five $100 bills in his wallet in case he met someone who had needs—especially a hurting employee or

18. See Smith, Emerson, and Snell, *Passing the Plate*, 41.

someone in Christian service who was facing a money crisis. That was the equivalent of three months' pay for a minimum-wage worker at the time. David's company was not large and, while having made some money, had not yet produced any wealth. Those five $100 bills were not the overflow of excess wealth. They were an expression of David's commitment to use all his money to bless others and extend God's kingdom.

I remember being concerned that, if word ever got out about this walking deacon's fund, Uncle David would get robbed every time he stepped out of his office door (which was in a rough section of Greensboro, North Carolina). My second reaction was to be impressed that a person would place that much importance on being prepared to help others. I did not yet want to be that kind of person, but David's practical financial dedication to God's work fascinated me with its down-to-earth reality.

God did bless David's business, which increased his ability to give. His childhood name "Buck" turned out to be correct. His first priority was to convert that financial blessing into significant giving. At the end of his life, the proceeds from the sale of his company were donated to mission agencies. For fifty years, he never moved from his small brick bungalow until his death in 2010, when he graduated to a home in heaven, which I am sure is more fitting for a prosperous business owner who worked full-time in business for the kingdom of God.

"Don't Saw Off the Boat!"

I was in my early teens when I looked out the window and was horrified to see my father sawing off six inches from our old, sixteen-foot wooden runabout. My dad and some other men of the church took that boat fishing every fall off the North Carolina coast, and this year they had launched it through the surf in a quest for speckled trout. All went well until they tried to return through the surf. A large wave swamped the boat and tore the transom (back) off of it, which, with the outboard attached, headed straight for the bottom. Since they were in the surf, the men were able to drag the boat ashore and retrieve the transom and motor.

I thought for sure that now was the time for Dad to buy a proper fishing boat—a swanky Grady White or a handcrafted wooden Simmons Sea Skiff. But no—here he was with his saw, trimming off the rotten wood and preparing to receive a new makeshift plywood transom for the now fifteen-and-a-half-foot boat. I thought to myself, "The length of our boat is going in the wrong direction—and besides, wouldn't a bigger boat be safer?"

I thought that my parents were probably making enough money to buy a proper boat—but, of course, I could not prove it. Dad would just never make a purchase like that, even though he loved boats and fishing. Finally, during my college years, my brothers and I began to build our own wooden boats, since Dad was a "dry hole." He was very supportive. He even joined in the project with one of my younger brothers and paid for materials. But that was peanuts compared to what he would have had to spend for a "proper fishing boat." He never told me why he would not buy one.

My father died at age sixty from a heart attack. Through talking to my mother (whose family job it was to talk about things), I found out why we had no boat. Dad was neither cheap nor a miser. But by the time of his death, he and my mother were giving 40 percent of their income to the Lord's work, and they delighted in that privilege. I was stunned. Dad had never told me, and I was sad in that respect—but I was challenged to see that spending money on expensive optional items was not something that one had to do.

Giving had become my parents' highest financial priority—a higher priority than the expensive toys, cars, vacations, and travel they could have afforded. God did bless them finally with the ability to keep giving generously while also buying and fixing up a little beach house twenty-one rows back from the beachfront. They saw it as a ministry to our now scattered extended family. But I still fished in homemade boats.

The Engagement Ring

Why did these brothers both become givers? Both my uncle David and my father were reared by a mother who was an exuberant giver, though she was of very modest means. She (Ruth) and her husband (my grandfather Charles) lived in Clinton, North Carolina, where Charles started the town's first electric company. Unfortunately, the generating station burned to the ground and the enterprise largely failed. They were therefore not at all wealthy. Despite that, they raised their seven children to follow Christ, which was driven largely by Ruth's conversion. Charles, and particularly Ruth, became very involved in promoting foreign missions in the 1920s and 1930s.

Their church community evidently did not embrace foreign missions as eagerly as the Pettys did, so they held mission prayer meetings in their home. I get the impression that it was a kind of underground prayer group for foreign missions and for helping missionaries to raise support. Both my father (Jim) and David, as the two youngest children, sat on the floor for hours with the five older siblings, listening to missionaries from around the world tell the stories of God's kingdom.

One missionary couple came to their home in desperate financial straits. There was no money available to help with their very substantial needs. My grandmother got an idea—the kind that occurs only to givers. She asked her husband if they could sell her engagement ring and give the needy couple the money. He agreed, and this provided them the needed funds. This act made a profound impression on the seven children, who saw up close what it means to invest in eternity. The children went on to be deeply involved in foreign missions and in giving.[19]

There are hundreds of thousands of givers like these in our churches. These three are but examples from a long line of ordinary Christians (to use Luther's words) whose "purses" got converted along with their hearts and minds. For them, living and giving were deeply intertwined. A dollar earned was an opportunity to give. Since they were content with what they had to sustain their families, the final purpose of their money was giving.

Most of us are aware of wealthy evangelicals who gave from their

19. For more on this story, see James C. Petty, *Step by Step: Divine Guidance for Ordinary Christians* (Phillipsburg, NJ: P&R Publishing, 1999), 256–59.

substance, not just from their surplus. Business owners R. G. Letourneau, J. Howard Pew, Art DeMoss, and Anthony Rossi are some wealthy evangelicals from the last century who lived this value and spent a lot of time and energy each week administering their gifts and supporting missions. But for every Art DeMoss, there are thousands of middle-class Christians who give at the percentage he gave, or higher.

We also know that poor Christians give a higher percent of their income to God's work than the middle class do. As mentioned earlier, the poor and the extremely wealthy both give about 8 percent of their income. While we do not hear about many of the poor who give that way, Christ pointed out some of them in Scripture, such as the widow in Mark 12:42. Jesus was also delighted that Mary would be known for the gift of her perfume that anointed him for his burial. These will be the great ones of the coming age.

I know that for my uncle, father, and grandmother, money was more than a means of self-sustenance. But it was not something essential to their identity, nor was it something to be preserved for their children or stored or invested for their own comfort, sense of success, or security. Rather, as they found Christ and grew in the Lord, *all* their resources became a means of seeking to promote God's purposes in the world. For them, money was for giving—for blessing others and extending God's work in the world.

These are the "evangelical revolutionaries." They and thousands like them have gotten us to a certain point, by giving most of the money and pulling the rest of us along. They make our average giving look better—because, were it not for the 20 percent who are in this category, our giving would come out to be the same as that of the unchurched. This is where we are, despite knowing God's grace in Christ, sitting under sound teaching, and living in the richest society ever to inhabit the earth.

It is mind-boggling to think what would happen if the other 60 to 80 percent of Christians were energized to give and serve in this same way. Remember the "problems" of Pastor Bill and the church treasurer? Dare we dream of taking on such a challenge? Dare we pray for it—pray that *all* of God's work might be done using *all* of his provision? And, finally, dare we plan for this? Could it happen? If so, how?

I hope that this book will help you to see *that the final purpose of having money is to give.* I do not see this truth widely taught or believed in the church, but I believe that changing our view of the purpose of money is a big key to renewing the church's giving. This theme is not new to evangelical teaching. Brad Hewitt, CEO of Thrivent Financial, recently said, "I describe money as love or service in a storable or transferable form. That's really money's purpose—to demonstrate love or service—and we can either use it to serve ourselves, or instead to show love for our family and support our neighbors, community, and the world."[20] Hewitt is so right that money is simply our capacity for loving and serving others. Many writers on Christian giving have mentioned this principle, but I do not believe that any have made it their central focus and drawn on Scripture to illuminate this truth. That is what I pray we can do in this book.

What Is Your Money Identity?

In order to develop a theology of money, we need to understand its identity and purpose. We also need to understand who we are in relation to money. Christians are new creatures in Christ. We have put off the old man in order to put on the new. When it comes to resources and money, this means that we are changing from being takers to being givers. We are becoming like our God, who gave his only Son. We are becoming like our Lord, who, though he was rich, yet for our sakes became poor, that through him we might become rich (see 2 Cor. 8:9). Through Christ, we are undergoing a character change of an uncommon kind—at least according to the standards of today's culture. Let me illustrate.

The *Raleigh News and Observer* published an article called "Money Talks."[21] It was written to help spouses recognize that money means

---

20. Quoted in Susan Mettes, "Wait, What *Is* Money?" *Christianity Today* 61, no. 1 (January/February 2017): 31.

21. Olivia Mellon, "Money Talks," *Raleigh News and Observer*, May 5, 2007.

different things to different people, since most couples seem to have strong differences over their approach to money. In the article, Olivia Mellon divides people into nine basic categories based on the approaches they take to their money—what she calls "money types": "hoarder, spender, binger, ascetic monk, avoider, amasser, worrier, risk taker and risk avoider." Each of these identities, and its resulting behaviors that create spousal conflict, is built on something deeper: a belief about the nature of the world. That belief defines how we think money or possessions must function in the world to provide us with the security, significance, meaning, or experiences that qualify us as "really living."

I found it interesting that "giver," as a possible financial personality type, was not mentioned in this article—or, for that matter, in our culture at large. Yet for Christians, becoming givers is our primary financial destiny and identity. We need more than a new view of what money is. We need a new *self* so that we can use, in God's service, the money that he gives us. We need hearts that can faithfully steward the kingdom funds we have been granted. Thankfully, God can help us to understand the grace of giving and change us to be able to function within that worldview.

The idea that we are called to be givers should generate lots of questions. Are we still required to tithe by giving 10 percent? Why are so few Christians motivated to give at even that level? How do we change that? Can Christians be *really* wealthy? If so, how do they differ from wealthy unbelievers? How do we address the extremes of poverty and wealth among Christians today? Would God have us address poverty among Christians? What about non-Christians? If so, how? Does the church need to worry so much about the poor today, since we have tax-supported programs in the United States to help prisoners, orphans, immigrants, the elderly, the unlearned, and the sick? If the twenty-year track record of free market economic development continues, won't that take care of most of world poverty within the next twenty years?

Our beliefs about these topics will determine much regarding our giving. As Robert Wuthnow puts it, "The main conclusion . . . is that religious giving is part of a much larger cluster of beliefs and cultural assumptions and, for this reason, cannot be separated from how people think about their work, money, and materialism, any more than it can be cut off from beliefs about God, spirituality, and stewardship."[22] There is a lot involved in writing a check!

While there are many factors involved in giving, our purpose will be to focus on crucial (and often neglected) texts and themes that relate to our overall goals for money. We will work to make clear what it means to use our money first for investing in the kingdom of God. Fortunately today there are many good books on the general topic of the Bible as it relates to money. Many of them are listed for the reader at the end of this book. In addition, we should not forget the large amount of the Bible itself that is devoted to money-related topics. Wes Willmer reports that seventeen out of thirty-eight parables talk about possessions. Possessions and giving are mentioned 2,172 times in the Bible—more than believing (272 times), prayer (371 times), and love (714 times).[23]

After we consider the view of the purpose for money that was taught and practiced in biblical history, we will trace its themes through the post-apostolic church and up to our own era. The history of giving by evangelicals in the last 200 years is well-researched, and we will draw from that well. Finally, we will address the burning issue of how God's people should apply this theology of money to their lives today.

Questions for Review and Reflection

1. Do you sense that your congregation consists of a committed core group of evangelical "revolutionaries" and a less committed remainder of the congregation? What makes you think this?
2. How do you think your church's giving compares (or how does your own giving compare) to the 4 percent of their

22. Robert Wuthnow, *God and Mammon in America* (New York: Free Press, 1994), 249.

23. See Wesley K. Willmer, ed., *Revolution in Generosity: Transforming Stewards to Be Rich toward God* (Chicago: Moody, 2008), 26–27.

household income that evangelicals give generally? What brings you to this conclusion?

3. How would others who are close to you (your spouse, a sibling, or a parent) describe your money personality type? Would they be right? Why?

Part 1

UNDERSTANDING THE PURPOSE OF MONEY

1

Creation as a Gift of God's Goodness

Every good gift and every perfect gift is from above, coming down from the Father of lights, with whom there is no variation or shadow due to change. (James 1:17)

God is the original Giver. And because of the cosmic, unfathomable levels of gifting that God demonstrated as the Creator, the moral environment of the universe itself is one of giving. Giving turns out to be the *primary way* that God expresses his goodness and love to us humans.

This chapter will examine some ways in which the God of the Bible showed himself to be a good and giving God through his creation. I hope that considering some wonders of creation will work reverence, joy, and wonder in all who know that great Creator.

The Infinite-Personal God

Creation itself was a massive project of pure giving (see Gen. 1:1–2; 2:1–2). Before creation, time, physical laws, space, energy, and matter did not exist. Dimensional space itself did not exist. The Bible teaches that God created the universe *ex nihilo* (from nothing)—and so both its forms (like the laws of math and physics) as well as its substance (such as particles, waves, and all energy) were brought into existence by him. He did not just give form and order to already existing

33

material, as many mythologies depict. In the biblical narrative, when there was truly nothing, God spoke and brought to life a staggering diversity of structures, energy, environments, plants, animals—and, finally, mankind.

Creation was a free choice on God's part. The God of the Bible was and is infinitely satisfied in himself. He has no need to express himself in creation or to pursue relationship or feedback for himself. God simply determined to give us a good universe as a gift from him. Even today, we live our lives, take every breath, and experience every desire and dream within the reality of that original gift.

It was a gift not only because God freely gave it to us but because it was "very good" (Gen. 1:31). The heavens and earth are so full of goodness that none of us (even hardened atheists) can view the beauty of the cosmos or our "shining blue planet" without a sense of wonder at its majesty and design. Psalm 19 says,

> The heavens declare the glory of God,
>> and the sky above proclaims his handiwork.
> Day to day pours out speech,
>> and night to night reveals knowledge. (vv. 1–2)

Psalm 145 is a psalm to God's goodness.

> One generation shall commend your works to another,
>> and shall declare your mighty acts.
> On the glorious splendor of your majesty,
>> and on your wondrous works, I will meditate.
> They shall speak of the might of your awesome deeds,
>> and I will declare your greatness.
> They shall pour forth the fame of your abundant goodness
>> and shall sing aloud of your righteousness.

> The LORD is gracious and merciful,
>> slow to anger and abounding in steadfast love.
> The LORD is good to all,
>> and his mercy is over all that he has made. (vv. 4–9)

The apostle Paul makes it clear that God's revelation of himself in creation leads to more than our simply being wowed by the universe. It involves ongoing, visible joy and pleasure for us. In Acts 14:16–17 he says,

> In past generations [God] allowed all the nations to walk in their own ways. Yet he did not leave himself without witness, for he did good by giving you rains from heaven and fruitful seasons, satisfying your hearts with food and gladness.

He also reminds the Romans that, even for the person without a Bible, "God's kindness is meant to lead you to repentance" (Rom. 2:4). God is delaying judgment in order to give humankind a chance to repent and be forgiven. Despite our fall into sin, the universe is saturated in the goodness of the God who created this gift for humanity.

While creation is a gift of life to all its inhabitants, it is a gift to humans in a higher sense. We were given dominion over it, to rule and care for it. Man did not earn that position. Our position, and our equipping to rule and care for the earth and to know its Architect-Builder, are also gifts of God's goodness. Being made in the image of God means that we were endowed directly by God with moral excellence, and with the moral capacity to choose, in a way that set us apart from the animals forever.

A Planet Just for Us

The Bible says that God gave us the keys to the universe when his creation was complete, safe, and fully prepared for us. Preparing creation and the universe for mankind was a gigantic undertaking—from elusive subatomic particles to a cosmos that is billions of trillions of miles across. No one can fathom the magnificence, power, and complexity of what exists through his sovereign commands.

God positioned Earth and three other rocky planets in our solar system. They are protected from asteroid bombardment by the gas giants (like Jupiter and Saturn) that he placed in outer orbits as guardians of these smaller planets. Jupiter and Saturn regularly get hit by comets and asteroids with no ill effects. Based on current exoplanet research, this arrangement of rocky planets may be rather rare in our galaxy.

God created Earth to contain in its crust all the ninety-plus naturally occurring elements of the periodic table. None are missing. He gave Earth a magnetic field to protect its surface from radiation generated by atomic fusion in the sun.

He placed Earth in the narrow habitable zone for water-based life. He added oxygen and water to the planet, created DNA-based life, and sovereignly directed the development of this life through diverse means of reproduction, feeding, and self-defense as well as giving it many different shapes, sizes, and abilities. The suitability of our current environment (our planet, solar system, and sun) was the result of God working a carefully crafted plan to make a place just for us. From our limited perspective, he went to a lot of trouble to make this gift to us, which is full of life, beauty, and magnificent design. It was truly "very good" and remains an awe-inspiring gift to this day.

The Gift of Self-Consciousness

Another wonderful gift God has given us is the ability for us to step back and study, analyze, and reflect on the world and ourselves. Though we are embedded in the world, we have been given a perch from which to study it and even watch ourselves doing so. This makes exploration, research, and technology possible. In our minds, we can encompass a vision of the entire universe and how it works. Put another way, each human brain can think about the entire universe as an object—and also think about the fact that we are doing so.

As we contemplate the gift of our existence in the world, we see that God made us not only to inhabit it and use it (as the animals do) but also to know it, reflect on it, and begin to develop its potential. We humans share, in a creaturely way, God's quality of transcendence.

And it is quite a universe God gave us to reflect on! It is not a little universe, just big enough to hold us (like a crate for a puppy), but a gigantic universe of unimaginable power, design prowess, and awe-inspiring majesty. Only about 6 percent is matter we can see. The rest is mysterious stuff that we are still trying to figure out. The creation is currently thought to be 13.7 billion light years across—big enough and worthy enough for God himself to enjoy and for us to explore for eternity.

There are currently limitations on how far we can travel through space, but we get quite a view from our earthly window on the cosmos. Perhaps that inaccessibility of most of space reminds us that, while we can enjoy the cosmos and be dazzled by it, we should also be humbled by it. This helps us to resist the temptation to think ourselves equal to God just because we can know some things about his creation. Yet it does not mean we should measure our significance by our microscopic size compared to the scale of the universe. Our significance is better measured by the size of what God created for himself and for *us*, so that we can know and enjoy it for his glory.

The Gift of Personal Relationship

Another free gift from God is community. Adam and Eve were a gift for each other. Theirs was an arranged marriage *par excellence*. They were called forth from the ground by God's sovereign wisdom and creative power. The Bible does not tell us the details of how God did this. It affirms only that Adam was made from the same ground that was used to make the animals. We can know, however, from what God has said, that at a particular time and place in Earth's history, God created Adam as the first human and endowed him with his image. Upon his creation, Adam was introduced by God to a wonderful garden and a completed but undeveloped world. Adam was equipped to beautify it and was given an open relationship with its Originator-Designer.

Adam was then introduced to Eve—the first female to be made in the image of God. No dowry or work was required for him to "win" her. Eve was a beautiful gift to Adam—one who was neither lower nor higher than he. She was of his very substance—bone of his bone and flesh of his flesh (see Gen. 2:23). Together they were called to the proper use and enjoyment of this new world. They became capable of a relationship that had analogies to the love, unity, and community enjoyed by the members of the Godhead.

And this most exalted love they enjoyed could also tap into the most powerful of bodily pleasure experiences: sexual orgasm and physical intimacy. God invented and preserved the blessing of sex for us, and he still enjoys our experience of its goodness when we use it as he intends. Poetry, prose, and song still flow today in a never-ending stream that celebrates this "fire of Yahweh" injected into human love: "Set me as a seal upon your heart, as a seal upon your arm, for love is strong as death, jealousy is fierce as the grave. Its flashes are flashes of fire, the very flame of the LORD" (Song 8:6).

Man and woman are truly blessed and exalted over all creatures by the experiences and meaning they can bring to life through God's gift of the marriage relationship. There is nothing like it in the animal kingdom, anywhere in the universe, or in heaven among the angels.

Psalm 8 reflects humanity's thanks and praise to God for our position and calling. The psalmist asks how a small and puny mankind could have any significance in such an awesome universe (see v. 4). He answers his own question like this:

> You have made him a little lower than the heavenly beings
>   and crowned him with glory and honor.
> You have given him dominion over the works of your hands;
>   you have put all things under his feet. (vv. 5–6)

> O LORD, our Lord,
>   how majestic is your name in all the earth! (v. 9)

The Great Land Giveaway

But God had more goodness to give. From his hand, the whole planet lay open to this new family. All the natural resources, continents, forests, seas, streams, plants, and valleys were there for Adam and Eve's children to care for and use for life. This world, which was inherently and obviously very good, was a gift to humanity from God for his glory and was carefully crafted and developed for them.

Terrain on earth was not preassigned to certain persons, classes, or races (as Israel came to be). Nor were parts of it off-limits (except for the Tree of the Knowledge of Good and Evil). The goods and benefits of *all* the earth were for *all* Adam and Eve's children. All they had to do was arrive at a location, use it, and develop it. It was a free gift of 57 million square miles of land to human tribes and families for thousands of years as they filled the earth.

Humans (with some prodding from God in Genesis 11) pursued their destinations around the world and accepted the free lands from the goodness of their Creator. It is safe to assume that our ancestors claimed land and populated every habitable continent remarkably soon after their quest to do so began. All this land was given away—mostly to folks who quickly forgot whom to thank for it. That, of course, does not negate the wonder and goodness of the gift.

Our Response as Givers

As God's image bearers, we were created with the motivation to create for others. We find delight in designing, creating, and gifting to our families, our children, and our clans or communities. Even as sinners, we experience joy in giving good things to our children and to others we love.

In 2 Corinthians 9:7 Paul reminds the church that they should give not under compulsion but as each determines in his or her own heart, because "God loves a cheerful giver." I love Spurgeon's comment on why this is true of God.

Now observe, first, God loves a cheerful giver for He made the world on the plan of cheerful giving, and a great artist loves all that is consistent with his plan. I say God has made the whole world on this plan, so I will show you. Look at the sun; what an orb of splendor; what a glorious creation of God! Why is it bright? Because it is giving away its light! Why is it glorious? Because it is scattering its beams on all sides! Imagine that it should say, "I will give no more light"; where would be its brightness? If it should say, "I will no more scatter my beams"; where would be its luster? It is in the magnificent generosity of that great father of the day that his glory consists! It is the grandest of orbs to us, because it gives us so much of that vitalizing force which is heat, and light, and life. Behold the moon, the fair queen of the night. Why do we rejoice in her? Because what light she receives from the sun, she gives again to us! If she were not to give her light, who would speak of her? . . . Even yonder twinkling stars which seem so small to us—do not their brightness and their radiance consist in their giving? "One star differs from another star in glory," because one star differs from another star in what it is able to yield to us. So it is with the heavenly bodies. . . . The cheerful giver is marching to the music of the spheres, he is in order with God's great natural laws, and God, therefore, loves him, since He sees His own work in him.[1]

From Receivers to Takers

Though God showed himself to them as the original cheerful giver, Adam and Eve quickly joined the rebellion against this giving God. They doubted his good intentions—despite their glorious earth, a beautiful garden with that all they needed, free and unearned use of and dominion over creation, open fellowship and conversation with God, and the gift of companionship with each other.

Despite it all, they decided that God could not be trusted to tell the truth and act in their best interests. Satan convinced them that God was withholding knowledge from them in order to keep them from being like himself—that God did not want Adam and Eve to have their complete fulfillment. They ate of the Tree in defiance of God's command, and the world fell into sin and under the power of death.

Sadly, the marvelous gifts of God were quickly misused. Adam and Eve's son Cain brought forth the fruit of this attitude, taking his brother Abel's life out of jealousy and rage because Abel's sacrifice was

1. Charles Spurgeon, "A Cheerful Giver Is Beloved of God" (sermon, Metropolitan Tabernacle, London, August 27, 1868), available online at https://www.spurgeongems.org/vols13-15/chs835.pdf, pp. 4–5.

accepted by God and Cain's manipulative offering was not. But that was just the beginning.

Once land was claimed or settled by a tribe or clan, the sharing stopped and the wars began. War, oppression, and extortion became the rule of land acquisition, leaving it to the strong and wealthy— largely to the exclusion of the weak and poor. This horrible history forgets but does not negate the joyful gift of the "very good" earth to Adam and Eve and *all* their children. It reveals our covetousness of others' land and resources for what it is: the sin of living supremely for self and for what others can provide us.

In the Jubilee legislation in Leviticus 25, God pushed back against this attitude of personal entitlement. Through that legislation, God provided protection and security for the land people owned and opportunities for them to redeem it if it was lost for any reason. From this Christian view of land ownership, we have even today a sense that anyone born into this earthly family should have an opportunity for life, liberty, and the pursuit of happiness. Providing people with this has been a challenge in the face of stronger economic, criminal, and military forces.

Thankfully, there is still a sense of injustice we feel at the "occupation" of one country by another or at monopolies that crush small businesses through predatory behavior. The diversity of nations and freedom of markets under law have been providential blessings in many areas of the world. This is nothing but the legacy of God's original gift of the earth to all humans.

There is no record of humans learning to give in Genesis 1–11. In fact, the record is one of jealousy, violence, and hatred of humans for each other. These chapters show a dramatic contrast between the goodness of God in creation and the failed rule of mankind as it filled the earth with violence (see Genesis 6–9).

People's violence and self-glorying ethics replaced thankfulness for all God had given them. Trust was displaced by the notion that humans had the right and power to decide what was good for them— even if it took away their neighbor's life or welfare. The Serpent had claimed that Adam and Eve could even take secret knowledge from God by eating of the Tree. No longer thankful receivers, Adam and

Eve became takers of what they wanted by force—even from God, if necessary. They became friends of the Serpent and made God their rival and therefore their enemy. From then on, for humans, taking replaced giving as the default mode of operation.

But God responded in disciplined grace in Genesis 3 and 9. While confirming their eventual death as the built-in consequence of their sin, he promised to break up mankind's friendship with evil and to win them back to himself. He promised to put enmity between Adam and Eve's seed and the seed of the Serpent. He would also protect them from themselves, making it impossible for them to eat from the Tree of Life. God knew that this would confirm them eternally in the fallen state.

Instead, God promised to send his Son (a seed) to crush the Serpent's head, despite the suffering of that future Son (see Gen. 3:15). In the coming chapters, we will trace how God reclaimed his creatures from a life of taking in order to make them as loving and giving as he is. In order to support that initiative, he continues to shower both his friends and enemies with such blessings as harvests, marital love, children, language, and culture.

Conclusion

The Judeo-Christian belief in a God who is both good and infinite is unique—unknown in other cultures. This is reflected by the lack of charitable giving that is inherent in secular, pagan, and pantheistic cultures.

The God of the Bible, by contrast, has spawned the greatest outpouring of mercy in human history. It has reached into the homes, cultures, and lives of even its enemies. In the West, we forget the unique and powerful impact of God's inherent goodness on our cultural values. We forget that his majestic, awe-inspiring universe, and our magnificent planetary home, which is the setting for a dazzling diversity of flora and fauna, are God's *gifts*. They are not "just here." Beyond that, we are the recipients of his unique gift to humans: the capacity for the moral excellence and moral agency that only God has. And most wonderfully, we also receive the gift of himself, in Jesus, which he gave to redeem us and to restore our capacities for moral excellence and agency through a personal but cosmic salvation.

Every breath, every day, every reflective mud puddle, every mountain range, every cool breeze—all of these are gifts that show us the great Giver who bestowed them upon us. Despite our sin, our birth brings us into a giving-dominated cosmos, and Christ ushers us into reunion with the God who is the greatest and original giver.

Questions for Review and Reflection

1. Have you experienced the wonder of creation as being the free expression of God's goodness? If so, can you describe it?
2. What four aspects of creation does this chapter identify that reveal the "gift" nature of what God has created? Can you add any others?
3. Has science's description of the world (as operating under physical laws) reduced, or increased, your sense of being thankful to God for creation? Why?

2

Abraham and the
Blessing of the Nations

The king of Sodom said . . . "Take the goods for yourself."
But Abram said to the king of Sodom, "I have lifted my hand to
the Lord, God Most High, Possessor of heaven and earth, that I
would not take a thread or a sandal strap or anything that is yours,
lest you should say, 'I have made Abram rich.'" (Gen. 14:21–23)

Beginning in Genesis 12, God acted systematically to bless the fallen
human race by reintroducing to them the knowledge of his goodness
and love. What is more, he acted to make his sinful creatures the
agents of that blessing. Let's look at how he began all this through
Abraham.

Abraham is the father of all who believe. He lived by faith in a
grace-based covenant with God. Because we live as believers today
in the fulfilled version of that covenant, I am always struck by the
similarities we see between Abraham's life and the spiritual dynamics
we face today. Let's look at the role that the promised blessing of that
covenant played in Abraham's life.

To begin, notice all the references to blessing that God makes
in Genesis 12:2–3, when he first calls Abram. "I will make of you a
great nation, and I will *bless* you and make your name great, so that
you will be a *blessing*. I will *bless* those who *bless* you, and him who
dishonors you I will curse, and in you all the families of the earth

shall be *blessed.*" Abraham was blessed so that he could be a blessing. That we too are "blessed to be a blessing" is the essential thesis of this book. God was not calling Abram to move to Canaan so that he and his children would enjoy a better life because of Canaan's wealth and prosperity. He called him to experience a dramatic disruption to his life so that *all* nations would be blessed through him. The final purpose and meaning of Abram's life was to be a link in the chain of blessing to others—one that would bring them back to God and the blessings of that relationship.

God did not choose to make Abram prosperous in the livestock business for Abram's own sake. This prosperousness was related to Abram's calling to be a blessing to all the nations of the world. He lived in tents and built up his flocks so that he could be a blessing to the covenant people to come, and to his neighbors—such as Abimelech and the residents of Sodom.

In a very introductory way, this illustrates our thesis. Just as with Abraham, our spiritual father, our blessing comes with a purpose: that we might bless others. God does not bless us with every spiritual blessing in Christ for our sakes only. His blessings come with a new purpose for us: to give ourselves to the witness, good works, and love that God has prepared for us to carry out. This contrasts dramatically with the self-glorying and self-consuming life that emanated from the fallen Adam.

We are Abraham's descendants—he is our father through the covenant of grace (see Rom. 4:12). When we are in Christ, we carry the blessing of Abraham to all the nations of the earth. Our salvation, our children, and any prosperity that God may give us in addition come with that same purpose.

Abraham's wealth was at the disposal of his descendants, Isaac and Jacob, and their children and was meant for all who were circumcised into the covenant. Every member of Abraham's household, including Gentile servants, were grafted in to the covenant family in order to become heirs of Abraham's God.

This solidarity in blessing became more specific with the twelve children of Jacob. God chose Jacob and not Esau in order to show that his blessing was ultimately based on his election of grace and not on birth. Membership in God's covenant would be for anyone who accepted that gracious covenant, including neighbors and household servants of Abraham, Isaac, and Jacob. The fact that the blessings of God are intended for *all* covenant members is seen throughout Scripture and eventually reflected in the solidarity of all believers as they share the gifts and wealth of all the others.

Abraham: Living to Be a Blessing under Duress

But testing was to come for Abraham. God blessed Abraham and Lot with an abundance of livestock, so that there was not enough pasture for both of them if they stayed together. To resolve the problem, Abraham engaged in an act of amazing generosity that reflected the giving nature of God himself. He gave his nephew, Lot, the choice of the best land.

Abraham clearly had a right to make the choice as the older family member and the head of this new branch of the family. But Abraham believed God's promise. His future did not depend on his negotiating for or claiming the well-watered portion of the land, so he offered that part to Lot.

Lot was marching to a different drummer. Lacking faith in God's promise, he immediately took Abraham's offer. He settled where he could get the best pasture and a home city, Sodom, for protection. He saw the choice not as a chance to bless his uncle but as an opportunity to increase his wealth and security. His "money personality" showed him to be a taker, not a giver.

Abraham was a giver of monumental proportions, considering what was at stake. Yet by faith Abraham knew that he owned all the land, because God had promised it to him. He knew that God would sustain him and fulfill his promises in the right redemptive season.

In accord with his promise, it was Abraham whom God blessed. He became richer in the currency of the hill country of Canaan: livestock and servants to care for them. Lot, by contrast, was drawn to the city—probably to its wealth-creating machine of trade and to the greater earthly "security" it provided.

Abraham's Tithe

In Genesis 14:14–24, Abraham found himself forced to rescue his foolish nephew, at great risk to himself and his family. After a disastrous trip to Egypt for food (see Gen. 12:10–20), having to risk everything by going into battle for his nephew was probably not how Abraham envisioned being blessed by God and being a blessing himself. Being a link in the chain of salvation was not proving to be very satisfying so far. What happened, however, was astounding in its own right and powerfully promoted God's witness to the surrounding kings and their subjects.

A coalition of kings from city-states near Abraham's ancestral home of Ur had threatened Sodom and other cities of the plain. The local city-state kings gathered their own coalition to repulse the attack but were soundly defeated. Sodom was taken and looted. Lot, his family, and his possessions were taken captive. When Abraham heard this, he gathered three local "chieftains" (with only 318 men) and, in a surprise attack, recovered all the loot, along with Lot and his family. This was an amazing act of courageous compassion. Abraham risked his life to save his selfish nephew, the population of this pagan, violent city, and all their wealth. And, as became evident, he did not do it in order to gain but in order to give. He began to show himself as the blessing that God intended him to be to the cities and nations around him.

After the battle, Abraham led a procession of wagons that carried the recovered booty. He was met by the mysterious Melchizedek— King of Salem and "priest of God Most High" (Gen. 14:18). He was the priest-king of the city that was later known as Jerusalem (see Ps. 76:2).

The book of Hebrews points out that Melchizedek was not a priest appointed under the Mosaic law. Hebrews 7:1–10 says that he was commissioned directly by God. He shared bread and wine with Abraham and publicly pronounced God's blessing on him.

Abraham in turn gave Melchizedek a tithe (a tenth) of all the goods he had gained. This first tithe that is documented in the Bible was given to a representative of the true God. Until then, Abraham had no priest or representative of God through whom to give his gifts or wealth. Hebrews points out that through that act, Abraham recognized the reality of a divine priesthood that was higher than any appointed by man. Ultimately, it revealed the reality of the eternal priesthood of Jesus Christ—a priesthood of much more efficacy than the Mosaic one. Through this act of giving, Levi (the Mosaic priest)—who, though unborn, was "in" Abraham—tithed to Christ through Abraham's tithe to Melchizedek (see Heb. 7:9–10).

By the time the defeated kings met Abraham, he controlled the wealth of their cities. At that point in the story, they were not in a good bargaining position. Abraham could have destroyed them and set himself up to rule their city-states as king. As victor, he could have seized the land, the cities, and the enormous wealth to which he was now entitled. He could have established a base from which to conquer the land God had promised him. But instead Abraham explained that God had provided his protection, riches, and blessing and that he would take nothing from the booty.

He refused the wealth so that these kings would never be able to say, "I have made Abram rich" (Gen. 14:23). Abraham wanted to witness to the reality that his God was the true and living God—and that God, on his own, would keep his promises to bless Abraham and all nations through him. Prior to this conquest, Abraham may not have been considered rich compared to the nobles and kings of these cities, but he did not want to become rich at the expense of his witness to the promise God had made to *give* him Canaan, the cities, and the nations.

There are many unanswered questions regarding this account. Where did Melchizedek come from? Where did he go? Was he an Old Testament appearance of Christ? Scripture does not say explicitly why Abraham offered the tithe. It is implied that he offered it in thanksgiving to God for his deliverance from his enemies.

But here the concept of a tithe offered to God clearly enters biblical history. Its voluntary nature made it consistent with the unilateral graciousness of God's covenant with Abraham—and, most significantly, it was offered ultimately to Christ.

Jacob followed Abraham's example in Genesis 28:22 and offered a tithe of all he had to God when he was delivered from his enemy. In fact, the promise that Jacob made in this verse can be read as an ongoing commitment to tithe from his wealth: "Of all that you give me I will give a full tenth to you."

The rest of the accounts of the patriarchs emphasize the amazing riches, blessing, and protection that God bestowed on Abraham, Isaac, Jacob, and Joseph—even amid their episodes of sin and unbelief. Canaanites such as Abimelech (see Gen. 20, 26) recognized that the true God was blessing Abraham and Isaac. He sought to covenant with Isaac in order to secure blessing and protection under Abraham's Lord—the God of such abundant giving. So in that way Abraham's witness continued in Isaac—even to Abimelech, the Gentile.

The Gift of God Himself

Earlier we saw that creation was a spectacular gift from God to man but that Adam horribly botched his role as the covenant head of the human race. Instead of bestowing eternal life, he bestowed certain death. Yet God acted in costly mercy in order to redeem the situation. God's lavish giving in creation is now dwarfed by his giving of *himself* to Abraham and his descendants. In fact, he gives himself to all those who believe. This covenant relationship, mutual giving, and solidarity between God and his people go to astounding depths from their very inception. Theologians only scratch the surface of this profound transaction. In Genesis 15:1 God says, "'Fear not, Abram, I am your shield; your reward shall be very great.'"

God promises *himself* to Abraham as his shield and, by implication, as his reward. Abraham had only a foggy understanding of what it would ultimately mean for God to give himself to Abraham's descendants, but we fully understand it now. Jesus fulfilled this term of the covenant completely: "God so loved the world, that he gave his only Son" (John 3:16).

This relationship of utter giving between God and Abram was to be codified and secured in an unbreakable covenant. In that covenant, God legally committed himself to be Abram's God (see Gen. 15) and took Abraham and his children to be his people. God took an oath to fulfill his promises even if it cost him his own life. And that is exactly what it cost Jesus. He offered himself as a sacrifice to ensure that the blessings of eternal life were secured for Abraham's true children—despite and because of their sin.

This train of blessing was revealed gradually in history. It always involved God's giving. He freely granted Abraham all the land of Canaan for a future everlasting possession. This gift was just announced; it was not a negotiation between God and Abram or a trade of service for land. It was an outright gift—an everlasting one, in perpetuity. Abraham received the gift as a gift of grace. He did not earn it. He just had to faithfully hold it. He simply had to live in it and by it.

That, however, was not a task for the faint of heart or the unbelieving. It was a fearful thing for Abram to accept this God as his God and his great reward. Consider that there was little visible protection or security in Canaan compared to what Abraham would have had in Ur. In Canaan there were walled cities where residents could flee in times of danger. The countryside could be dangerous for nomadic folks without protection. Abram was living in tents. It was a bit like camping on a city sidewalk with bags of money sitting around your tent and very little to protect you. There was no way this was going to work without God's supernatural protection.

Not only that, but Abraham had no rights, no title to land, and initially no treaties. He was an alien, an undocumented immigrant, who was there only by the goodwill of those who currently controlled the land. He waited for a future city that would be built and inhabited by God (see Heb. 11:10). It was thus a poor place to plan to accumulate riches for himself. He had to view everything in his life—wife, children, livestock, servants, and any accumulated wealth—as part of God's plan to bring redemption to that dark land and from there to the world. These things were God's provision—a provision that was enough for Abraham's task. God would protect that provision and bring everything to fruition through it.

Abraham was a religious minority. He was to live in Canaan in peace, bless its inhabitants, and allow God to witness through him that he was indeed the true God. He had to invite the Canaanites to come under the hope of the covenant. We don't know whether Abram shared with them that God would eventually give him their land. That information might have created some real danger, or at least misunderstanding—especially if the local clan chiefs (like Abimelech and the four kings) inquired into how this blessing was supposed to work out.

I wonder how many of us would accept such a missionary calling. Let's summarize the terms of this job offer from God.

- Leave family, friends, business, and personal security, never to return.
- Go to a place and culture that will still be undesignated by God at the time of your departure.
- Live in tents out in the open, in a land that has walled cities for a reason.
- Live by the goodwill of local landowners and never own or control any land yourself—except for your grave site.
- Accept the job of carrying God's blessing to pagan nations that are corrupt, hostile, and entirely ignorant of the true God.

It turns out that we do serve under analogous conditions. We are called to seek first the kingdom of God and to invest everything in its pursuit without regard to the cost. We are part of a counterculture, neither understood nor accepted by the world, as we wait for God to inaugurate his culture at some future time. Like Abraham, we do not position ourselves first of all for security, wealth, acceptance, or earthly meaning, but for service where God has placed us. We find peace in knowing that we have received the promised kingdom and that God knows that we have needs now, before that kingdom fully comes. We, like Abraham, still wait for that "walled" city where we will find lasting peace, prosperity, and security.

We are called not to protect ourselves from our enemies by force but to love our enemies and do them good, announcing to them the good news of God's mercy available in Christ. While Christ has absorbed the curse of death for us, we are still called to lose our lives for his sake, that we may save our lives and the lives those to whom we minister. It is remarkable how the root challenges and spiritual issues are similar in both cases.

Abraham and Sarah most likely did not know how the Lord would give their children the land. They just obeyed by growing herds that would provide for them, their children, and the covenant household in that day. They did not build cities, palaces, or kingdoms by which they could store up and protect wealth. In fact, they continued to live in tents, without property ownership and at the mercy of their Canaanite countrymen. They became rich, but their wealth was not what it would have been if Abraham were a king in the cities. During the three famines in patriarchal times, they were unable to sustain themselves, although they did have enough cash to buy grain in Egypt.

Abraham saw that his life purpose was to be a conduit of God's blessing to God's people. Through them, he was to offer the nations adoption into God's family. He was not there to take from the people around him, nor was he there to isolate himself from them in a selfish personal peace. He worked and waited for his seed (the Son) to bring God's blessing to fruition. He freely tithed to God when he met the priest of God, and gave away his windfall wealth to those who had lost their own, so that *they* might see the witness of God's promise.

Having already consecrated himself to God and to his purpose to bless all the nations through him, he understood the purpose of his wealth. It was the same as the purpose of his life: to bless others with the blessing God had given him. Abraham was a giver, like the God he served.

Questions for Review and Reflection

1. Do you think you would have been willing to relocate to a potentially hostile foreign country and depend totally upon God to bless and protect you for the sake of providing a means of blessing and redemption for others (i.e., the nations)?

2. Why did Abraham not take the opportunity to provide riches, cities, and security for himself and his promised family line

after he liberated the wealth and the people of Sodom and of the other cities of the plain?

3. To what extent do Christians today live with the mentality that our lives, families, and wealth are given to us by God that we might be a means of blessing to others (i.e., the nations)?

3

Giving under the Law

Every seven years . . . you must cancel any debt your brother owes you. However, there should be no poor among you, for in the land the LORD your God is giving you . . . he will richly bless you, if only you fully obey the LORD. (Deut. 15:1, 3–5 NIV)

Abraham's response to his work, wealth, and family reflected his faith in God's promise to build an everlasting land and city. All Abraham's resources were dedicated to securing the path to that future kingdom. Were his sojourn and his orientation to wealth unique? Was his situation unique? How do the remainder of the Torah (the five books of Moses) and the rest of the Old Testament view the purpose and use of money?

The book of Exodus gives us a look at Moses and his personal experience with these issues. Acting on his promise to Abraham in Genesis 15:13–16, God hears the cry of his people, who by then have been enslaved for four hundred years (see Ex. 3:7–8). The time is right for God's deliverance. The Israelites are now numerous enough to occupy and farm the land of Canaan, and the Canaanites are now so wicked that God can justly wipe them out of existence. Neither of these conditions prevailed during the time of the patriarchs.

Yet even Israel's enslavement occurred in connection with Abraham's seed being a blessing to Egypt and to all the nations around it (see Gen. 45:7; 50:20). Through Joseph, these nations were saved from starvation, and Egypt was greatly enriched. Joseph was a blessing and a witness to all nations, as Pharaoh saw the prophecies of the true God come to pass before his eyes. This was the first of many instances when God made the truth of his nature and covenant public at the centers of world power and, therefore, to the kings of the ancient Near East.

Joseph's witness was extinguished within a few generations, when Egypt enslaved his descendants. Still, God continued to bless his people even in their slavery. He gave them many children, and they flourished under the dome of Egyptian protection, economic productivity, and cultural power. In God's wise plan, they were shielded from the outside aggression they would surely have encountered in Canaan. They (along with other slaves) became the labor force that helped to build the mighty empire and economy of the Nile River.

However, as Moses reports in Exodus 1–3, the Egyptians became afraid of the Hebrews. As their numbers grew, God's promise to multiply them as the stars of the sky became a reality—and a liability in the eyes of the Egyptians. They decreed that each baby boy was to be drowned. The female babies were not considered a threat. This cruelty, added to centuries of suffering and oppression, was the final straw that led to God's reaction.

God put it into Moses's heart to visit his people, understand their suffering, and seek to secure greater justice for them as slaves. Moses failed and ended up a fugitive in Sinai, but there he received God's call to return to Egypt and bring the Hebrews out so that they could meet their God, renew the covenant, and restart a life with I Am. God would go with them to a new land, where they would live in everlasting fellowship.

Moses had as much to lose by leaving Egypt as Abraham did by leaving Ur. The book of Hebrews reminds us what Moses left behind for the sake of God's purposes.

> By faith Moses, when he was grown up, refused to be called the son of Pharaoh's daughter, choosing rather to be mistreated with the people of God than to enjoy the fleeting pleasures of sin. He considered the reproach of Christ greater wealth than the treasures of Egypt, for he was looking to the reward. By faith he left Egypt, not

being afraid of the anger of the king, for he endured as seeing him who is invisible. (Heb. 11:24–27)

Moses believed that God would fulfill his eight-hundred-year-old covenant promise to give them the land of Canaan as an everlasting possession and to dwell there with them. He "bet" his life, his accumulated wealth, and his family on that hope. By faith, Moses let go of the wealth of Egypt in favor of the greater wealth connected to God himself. His life, education, relationships, energy, and resources were dedicated to God's purposes: mediating God's blessing to the covenant people and then, through them, to the world.

With great power, humiliating Pharaoh and all the gods of Egypt, God brought his enslaved people to meet him for the first time. He did this publicly so that all the nations would know that Israel's God was the true and living God. The exodus was seen by biblical writers as the greatest evangelistic event of the Old Testament. Sadly, it fell largely on the deaf ears of the kings and leaders. These city-states were strong, arrogant, and rich. They were blinded by the false security related to their riches and by the greed, profitable oppression, and hedonism of their culture.

The Canaanites were particularly evil and cruel. They were now ripe for judgment. While that was a tragedy for them, it also represented an opportunity for them, if they would but recognize the "I Am" of Israel as the true God.[1] They were in the best position to see the destruction of Egypt's gods and to be confronted with the ultimatum to repent and surrender to Israel's God, in the hope that he might have mercy on them. Some individuals (such as Rahab), and one city-state (the Gibeonites), did accept Israel's God as the true God and sought to make peace. Both were incorporated into the people of God. But the rest sought to crush Israel and suffered the devastating consequence of the annihilation of their people and culture.

The biggest sacrifice Moses made for God was in leading Israel

1. "I Am that I Am" is the covenant name of God that was given to Moses in Exodus 3. It emphasizes his self-existence (aseity) and absolute sovereignty. I will refer to God's covenant name as "I Am" in this chapter because I believe it is more helpful to English speakers than the usual rendering as *Yahweh*.

through this traumatic calling. His biggest problems were never the Canaanites but the unbelief and rebellion of the Israelites. His spiritual babysitting, frustrations, emotional suffering, and stress lasted forty years as he mediated between a holy God and his unfaithful, insulting, and unthankful people. His life was a gift to God's people.

Moses's example prefigured that of Christ and so comes to us as our example. Christ does not call us to retire from the world and quietly wait for our reward. We are on his mission—a mission for all the nations of the earth to find blessing through the covenant of grace. We, like Moses, Jesus, and all other Christians, have a calling to turn away from self-interest and to live out the love before others that we have received from Christ. Would that we could consecrate our lives the way Moses and Christ did! Our time, talents, and money come as part of the package when we enter into God's mission to bless all the peoples of the earth.

A Personal Meeting with "I Am"

Under Moses, a new era of giving was introduced to the new nation. Giving and generosity would now be taught by law. They would display the mercy, wisdom, and justice of God in a tangible, measurable way. But biblical giving never stands on its own *as law*. It starts with a personal meeting with God. Prior to Sinai, the people had never met God or spoken to him. The Lord was a distant memory. God led them to Sinai in order to speak to them directly, personally, and audibly. He did it in a way that would enable them to answer him and to state their intention to keep and renew the covenant. Abraham's, Isaac's, and Jacob's direct experience of God would now be experienced by over 500,000 men, along with their wives and children.

However, God begins with some shuttle diplomacy. His initial words to the people, sent privately through Moses, were gracious words. They were remarkably like the words God had spoken to Abraham, with the addition of a promise that the people would be treasured and would become a whole kingdom of priests (and, thereby, would all have access to him):

You yourselves have seen what I did to the Egyptians, and how I bore you on eagles' wings and brought you to myself. Now therefore, if you will indeed obey my voice and keep my covenant, you shall be my treasured possession among all peoples, for all the earth is mine; and you shall be to me a kingdom of priests and a holy nation. (Ex. 19:4–6)

The people, through their elders, received the message and affirmed to God that they would keep the covenant and do everything the Lord had said. God responded that he would now speak directly with them.

And God did speak audibly to over a million people. He reintroduced himself to them and reminded them of his redeeming love and gracious care for them. He said, "I am the LORD your God, who brought you out of the land of Egypt, out of the land of slavery" (Ex. 20:2). In short, he told them that he had loved them, and then he laid out for them exactly how they were to love him and one another.

We might think that the people would be thrilled to hear from their "long missing" Creator-Savior God. Instead, they were terrified, and they begged God not to speak to them directly but rather through Moses. God agreed and invited Moses to play this role on a permanent basis. As far as we know, God never spoke directly and publicly to all Israel again, until he addressed the crowds when Jesus was baptized.

A Life Given to Giving

Moses agreed to this new position because of his love for the people. As with most ministry commitments, he had only a glimmer of how difficult it would be. It was an often frustrating job. It even reached the point where God considered wiping out all the Israelites and offered to Moses the option of starting over and building a new people from scratch—from *his* children. That would have been much less complicated for Moses. But his zeal for God's reputation and his reluctant but real love for Israel moved him in the Spirit to intercede and to convince God to carry on with these difficult folks.

Moses, like Abraham, was called to live for God's purposes. While he understood something of the stage of redemption on which he was to lead, he clearly looked beyond it. By faith he saw Canaan as an everlasting possession and the people as true priests before God. Like Abraham, Moses knew that somehow this would open doors for all nations to participate in the blessing through Abraham's seed. Moses consecrated all that he had (indeed, his whole life) to this vision and to his immediate task in that vision. He reluctantly but clearly offered himself as a consecrated offering for God's purposes: to love and save a lost world.

We do not have a record of Moses's financial giving, but it is clear that he consecrated himself as well as his family, reputation, lifestyle, wealth, and power to the fulfillment of God's larger promises on earth. In that sense, he was like Abraham. He left his pursuit of security, power, and wealth in order to live for others. Everything that he was and possessed was for them. While we can be sure that he gave a tenth of his possessions as instructed, he did not look upon the other 90 percent as his private possession. It was all used as a resource in the work God called him to do.

By doing so, Moses reflected his greater Lord, Jesus Christ. Messiah is the greater prophet, one "like unto Moses" (see Deut. 18:15–22; 34:10; Acts 7:37), who would bring God's word and salvation to an equally rebellious world. Through our union with Christ, each of us carries on that work as his prophets, priests, and kings, bringing truth, mercy, and the embodiment of God's rule to our circumstances in life. As God sent Moses, so he sent his own Son, Christ. And as God sent Christ, so he sends each of us.

Kingdom Economics 101: Give Us This Day Our Daily Bread

The processional out of Egypt did not travel far before they came to the end of the food they had packed in Egypt. Exodus says, "The whole congregation of the people of Israel grumbled against Moses and Aaron in the wilderness" (Ex. 16:2). They said they wished that God had killed them rather than letting them experience hunger.

They had suffered in Egypt but had a high degree of food security, which was built into Egyptian agriculture. That security was now gone, and it was not clear how they would eat under the rule of "I Am." Rather than asking God, they "tested" him. They complained and threatened mutiny, demanding that he feed them or else sacrifice them in the desert.

In response, God told Moses that he was about to rain bread from heaven (see Ex. 16:4). The people had to pick up a day's portion of bread (manna) each morning. On the sixth day, they were to gather twice the amount and keep half to eat on the Sabbath. This would be a test for each person's heart regarding whether or not they would trust God for food on a daily basis. Some gathered more than they needed, in case God did not supply it the next day. That surplus rotted. But the extra that was gathered on the sixth day kept perfectly so that God's people could eat on the Sabbath.

This event is seen throughout Scripture as a reminder to *both* pray for our daily bread (see Matt. 6:11) and seek to gather it, rather than complaining or accusing God. It also reminded the people that under God's rule it is unnecessary and actually wrong to hoard resources out of fear that God will not provide. Yet it also demonstrated that it is appropriate to gather extra in order to store up properly for our future rest. Perhaps the lesson is that we should save for when we cannot work—but not more than we need.

The details of these self-adjustable portions (see Ex. 16:16–17) are used by the apostle Paul to demonstrate the unique economic equality that love for one another produces. Each Israelite gathered as much of the manna as he needed. Some gathered more, and some less, but when it was measured, it always seemed to divide equally. This detail is applied in 2 Corinthians 8 and 9 to show that God desired starving Jews in Jerusalem not to have "too little" and wealthy Gentiles in Corinth not to have "too much." This profound principle is implemented through the offering that Paul sponsored for the famished Jerusalem saints. It documents that there can be different levels of provision without the evil of "too much" or the evil of "too little." We will revisit this discussion in chapter 9.

Pre-positioned Resources

After God renewed the covenant with his people and gave them the heart of the law, he gave instructions for building the tabernacle and directed Moses to raise the money. So Moses called for gifts and for volunteers to construct a "tent of meeting," where God could dwell with his people.

Providentially, Israel was loaded with materials, treasure, and skilled craftsmen because of their time in Egypt. The craftsmen were trained in the Egyptian decorative arts, and the materials and treasure they had received as they left Egypt were payment for their four hundred years of work. God then poured out his Spirit on the people so that they were powerfully motivated to give generously and serve skillfully in order to advance his kingdom.

The Exodus record emphasizes that this was a completely freewill offering given by willing hearts. The materials needed for the tabernacle were the very kinds of gifts they had received from the Egyptians—gold, silver, precious stones, fine linen, fabrics, and valuable wood. God had "pre-positioned" these resources into their hands because he knew that the tabernacle would need to be built. He provided for his own work by pre-equipping the Israelites with the resources and skills that were needed.

Exodus 35 and 36 describe the exciting process of God's Spirit moving hearts to contribute and motivating artisans to create. Soon there were more than enough materials and workers to complete the tabernacle, and the builders asked Moses to tell the people to stop giving. The wealth and skills that God had provided were more than equal to the need.

Now, as then, *God's call always comes with God's provision.* His provision comes from the wealth and skills that he has already given to individual believers. Christ, even more so than Moses, has fitted the body together so that each member contributes to the building up of the whole.

We shall see this dynamic of Spirit-led giving again at the fundraising for the temple under David and yet again at the founding of the church at Pentecost. In all three instances, the Spirit moves hearts to give for his kingdom. It is faith-building to see God providing the wealth and resources that enable his people to joyfully give to his work. In the era of the Spirit, this becomes the predominant dynamic of all giving: each determines what to give from the wealth and resources that have been given them by God. As Paul says, we were created for these good works, which God prepared for us before the creation of the world (see Eph. 2:10).

Giving as Spiritual Formation under the Law

At Sinai, God began the work of spiritually forming his own people. He gave the law to teach them how to know and obey him, and it included scores of commands about giving, offerings, and sacrifices. Let's review the main features.

The life of a faithful Israelite was characterized by giving. The people received God's blessings and gave back to him and to others. The *NIV Study Bible* has a helpful chart of the five types of offerings in its notes.[2] Offerings were required of the firstfruits of every harvest, of the last fruits of every harvest, for the redemption of all firstborn animals, and for all sins, both intentional and unintentional. There were freewill offerings for ceremonial occasions as well as offerings and gifts that were related to the twelve Old Testament feasts and sacred days.

Taken together, these offerings constituted a holistic teaching strategy regarding the offering of one's resources to the Lord. Making offerings to God was a significant part of the economic life of God's people under the law. It is not surprising that the Old Testament saints found the task of observing all those gifts, offerings, and sacrifices to be challenging but doable.

---

2. See R. Laird Harris and Ronald Youngblood, "Old Testament Sacrifices," in *The NIV Study Bible*, 10th anniversary ed., gen. ed. Kenneth Barker (Grand Rapids: Zondervan, 1995), 149.

Tithes

The most well-known of the laws about giving were the tithe requirements. Tithes were brought each year from the increase of the herds and claimed the first 10 percent of the crops that were harvested (see Deut. 12:1–19; 14:22–29). Leviticus introduces the principle.

> Every tithe of the land, whether of the seed of the land or of the fruit of the trees, is the LORD's; it is holy to the LORD. . . . And every tithe of herds and flocks, every tenth animal of all that pass under the herdsman's staff, shall be holy to the LORD. (Lev. 27:30, 32)

There are several distinctive features of the tithe laws.

The Tithe Was Made Holy by God

Even though the tithes were brought *to* the Lord, the Israelites were not giving from what was theirs. Rather, they were giving (returning) the 10 percent that was already owned by God and that he had entrusted to them. John Kelly concludes that tithing was actually a *rent* that was charged by God—the real owner of the land that was assigned to each Israelite family. This is why landowners were expected to tithe on herds and crops, but Levites or those who became landless were not.[3] To not pay this rent was to steal from God. It was consecrated to God because it was already holy (set apart for God's use) by God himself.

The Tithe Was a Discipling Tool

The reason for the tithe is given in Deuteronomy 14:23: "that you may learn to fear the LORD your God always." It was a means of spiritual formation, even as it provided a living for the Levites (who then tithed on those tithes in order to support the temple priests). Learning to trust God for his provision and thus fearing (revering) him is something that givers still experience today. The command to

---

3. See John Kelly, "The Tithe: Land Rent to God," *Religion & Liberty* 14, no. 4 (July–August 2004): 6–9, cited in Victor V. Claar and Robin J. Klay, *Economics in Christian Perspective: Theory, Policy and Life Choices* (Downers Grove, IL: IVP Academic, 2007), 86.

give proportionally from our wealth while trusting God to supply for us in the future teaches a lesson that all believers need to learn. A tenth was a substantial amount for the Israelites—well beyond spare money, which would not test or refine the heart of a believer.

The Tithe Was Proportional

There were no exceptions or exemptions to the general tithe, unlike options that were offered the poor for presenting sin offerings and sacrifices. Everybody was expected to participate in a proportional way—to give as he had been blessed. This is echoed in the New Testament, when Paul tells believers to set aside offerings in proportion to what they have, not in proportion to what they do not have (see 2 Cor. 8:12).

The Tithe Was Shared with Others in Need

Every three years, the tithe was not taken to the temple (tabernacle) but was stored locally so that it would be available to the Levites, and to the poor and destitute, for three years. There were other laws for assisting the poor, but it is important that the most basic source of giving in Israel included a substantial portion for sustaining the poor.

The tithe was inconsistently but widely practiced during times of Israel's spiritual health—at least at a level where it sustained the tabernacle, the temple, the Levites, and the priests for almost one thousand years. While the tithe was deeply embedded in the Old Testament structure, I will argue that it is no longer required in the New Testament. Today, rather, the tithe challenges us with where to *begin* our stewardship and enables us to compare our giving to the sincerity of the Old Testament saints.

The More Difficult Giving Commands

The tithe was not the most challenging form of giving that God instituted among his people. Those were the laws directed at the landowners and wealthy, which were most widely ignored. Landowners and those with money were to help the poor in at least four unique ways.

Gleaning

Farmers who harvested crops could not pick up any fallen produce but were to allow the poor to come onto their land and "glean" any fallen fruit or crops. The book of Ruth illustrates this provision because the field owner, Boaz, was a godly man (see Ruth 2). Farmers also had to leave the corners of their fields unharvested and allow the poor to harvest them for their own use. They had to allow the poor into their fields to hand-pick ripe crops and eat them, as long as they did not carry any crops out of the field with them. Jesus and his disciples took advantage of this provision in the Gospels (see Matt. 12:1). Finally, every seven years, each farmer was not to plant his field but to leave it fallow. If crops sprung up anyway, they could be eaten by the farmer, the alien, the poor, and the animals (Lev. 25:1–7).

These benefits were regular and ongoing and were in addition to the offerings and tithes offered to the Lord. God's economic system had a visible means of "trickle down" sustenance for those in dire need. This was not a primary provision for workers but a minimal provision for those who were unable to generate income. Yet notice that even this support required recipients to do meaningful and productive work (thoroughly scouring the fields) in exchange for a small living.

Loans

God forbade the charging of interest on loans to other Israelites. Loaning was not, therefore, a profit-making business. It was undertaken because of God's command to show love and loyalty to fellow members of the covenant people. Loans to outsiders could earn interest. All these loans had to be made from real personal wealth and for charitable reasons.

This system gave the poor a *common interest* in the wealth that was held by Israel's more prosperous citizens. The wealthier were to lend it to others to the extent of their need. This was not socialism, much less Marxism, since the lender retained ownership of the property (or money) prior to, during, and after the loan. But heart-motivated compassion was the conduit by which the poor had access to capital. The Old Testament gave an *unconditioned* and divine command to the wealthy to use their wealth to loan to the poor.

Every seven years, all Israelites were required to cancel, without penalty, all unpaid debts (see Deut. 15:1–6). This gracious provision, along with the interest-free nature of the loans, protected the poor from a spiraling mountain of debt. For Israel, this freedom from enslavement to debt reflected the freedom God gave his children when he brought them out of Egypt. Our bankruptcy laws today are an attempt to systematize this provision for our economy.

If a poor man asked for a loan near the end of the seven-year period, the lender could not allow that fact to deter him from making a shorter-term, interest-free loan to him (see Deut. 15:7–11). God anticipated the temptation of self-centered thinking and quoted what the lender might say to himself in an effort to avoid responsibility for making the loan: "Take care lest there be an unworthy thought in your heart and you say, 'The seventh year, the year of release is near,' and your eye look grudgingly on your poor brother, and you give him nothing" (Deut. 15:9).

The emphasis is on the state of the heart—whether it is grudging or generous. The heart, both today and three thousand years ago, is where the battles over money are fought. Generosity is a heart attitude that connects to all our behaviors regarding money.

Release for Indentured Servants

After seven years of service, each Israelite slave had to be *offered* his or her freedom and sent away with a substantial gift (see Deut. 15:12–18). Owners were warned not to withhold this, because (in that economy) the slave provided 200 percent the value of a hired servant. Godly owners were not even to consider it a hardship to release such slaves, since God had released them from Egypt and sent them out laden with treasure.

Foreign slaves were not offered such release. They, presumably, would need to become members of the covenant people in order to benefit from this provision. This involved circumcision and an oath of loyalty to "I Am." Many doubtless did become Jews and discovered a deeper release than they had ever dreamed of. Abraham's non-Jewish slaves and servants all became members of the covenant people and were subject to its wonderful protections. There appears to be nothing similar to this legislation in similar cultures, such as the Code of Hammurabi.

The Recycling of Real Estate

The most far-reaching (and least obeyed) provision was the "Year of Jubilee" (see Lev. 25:8–54). This law had many facets, but its most basic provision was that every fifty years, land must be given back to the descendants of its original owners. It did not matter how the land was lost originally—whether through sickness, laziness, crime, fraud, drought, famine, or lack of offspring. It now had to be restored (redeemed). This provision helped to ensure that there was never a multigenerational, disenfranchised underclass in Israel. It was a failsafe provision if other Mosaic provisions (such as the privilege of redemption [repurchase] of the land by family members) were unsuccessful.

To protect the Jubilee provision, God forbade the selling of land in perpetuity. He claimed ultimate title, reminding the Israelites that they were his tenants. When the Jubilee trumpet sounded, each family and clan was to gather on its ancestral grant and begin again—the poor with a new franchise of life and dignity and the rich on a level playing field with others.

As with all agrarian economies, land was the Israelites' means of sustenance. Without land, there was no way for a person to sustain his family except by servitude. Such servitude was seen by God as something that had to be corrected every seven years, along with a fundamental renewal of land ownership every fifty years. Control of land was the capital of their society. It represented opportunity. God's plan was to provide opportunity and see it redemptively renewed when lost.

This provision seems to be more than just an unattainable ideal to be used as a teaching tool. It was the way that Israel was to actually recycle the opportunity of land ownership. Israel's God was deadly serious about the Jubilee laws. The people's flagrant disregard of these laws, and their oppression of the poor, helped to precipitate the Babylonian captivity.

To be sure, the Year of Jubilee prefigured the reality that God will restore eternal ownership in the everlasting promised land to his people on the last day. He will pay all debts for sin and end all servitude to evil and death. But, while it pointed beyond itself, the Year of Jubilee was meant to renew the opportunity that land owner-ship provided in Israel. It was a tangible down payment and foretaste of the inviolable title that God will grant his people in the everlasting life of his kingdom.

A Jubilee Vision for the USA

The inscription on America's Liberty Bell is God's command to "proclaim liberty throughout the land" (Lev. 25:10). The freedom that the American Revolution promised was largely understood as a freedom of opportunity. Most people migrated to the United States because of economic opportunity, not religious freedom. Freedom from unjust taxation and from serfdom to lords and kings, as well as a free-market economy for all, were the driving forces behind the Revolution. The political and religious freedoms that the colo-nists sought were important to safeguarding economic opportunity. Unfortunately, much of that opportunity came at the expense of Native Americans, who were driven off their land by residents of the new country, and African Americans, who were enslaved as property and held in perpetuity.

Most useable land has now been appropriated in the United States and in most developed nations. Education is now the closest thing we have to free opportunity for our children. It is seen as a means by which the poor may sustain themselves in our manufacturing and information economy. Especially since the early 1900s, it has been hoped that free public education may provide people an open-ended path for upward mobility and development. That seems to have been the case for the middle class, but even after the legal desegregation of schools it has become painfully evident that public education has not produced this effect for most of our low-income urban and Native American families.

Despite the fact that neither we nor the Israelites sustained this ideal, it is significant for us to note how deeply the renewal of oppor-tunity was built into Old Testament economics. It is probably obvi-ous why we do *not* have much debate today about applying the Old

Testament standards that governed the Jubilee laws of Leviticus 25 and Deuteronomy 15. They seem hard to apply in our economy of perpetual ownership and intergenerational wealth and poverty. We shall see, however, that these laws led to a surprising development in the practices of the New Testament church.

How Israel Could End Poverty

In stark contrast to the laws of other nations, the law of God made wonderful provision for those who had become poor, enslaved, bankrupt, or landless to renew their opportunity. God used the strongest language to promise that he would bless the economic and social prosperity of Israel if they obeyed these laws. Moses restated this promise as motivation for the people to grant the release from debts, but he applied it to "all the commands" of the Lord.

> But there will be no poor among you; for the Lord will bless you in the land that the Lord your God is giving you for an inheritance to possess—if only you will strictly obey the voice of the Lord your God, being careful to do all this commandment that I command you today. For the Lord your God will bless you, as he promised you, and you shall lend to many nations, but you shall not borrow, and you shall rule over many nations, but they shall not rule over you. (Deut. 15:4–6)

These blessings on the land and people would substantially end poverty in Israel. If Israel obeyed, not only would they be blessed, but they would be in a position to loan to other nations with interest and to demonstrate the reality of God's blessing. This was to be a witnessing and evangelistic endeavor before the watching world—one that had a profitable byproduct for Israel.

Yet God also knew that, until Messiah would come to rule, Israel would not obey. There would always be a need for those with wealth to lend, release, and restore. The end of poverty would never become systemic in Israel—even though it could have been the case. Therefore God went on to command:

You shall give to him freely, and your heart shall not be grudging when you give to him, because for this the LORD your God will bless you in all your work and in all that you undertake. For there will never cease to be poor in the land. Therefore I command you, "You shall open wide your hand to your brother, to the needy and to the poor, in your land." (Deut. 15:10–11)

Jesus quotes from this passage when he says that "the poor you will have with you always," reflecting on the way that the sin of the people still reigned over their economic life. He is not saying that there is nothing we can do to reduce or eliminate poverty. Even if there is hardship around us and many are poor, Deuteronomy 15:10–11 shows us that individuals who are blessed by God with money can and must lend it to others in order to diminish poverty.

Here is a short list of the main features of economic life under the law of Moses and the functional equivalents that we have in our society, which is so heavily influenced by Old Testament law and Christian ethics.

OLD TESTAMENT	TODAY
Tithes and offerings of crops and animals	Maintenance support for religious workers and facilities
"Freewill" offerings of gold, silver, and commodities	Freewill capital drives for religious facilities
Gleaning and eating in the fields	Emergency food aid of all sorts
Food storehouses in each town for the poor and the Levites	Longer-term food provisions for maintaining the poor

A seven-year cap on indentured servanthood	Short-term unemployment benefits and other support for those who are out of work
Return of ancestral agricultural land every fifty years if it was lost for any reason	Public access to capital markets, for those who have declared bankruptcy, seven years afterward
Release from debts that the debtor is unable to repay every seven years	Bankruptcy relief
Land ownership and ongoing support for childless widows by Levirate marriage (see Deut. 25:5–10)	Social security for widows
Renewal of land	Universal free education, designed to enable anyone to access the economic potential of our culture
Command to love needy neighbors	Charitable giving

Outright gifts of money to the poor were not nearly as prominent in this period of Israel's history as they have become since. Under the law, interest-free loans were the gold standard. Giving alms to the poor through personal donations to those who were begging and through the temple treasury became more prominent in New Testament times as older institutional forms of assistance for the poor came to an end. Some of this changed as a result of the Babylonians, Persians, Greeks, and Romans occupying the land. This made the charitable giving of the new era even more important.

What do all these Mosaic provisions mean for us? After Christ's ascension, the need for so many specific cultural, ethnic, and economic rules were and are largely replaced and fulfilled through the transformed hearts of God's people. They were no longer needed or applicable in the diverse cultures of the Gentile church. In the New Testament, generosity in all its forms is a way we live out the Great Commandment to love one another as God has loved us. However, these Old Testament examples of mutual care and relief still illuminate the principles and values that we are to apply in our love for each other in the New Testament era. We will explore this in chapters 7–9.

Obey God and Get Rich?

This brings us to a question: does God promise to bless the righteous with prosperity and wealth in this life? It seems that he did in the Old Testament, because there is a set of "laws" that impacted Israel's financial welfare both corporately and individually. God promised them protection and prosperity if they obeyed. We saw the positive side of that in Deuteronomy 15. But there is an important negative side, too: destruction, misery, captivity, and death are promised as consequences for persistent and unrepentant disobedience. This dynamic is called the Deuteronomic Principle.

Hear it in Moses's own words.

> See, I have set before you today life and good, death and evil. If you obey the commandments of the LORD your God that I command you today, by loving the LORD your God, by walking in his ways, and by keeping his commandments and his statutes and his rules, then you shall live and multiply, and the LORD your God will bless you in the land that you are entering to take possession of it. But if your heart turns away, and you will not hear, but are drawn away to worship other gods and serve them, I declare to you today, that you shall surely perish. You shall not live long in the land that you are going over the Jordan to enter and possess. I call heaven and

earth to witness against you today, that I have set before you life and
death, blessing and curse. Therefore choose life, that you and your
offspring may live, loving the Lord your God, obeying his voice
and holding fast to him, for he is your life and length of days, that
you may dwell in the land that the Lord swore to your fathers, to
Abraham, to Isaac, and to Jacob, to give them. (Deut. 30:15–20)

Lest there be any thought that such "Deuteronomic obedience"
brought the people righteousness before God himself, this promise
comes against the background of Deuteronomy 9, where God states
in the clearest terms that the people deserved none of God's blessings
(the exodus, manna, water, protection, and so on) because of any
righteousness of theirs before him. That chapter ends with the story of
Moses's interceding for the people for forty days and nights—pleading
with God not to destroy them because it would tarnish his reputation
among the nations. So, for his own name's sake, God determines not
to destroy them but to redeem and save them in a way that reclaims
the righteousness and powerful grace of his name (see vv. 25–29).

In redemptive history, the "default setting" for God's people was
blessing, as God promised unconditionally to Abraham and demonstrated in the exodus (see Ex. 20:2). Yet, as they rested upon this rock-
solid foundation of grace, they were called and required to live the
"Christian life"—one that was rooted in the same repentance and faith
as that of the New Testament saints but was composed of more laws
and ordinances, which embodied and taught the holiness and love of
God to his people. As we have seen, heart-driven obedience to the
moral, ceremonial, and civil laws trained and nurtured the Israelites
to understand who God was, how he saved them, and how they were
to love him and one another.

The apostle Paul reminded the Galatian Christians that, under
Old Testament law, they were like children, under a tutor and subject
to the "elementary principles of the world" until they attained their
full adulthood and inheritance (see Gal. 4:1–3). These elementary, or
elemental, principles of the world are the rewards and punishments
that were tied to law- or ceremony-keeping.

Yet Paul also declared that biblical Deuteronomic law rests on the unconditional Abrahamic promises. Ultimately, blessing will triumph over the curses brought on by sin. Paul emphasized this point when he said that "the law . . . was added because of transgressions" (Gal. 3:19). First came the promise and then the law. Under Moses, the administration of earthly blessings or curses was a spiritual discipline to teach the people about God's holy name.

There was a second reason for the Deuteronomic Principle: God's military protection and earthly blessings were a witness to the nations at that time. Israel's God was to be seen by the world as different from national deities. Moses asked, "What other god has done anything close to this?" (see Deut. 4:32–34). The blessings were to help Israel understand the great privilege they had in having a God who humbled the gods of the nations. He was a God who would march Israel out of Egypt after four hundred years of slavery and destroy its army, which would send a clear message to the nations that the true and living God had chosen Israel to reveal himself and that therefore the nations should seek him there. Other kings did come to see the blessing of God on Abraham, Moses, David, and Solomon.

Yet the flip side was also true. When Israel disobeyed, it sent the wrong message to the nations about their God. If God had continued to bless an immoral people based on tribal loyalty, his holiness would have been impugned. God's discipline of Israel declared to the nations that he was *not* like their national gods. They demanded to be offered food, drink, and forms of assistance, but they were often as immoral as the humans who they dealt with. The biblical God was the only holy God who made moral demands upon his worshippers. He punished his people and even had to turn away from them for a season because of their sin. Just as the blessings of obedience were corporate, so were the judgments—and they were visible at the national level, so that Israel and other nations might fear the Lord.

It was puzzling to Old Testament saints how God would reconcile these seemingly contradictory promises. The New Testament records the resolution of these two poles of promise and law: they were stunningly and exactly fulfilled in Christ. Jesus obeyed the law perfectly as the perfect Prophet, Priest, and King and was therefore justified and exalted to bring us our guaranteed life. But he also absorbed the full impact of the curses for our sin and bore it away in his own body on the cross.

Christ thereby introduced a new order in a kingdom that was ruled through his Spirit. Both the Deuteronomic blessings and the curses are now fulfilled in Christ. Those Old Testament measures were temporary and weak, and they only looked forward to the work of the Anointed One to come. In place of Deuteronomic blessings centered on earthly flourishing, Christ brings us the personal presence of the Holy Spirit—a full revelation of the glory of his coming kingdom—and yet also promises that his Father will always provide the daily bread that his children need in order to complete their walk of salvation on this earth (see Matt. 6:25, 33).

Christ also warns us that in the New Testament age he will not reduce trials or testing in our lives because we are believers. Instead, he will powerfully redeem us amid suffering and loss in order to make us more fully into his image and to advance his kingdom (see Rom. 5:3–5; 8:28). This is prefigured powerfully in the Old Testament through the sufferings of Israel in Egypt, the sufferings of David, the sufferings of the poor and the prophets. Ironically, it is the presence of God in our lives that sometimes generates significant suffering, opposition, and discrimination in the old world system that has yet to pass away. But we have a wealth in the Lord's presence, saving rule, and revealed grace that would make any Old Testament saint envious.

Questions for Review and Reflection

1. While the enslavement of the Israelites by the Egyptians was a great evil, how did God use that time of enslavement to begin to realize the promises he had made to Abraham?
2. How many ways can you recount in which God provided for his people in the wilderness so that they could fulfill the purposes he had spoken to Abraham? Did they ever lack his provision?
3. What were some ways the Old Testament law provided for the renewal of economic opportunity for those who fell upon hard times? Is that relevant to God's people today? How?

4

Kings, Sages, and Prophets

*The wicked borrows but does not pay back, but the righteous
is generous and gives. . . . He is ever lending generously,
and his children become a blessing. (Ps. 37:21, 26)*

We have seen how Abraham viewed himself as holding his possessions
in trust, to be used for God's purposes of blessing all the nations
through his seed. Moses followed Abraham in that faith. The law
was added at Sinai so that Abraham's children could be systematically
discipled into fearing, trusting, and loving their God, and thereby
could grow into a righteous nation for all the world to see. After the
conquest of Canaan, Israel tried but largely failed to live this out.

God granted them the land and every family a place in it. He
continued to dwell with them in a humble tent and sent judges to
rule them and deliver them from enemies. But Israel proved fickle
in its allegiance to the great I Am. During times of faithfulness they
prospered, and during rebellion they suffered, but they never got off
their spiritual roller coaster until David was appointed king. Let's
now consider the financial practices and attitudes reflected by David,
Solomon, and the prophets.

David, the Giver after God's Own Heart

David, Israel's second king, clearly embodied the thesis that God
gives wealth to us in order to fund his work and mission. David was
chosen by God as a king who would display a heart of righteousness—a

heart after God's own heart. He led the people into a golden age of covenantal blessings through his trust in God and his obedience to the covenant. Under David, justice prospered, security was assured, and economic prosperity was the norm.

As a Hebrew king, David was subject to Deuteronomy 17:15–17, which commanded that the kings of Israel should not accumulate gold, silver, wives, and war horses from Egypt. However, David did acquire great wealth from Israel's conquests. Trade developed under his leadership, and God blessed his work wherever he turned. It was what any godly king of Israel might have experienced.

But David did three things that were unheard of in the ancient world. He did not use his wealth to try to expand Israel's empire beyond the boundaries that were set by God. Neither did he appropriate riches for himself nor begin public works that would be memorials to his greatness and power. Any of those three endeavors could have absorbed most of the wealth of a king who was looking for greatness.

God did not forbid David from creating wealth. He actually brought wealth to David through his victories in combat. But God did forbid his kings to accumulate wealth beyond their needed reserves. This is a profound distinction and a principle that holds even today. Christians are to earn money but are not to accumulate it beyond what they need to provide for themselves and their families. We are not to seek wealth—and, when it comes to us through God's blessing, we are not to store the excess for ourselves. We are to see ourselves as God's trustees of those funds. Some will be blessed with great income, and others will reap more sparingly.

David did build an attractive cedar "White House" for himself and his wives, staff, and guard. It was a palace where he could rule in efficiency and beauty, reflecting God's blessing on Israel. But there was a great excess of funds left over. What was David to do with it? His passion was to use the funds so that he could build a house for God—a much larger and more expensive undertaking.

But God reverses David's expectations, telling him that he will not be allowed to build a house (see 1 Chron. 17:4–10). Rather, God talks about the house that *he* will build for David—a house to be built by David's greater Son, who would establish an everlasting kingdom for him. God would, in short, build David's house, not the other way around. He emphasizes to David that since the days of Abraham he has not asked anyone to build him a house. God has been like a migrant, going "from tent to tent and from dwelling to dwelling" (1 Chron. 17:5). He certainly does not need David to build him a house.

He also reveals to David that he will not be allowed to build because he has been a man of war and bloodshed (see 1 Chron. 22:6–10). Instead, God would call David's son Solomon to build the temple. It would be a place where all nations could come to inquire of God.

Though this disappoints him, it does not stop David from saving an enormous amount of gold, silver, wood, and other commodities to assist in the building. He also leads his officers and the people in a visionary "capital campaign" to encourage them to give themselves to the Lord and provide for the temple. He says, "I have provided for the house of my God, so far as I was able" (1 Chron. 29:2); "With great pains I have provided for the house of the LORD" (1 Chron. 22:14). The rich usually give a lot, but from their excess. David gave until it was painful.

In today's economy, David's personal contribution of gold would be about $6 billion. He raises another $10 billion from his leaders. First Chronicles 22:14 reveals the real surprise, as David gives an enormous amount of gold, silver, and other wealth from the national treasury. One calculation of this adds up to $216 billion in gold and silver. The Chronicles narrative declares that the quantities of bronze, iron, and other commodities were too extensive to be weighed. In addition, David paid for tens of thousands of craftsmen to construct the temple. I am certain that this was the largest amount ever raised for one project in the kingdom of God—including the 6.1 billion in today's dollars that are estimated to have been spent on St. Peter's Basilica.[1]

---

1. It is outside the scope of this book to research this carefully, but Wikipedia lists 46.8 million ducats as the cost of St. Peter's construction. A ducat equals about 0.1107 Troy ounces of gold, which in 2018 sells for $1,200 per ounce. That comes to $6.1 billion. See "Specifications" under Wikipedia, s.v. "St. Peter's Basilica," last modified June 4, 2019, 23:20, https://en.wikipedia.org/wiki/St._Peter%27s _Basilica#Specifications. This figure was gleaned from R. A. Scotti, *Basilica: The*

This temple fundraising campaign was the second of two occasions (along with the building of the tabernacle) when God invited large, direct capital gifts. Both offerings were totally voluntary; people were to give joyfully from the heart—a theme that is characteristic of *all* giving in the age of the Spirit. Through both offerings a great abundance was collected—a witness to the startling blessing of God on the people and to his Deuteronomic blessing on their successful economy in particular. It was revolutionary that David emptied his own coffers and those of his nation for this enterprise. He desired God to dwell with his people so that they would have access to his mercy and presence. God wants the nations to recognize and worship the God whose name is "I Am."

David said,

> Yours, O Lord, is the greatness and the power and the glory and the victory and the majesty, for all that is in the heavens and in the earth is yours. Yours is the kingdom, O Lord, and you are exalted as head above all. . . .
>
>   But who am I, and what is my people, that we should be able thus to offer willingly? For all things come from you, and of your own have we given you. For we are strangers before you and sojourners, as all our fathers were. Our days on the earth are like a shadow, and there is no abiding. O Lord our God, all this abundance that we have provided for building you a house for your holy name comes from your hand and is all your own. (1 Chron. 29:11, 14–16)

David was aware that without God's electing love and covenant, he would have nothing. He understood that God had invested his own divine wealth in him, his leaders, and his kingdom so that they could give it back as a joyful offering for God's purposes. David says in 1 Chronicles 29:2 that he had provided all that he was able for the house of the Lord. In other words, David did not ask, "How much do I have to give?" but "How much can I give?" And he gave it. That is the mark of Spirit-driven, cheerful, willing generosity. In verse 18

Splendor and the Scandal; Building St. Peter's (New York: Plume, 2007), 241.

David prays that God will "keep forever such purposes and thoughts in the hearts of your people." He is referring to the attitude he held, that all that he had was God's investment in him to be used for God's work "so far as [he] was able." As we shall see, Paul picks up this theme and makes it central to New Testament giving, expounding on it in 2 Corinthians 9.

David saw himself, as Pastor David Harvey has rightly commented during his speaking ministry, as God's ATM. He was disbursing God's money for God's purposes. Behind all giving is God sharing his wealth *with* his people *for* his people to be able to do his work. Certainly David, without God's investment in him, would not have had $6 billion to give from his personal store, in addition to the more than $200 billion that he gave from the kingdom treasury.

David's prayer shows that God's purposes were central to all that wealth meant to him. Sustaining the lives of himself and his court, or keeping himself in power, were not the purpose or meaning of the money he had been given. He did not keep a great deal of it, compared to the amount that the nation had in its own treasury. What he did save for himself he dedicated to a "palace" for God and felt incredibly blessed to be able to invest in that endeavor.

In Deuteronomy 17:15–17, Israel is told that any king God chooses must not store up wealth for himself. For David, money was given to be used for God's purposes—worship, witness, and edification—and that is where he expended it.

But not all of Israel's kings followed in David's footsteps or took this command from Deuteronomy to heart. David's son Solomon accumulated forbidden foreign wives and great riches while burdening the people with permanent conscripted service and higher and higher taxes. Solomon did not recycle his windfall wealth back into the economy and the lives of the people. In Solomon's mind, money became increasingly money for *him*—his security, glory, influence, and pleasure. Solomon's son Rehoboam put even heavier taxes on the people (see 1 Kings 12:1–15)—a decision that split the kingdom into Israel and Judah. Jeroboam took over as rival king of the northern tribes.

David, however, was not a taker like Solomon or Rehoboam. His giving foreshadowed the giving of his greater son, Jesus. Christ was rich, as the Son of God, but he set aside his privilege, glory, and wealth (see Phil. 2:6–11) in order to come and build us into his temple (see 1 Peter 2:4–5). The sacrifice of his body was, as it were, the "raw material" for the construction of a living temple by the gift of the Holy Spirit.

We are the body of Christ, built into that holy temple of kings and priests (see 1 Peter 2:9) by the Holy Spirit (see Eph. 2:21–22). We too are not to accumulate wealth for ourselves but are to be stewards of it for God's purposes.

Teaching from Ecclesiastes

There is a sense in which Solomon had too much money, as he raised taxes and enslaved sons of Israel. Solomon bypassed the hard military life of his father and experimented with how much meaning and value he could extract from pleasure. Ecclesiastes is the account of Solomon's experimentation with every kind of pleasure, luxury, intellectual and artistic stimulation, and financial success. It looks at life "under the sun," without reference to the values and promises of God. Solomon determined that while earthly blessings are enjoyable, they do not satisfy or give life. They have no lasting meaning or redemptive power. They are "vanity"—empty of power to save the soul.

At the end of his investigation, he writes,

> The end of the matter; all has been heard. Fear God and keep his commandments, for this is the whole duty of man. For God will bring every deed into judgment, with every secret thing, whether good or evil. (Eccl. 12:13–14)

In other words, loving God and neighbor is the overriding purpose of life. Each of us will be judged on that alone, and the outcome will have long-term impact.

We do not have to repeat Solomon's experimentations. We can instead focus on learning to express love and obey Christ's commandments with the wealth, position, and influence we have been granted. Despite this, many of us do what Solomon did. We experiment with life apart from God in order to see for ourselves whether we can find true treasure outside of him. Some, by God's mercy, emerge to find God. Others, sadly, find their life choked out by the deceitfulness of riches (see Matt. 13:22).

Ecclesiastes reminds us that the purpose of money is *not* to fill our lives with meaning. God gives us money so we can meet our necessities, enjoy his provisions without putting our hope in them, and bless others.

Proverbs: Wisdom and Foolishness Regarding Riches

The book of Proverbs also reflects the life and thought of Solomon. While his proverbs form its core, other proverbs from the wise are also included, down to the time of Hezekiah. They provide moral teaching about wisdom—the application of God's commands to life. The book memorializes, in simple, two-line, contrasting or reinforcing verses, principles of wise (good) behavior and attitudes as well as foolish (evil) ones. The foolish are not just ignorant, as the "simple" are; they are those who choose to disregard all that they know to be righteous, loving, truthful, and constructive.[2]

Money is mentioned frequently in Proverbs, and attitudes and behaviors related to money are tied back, ultimately, to the two character types of the wise and the foolish. Therefore, Proverbs contains sayings for both the rich who are wise and the rich who are foolish.

The precepts of Proverbs reflect an ideal life being lived under the rule of God. David and Solomon brought much of the Deuteronomic blessings (see Prov. 22:4; 28:20) to a high-water mark in Israel. Under King David and in the early years of Solomon, Israel was indeed a light to the nations, and it demonstrated its divine wisdom as the true source of peace, prosperity, and stability. David and Solomon's kingdom gives us a foretaste of the final glory and justice of Christ's

---

2. See Duane A. Garrett and Kenneth Laing Harris, "Introduction to Proverbs," in the *ESV Study Bible*, exec. ed. Lane T. Dennis, gen. ed. Wayne Grudem (Wheaton, IL: Crossway, 2008), 1132.

fulfilled kingdom. In that kingdom, righteousness will become fully realized through the fruits of wisdom, and the folly of wickedness will be exposed and punished.

Proverbs is unified in the analysis it offers of the heart: the wise and discerning person has a heart that fears the Lord, and the fool does not. This difference in the way people's hearts are orientated is like a continental divide, which leads all of life to flow in one or the other of these directions. In Proverbs, people's attitudes and behavior regarding money reflect and demonstrate this deep divide between wisdom and foolishness. Wisdom leads to honor, riches, and happiness, while foolishness leads to punishment, misery, and loss.

So what money-related themes in Proverbs directly impact our thesis that the final purpose of money is to bless others? The first theme is that wisdom is the most valued of all possessions. The wise man thus values wisdom above money. He knows that wisdom (not riches) is the door to all other blessings. Proverbs 3:1–20 is a vast catalog of the benefits of acquiring wisdom. Wisdom begins with the fear of the Lord (see Prov. 1:7), heeds the self-disclosure of God (see Prov. 2:5), and equips a person to apply God's will in the specific situations of his or her life. The wise will be content with and obedient to God's purposes and will let God add riches to him or her in his timing (see Prov. 11:28).

The fool (who rejects learning from God) will hasten to get rich (Prov. 23:4; 28:20, 22), will ignore the pleas of the poor (see Prov. 21:13), and will mock and despise them (see Prov. 14:21; 17:5) as well as oppressing them in order to get rich (see Prov. 14:31; 22:16; 28:8). God promises to punish and bankrupt such a person (see Prov. 17:5; 22:16; 28:22). The fool thinks he is pursuing life by following the driving pursuit of money, but he ends up losing it all. We will see how Jesus picks up this theme in the Gospels.

A second related theme in Proverbs is that the wise (the righteous) are always generous. They see their money as a source of generosity to those in need (see Prov. 11:24; 19:17). They do not despise their poor neighbors or ignore their needs; instead, their habitual response is one of generosity, which honors God (see Prov. 14:31) and is motivated by his reward. Fools use their money to pursue their pleasure, but the wise have a "bountiful eye" and share their bread with the poor (Prov. 22:9). Generosity is an outlook on life—a way in which someone sees the world in terms of his or her capacity to help. It involves an eye that scans for how to help, not for ways to get. This is the opposite of the covetous eye that is referred to in the tenth commandment and in Jesus's teachings in Matthew 6:23.

A third theme in Proverbs that is related to money is its command for us to work with patient diligence. Faithful diligence in whatever work we have is taught as being the path to God's blessing and reward (see Prov. 12:27; 13:11). Fools are warned that laziness and indulgence will lead to poverty (see Prov. 10:4; 13:4; 21:17). A heart that is engaged in work will lead the worker to prosper and thus to be able to give or lend to the one who is in need. It is from such resources that the wise are exhorted to "honor the LORD with your wealth and with the firstfruits of all your produce" (Prov. 3:9). While God rewards work, the wise are told not to "toil to acquire wealth" (Prov. 23:4). Wealth is not the purpose of our work. We toil in order to provide for the necessities of life and to give to God and to others in need. This theme is picked up by the apostle Paul in Ephesians 4:28 and Acts 20:35. As we will see, Paul commands Christians to work so that their dependents will not be a burden on the church and so they can give to those who are in need.

These three themes provide a good foundation for us to move forward with our understanding of the biblical theology of money and wealth.

Money and the Prophets

While the wisdom books describe values, attitudes, and practices that flow from the heart of both wisdom and foolishness, the Prophets document it throughout Israel's history. They predict the real-life consequences that would come for Israel, her kings, and her people, and they call the people to new obedience and faith in I Am.

In chapter 3, we outlined the dramatic place that tithing, giving, offering, sacrificing, lending, and releasing capital held in the life of Old Testament believers. The provisions of Mosaic law were extensive and relatively expensive, especially for the wealthy. Of course, that was more than offset by God's promise of more blessing for those who obeyed.

Unfortunately, the people of God (with some exceptions) did not do well with following even the most basic provisions for giving. As a result, God sent dozens of prophets to document their disobedience, idolatry, and oppression and to lay out the cataclysmic consequences if there was no repentance. No repentance was exactly what was forthcoming.

After Solomon, the poor fell into intergenerational poverty and were ruled by an order of rich, self-centered landowners who doubtless sponsored priestly leaders and prophets who would not criticize them. In Amos 4:1–2, the prophet says, "Hear this word, you cows of Bashan . . . who oppress the poor, who crush the needy, who say to your husbands, 'Bring, that we may drink!' The Lord GOD has sworn by his holiness that, behold, the days are coming upon you, when they shall take you away with hooks."

The rich could never bring themselves to give the land back to the poor for the Jubilee or to release their slaves or debtors. It was just too hard to "give" so much away. Occasional offerings and low-value sacrifices were less expensive and therefore more frequently brought, but even these were often offered to local (more convenient) gods instead of to the Lord.

This brings us to the powerful passage in Isaiah 58. There God calls his people to fulfill the vision of Jubilee and release, as outlined in Leviticus 25 and Deuteronomy 15, in their day. In this moving passage, God confronts Israel with their current works, which were a cover for oppression, apathy, and greed. He shows them what true service to the Lord looks like. The passage documents what was wrong, what had to change, and the exalted blessing that would come from the people's faithful service to God.

Note the things that were wrong with their service. They were careful (even zealous) to observe the daily worship aspects of their faith and professed a desire to know God's ways and apply them to their lives (see Isa. 58:2). Their local assemblies seemed to "have it together." Yet while they were fasting, they were oppressing their indentured servants for the sake of their own ease and riches. They were violating the commands of Deuteronomy 15 about the release of slaves and the forgiveness of all debt every seven years. They did not send their servants out with payment, as required by God, but bound them (see Isa. 58:9) to perpetual slavery without hope or compensation and engaged in cruel fighting and hitting (see vv. 3–4). When the slaves cried for justice, they would be defeated in court by the deceit of their owners (see Isa. 59:4), who ended up shedding innocent blood. They covered this disobedience with extreme shows of outward repentance and public demonstrations of fasting and long prayers, thinking that they could please God in this way. They apparently forced their slaves to work on the Sabbath so that the owners could pursue their own economic goals and have a life of ease. Their hearts were mastered by the goal of making and protecting their money, even if doing so meant direct disobedience to the Lord.

In contrast, look at how God describes the "fasting" that he desires. This kind of fasting might have actually cost the people some money.

- The people were to "loose the bonds of wickedness, to undo the straps of the yoke, to let the oppressed go free, and to break every yoke" (Isa. 58:6). The landowners had no desire or intention to free those who served them. They held them captive for their labor, as the Egyptians had done. If the owners were generous, as God had been to Israel, they would have wanted to liberate them from the servitude that resulted from their poverty.
- God said, "Is it not to share your bread with the hungry and bring the homeless poor into your house; when you see the naked, to cover him, and not to hide yourself from your own flesh?" (v. 7). I wonder if these landowners refused to open their farming enterprise to the current poor, homeless, naked Israelites. They could probably make more money by keeping the previous generation of slaves and never letting them go. Thus they had no room in their farms or hearts for the merciful role that indentured servanthood could play in giving the

poor a way to survive and then freeing them to start again. These landowners drove away gleaners and other poor who might feed themselves from their fields in accordance with Mosaic law.

- These Israelites needed a change of heart to compel them to "pour [themselves] out for the hungry and satisfy the desire of the afflicted." God promised that "then shall your light rise in the darkness and your gloom be as the noonday" (v. 10).

The chapter ends with one of the most exalted promises in Scripture: "Then you shall take delight in the LORD, and I will make you ride on the heights of the earth; I will feed you with the heritage of Jacob your father, for the mouth of the LORD has spoken" (v. 14).

Giving Dies a Slow Death in a Restored Israel

Such sin led to captivity in Babylon for seventy years. Then, after the return of a small contingent to Jerusalem, Malachi was sent to again rebuke Judah—not so much for a lack of orthodoxy as for an unwillingness to positively follow God's commands. The people had decided that they were desperate economically and could therefore ignore God's law about tithing. Their stingy giving did not reflect a trust in God to provide for them or a desire to be in relationship with him. To them, the tithe laws were just Jewish window dressing.

In Malachi 3:7 God complains, through the prophet, "From the days of your fathers you have turned aside from my statutes and have not kept them. Return to me, and I will return to you, says the LORD of hosts." The people then ask, "How shall we return?"

Will man rob God? Yet you are robbing me. But you say, "How have we robbed you?" In your tithes and contributions. You are cursed with a curse, for you are robbing me, the whole nation of you. Bring the full tithe into the storehouse, that there may be food in my house. And thereby put me to the test, says the LORD of hosts, if I will not open the windows of heaven for you and pour down for you a blessing until there is no more need. (vv. 8–10)

After being cleansed of overt idolatry, though they had a small rebuilt temple, restored walls, a reconstituted people, and a renewed teaching of the law, Jerusalem was still an insignificant, poor town, that was lost in the vastness of the Persian Empire. God had not yet exalted them as a light to the nations or come to his temple as he had done under Solomon. The people waited a few months but quickly lost hope and drifted into a survival mentality. "Worship degenerated into a listless perpetuation of mere forms, and they no longer took the law seriously."[3]

They sought financial and social security elsewhere. They brought forth corrupt fruit—intermarrying, defrauding widows, oppressing aliens and orphans, cheating laborers of their wages, and discriminating and committing perjury at law. The people withheld tithes and offerings—and even blamed God (see Mal. 3:14). The storerooms of the temple (from which the Levites on duty were to live) were empty. The people offered God what they thought he deserved: the blind, diseased, and lame animals that had little economic value.

God, through the prophet, sarcastically suggests that they try offering these animals to the Persian governor as tax payments and see what kind of response they get (see Mal. 1:8). "Cursed be the cheat who has a male in his flock, and vows it, and yet sacrifices to the Lord what is blemished" (Mal. 1:14). Their hearts were not in their offerings. They saw giving to God as a burden that compromised their economic progress and even their survival.

Yet despite this low point at the end of the Old Testament, God promises to send a messenger (see Mal. 3:1) who will prepare the way for the Lord himself to come and bring in his rule. He will suddenly come to his temple and cleanse it like a fiery furnace, consuming the wicked but becoming a sun of righteousness and healing joy to those who fear him (see Mal. 4:1–2).

That messenger, John the Baptist, did come in AD 27. He called the people to repent from their sin and to turn to the mercy of God. John prepared the way for Jesus, who then came to make an end to

---

3. Herbert Wolf and John H. Stek, *NIV Study Bible* notes (Grand Rapids: Zondervan, 1985), 1423.

the sin of his people and to bring in the rule of the greater kingdom of God.

Lessons Thus Far

Our thesis that money is for giving is reflected in the lives and thinking of all the Old Testament heroes. We have seen that God himself is the original and greatest giver. He gave the Earth and its universe to mankind. After mankind's rebellion and the entry of sin, God did not abandon us in disgust. He called Abraham to leave his comfort and security and to live as an alien in a hostile land so that through him God could give blessing to all nations of the earth. Abraham received blessing so that he could give blessing. Every last one of his sheep, his goats, and even his children were dedicated to pursuing that blessing on his seed and then on the whole world.

God formed a nation from Abraham and met with them at Sinai, speaking to them as he had to Abraham. He gave himself to Israel as "their God" and took them as "his people" in an everlasting covenant relationship of mutual giving, still with a view toward blessing the nations.

The reigns of David and Solomon marked the high point of God's bringing his message to the nations. Royalty from around the world came to see and sample what God was doing in Israel and how they could align themselves with it. David saw all that he had as an investment in that process of proclaiming the glory and greatness of the Lord before the nations.

Sadly, Israel quickly turned from God to enjoying the blessings as theirs alone and attributed the blessings to fabricated false gods who made no demands on them to love God and their neighbors. To fulfill his plans to bless the nations through Abraham, God was forced to discipline his people by cutting them off from the land and putting them back in captivity. But he did so with a view toward preserving a remnant (a shoot from the stump) from which his own Son would come to fulfill the promises singlehandedly.

God never turned away from his purpose of giving. He gave his only Son in order to keep his giving program alive. We can now turn and see how this redemptive program was launched and how it pre-vailed in fulfilling God's commitments to give renewal and blessing to his sinful creatures and, even more dramatically, to transform their character to conform to his own—the original love-motivated Giver.

Questions for Review and Reflection

1. How did David's life demonstrate an attitude of conscious stewardship of his wealth?
2. Why is wisdom described in the Bible as being the most prized possession on earth?
3. Since Christians do not serve under Old Testament economic and civil law, does this increase or decrease their requirement to be generous and help the poor? Why do you think that?

5

Jesus and the Economics of the Heart

*Sell your possessions, and give to the needy. Provide yourselves
with moneybags that do not grow old, with a treasure
in the heavens that does not fail. (Luke 12:33)*

When Christ announced himself to the synagogue at Nazareth, he
quoted an adapted version of Isaiah 61:1–2, saying,

> The Spirit of the Lord is upon me,
>   because he has anointed me
>   to proclaim good news to the poor.
> He has sent me to proclaim liberty to the captives
>   and recovering of sight to the blind,
>   to set at liberty those who are oppressed,
> to proclaim the year of the Lord's favor. (Luke 4:18–19)

Isaiah had announced to Judah and Israel the coming of a radically renewed and powerful "Year of Jubilee" (cf. Lev. 25). It would be
ushered in by the Messiah (the Anointed One) and would offer universal justice and everlasting joy. This good news, as in Leviticus 25,
was for the poor and was to be announced to the poor, but it greatly
expanded the scope of redemption beyond the realm of the financial
to include release, comfort, joy, justice, and righteousness in place of
all despair, ashes, and mourning. It described a renewal of economics,

city building, and trade that would allow the people to feed on the wealth of the nations. It was capped with the promise that the people would be called "priests of the LORD" and "ministers of our God" (Isa. 61:6). The Messiah's Jubilee would be (if you'll excuse the expression) a Jubilee "on steroids."

The "Year of the Lord's Favor" was already the most radical renewal of all the civic institutions in the Old Testament economy. It was the greatest news for the poor and was tied to the greatest redemptive event of the year: the Day of Atonement. On that day, Israel made atonement and received forgiveness for all its sins and was released from punishment. The Jubilee combined spiritual release with economic renewal when slaves, debtors, and the landless were freed, paid, and re-endowed with their portion from God.

It was a liberty so important that it had to be "proclaimed" by trumpet throughout the land. This gave it a clear declarative quality as God's proclamation. Freedom and restoration were not earned but simply given—proclaimed by God himself through the priest.

While the priests had probably proclaimed the Jubilee numerous times since it had been instituted by Moses, it was evidently rarely implemented by those who were to do the releasing. The rich kept the debt, the slaves, and the land for themselves, in direct contradiction to God's command. That amount was just way more than they wanted to give; they loved the money more than God and were not about to let go of such a substantial part of it. By the time of Jesus, almost all Jews had lost their land to a small group of rich and powerful landowners. It was for this landowning group that average Jews worked, as tenant farmers or in some form of indentured service (or even slavery).[1]

After Jesus read Isaiah, he sat down (probably in the teacher's chair) and said, "Today this Scripture has been fulfilled in your hearing" (Luke 4:21). His hearers were familiar with the "year of the Lord's favor" described in Isaiah 61:1–2, so his announcement was a bombshell.

---

1. See Craig L. Blomberg, *Neither Poverty nor Riches: A Biblical Theology of Possessions*, New Studies in Biblical Theology 7 (Downers Grove, IL: InterVarsity Press, 1999), 87–89.

The audience in Nazareth would have understood that Jesus was announcing the almost unimaginable Jubilee that Isaiah had predicted. And he would do more than make empty announcements like the priests in Jerusalem—the Messiah's Jubilee had arrived! Jesus would signify his authority to bring in this kingdom, both by the power of the Spirit upon him and by the signs of the kingdom that he performed. The messianic Son of God would actually bring in the Year of the Lord's Favor.[2] Jesus immediately began an intense healing and teaching ministry, proclaiming the good news to the poor and healing many.

His commands were the ethics of this new Jubilee kingdom—the fulfillment of the law. In his kingdom, his subjects were to love one another as he had loved them. They were to give as he gave—and he laid down his life as a ransom for many. They were to live for others, as he lived, with the Spirit that he would give them. They would continue to spread the teaching and acts of Jesus and would announce to the world the Year of the Lord's Favor. Within three years, they would invite all nations to reclaim their lost inheritance in God.

Jesus's commandments fulfill but do not destroy the law. The law is focused, reformed, and empowered for the age of the Spirit under the terms of the new covenant. The scaffolding of the ceremonial, civic, and ethnic law falls away, revealing the essential glory of a kingdom ruled by Jesus Christ. It brings all the blessings of the old covenant to a higher level of fulfillment—one that is laden with the fuller weight of the glory of God's grace, presence, and transforming power.

Where Is Your Treasure?

Money figures prominently in Jesus's teaching. In fact, Jesus has more to say about money-related issues than about any other topic. Matthew 6 is a good place to begin.

Do not lay up for yourselves treasures on earth, where moth and rust destroy and where thieves break in and steal, but lay up for

---

2. See N. T. Wright, *Jesus and the Victory of God*, Christian Origins and the Questions of God 2 (Minneapolis: Fortress Press, 1996), 294–95.

yourselves treasures in heaven, where neither moth nor rust destroys and where thieves do not break in and steal. For where your treasure is, there your heart will be also. (vv. 19–21)

Jesus commands his followers not to lay up treasures on earth but to invest them in the newly arrived kingdom of God. It has been well said that "we cannot take our treasure with us, but we can send it ahead." We store up our treasures in the heavenly kingdom by giving them to advance that kingdom on earth. We do this by obeying Christ's rule—dedicating our time, talents, and treasure to assist the needy, publish the good news, and love our neighbors.

This seems to be a direct development of Proverbs 19:17, which expounds the ideal ethics of the kingdom:[3] "Whoever is generous to the poor lends to the LORD, and he will repay him for his deed." Jesus pleads with and commands those with riches to give and lend to the poor, as a way of investing with God. God, as it were, keeps a ledger of debts; and when we give to the poor, God puts it on his ledger to repay. His people were not permitted in the Old Testament to charge interest, because it is God who will repay with interest—and much more.[4] The investments we make are also secure with God—so those in his kingdom should invest for the age to come.

Whether or not people invest in such a wise way is not a matter of intelligence but one of wisdom and love. If someone's heart (and therefore treasure) is in this age, he or she will not send it ahead to the next. It will be lost forever, and the person will end as a fool. Yet if someone's treasure (and therefore the love of his or her heart) is not in this current earthly economy but in the work of the future kingdom, he or she will invest there, gaining everlasting security and an extravagant rate of return when the kingdom becomes visible and fulfilled.

This is like the decision a Confederate soldier would face if, having just been defeated and wounded at the Battle of Gettysburg, he

---

3. See chapter 4 for a discussion of this perspective in Proverbs.

4. See Gary A. Anderson's excellent work, *Charity: The Place of the Poor in the Biblical Tradition* (New Haven, CT: Yale University Press, 2013). He shows the considerable buildup of inter-testamental rabbinic teaching that he believes can be traced to this proverb, so that when Jesus mentions this topic it is not new to his hearers.

found in his retreat a stash of US money on a fallen Union soldier. After taking the money, should he exchange it for Confederate money to use in the future, victorious South? Or should he save it because he sees that the Confederates will lose not only Gettysburg but the entire war? In the same way, through Christ's death and resurrection, we realize that Satan's rule has been broken and he will lose. But we are still tempted to hold on to our present world's currency instead of trading it for what will last into the future.

Jesus gives us a very elementary choice. Our hearts will be located where our treasure is located. If our treasure is not in heaven, our hearts will not be there. We will not have loved God with all our hearts.

Back to the Civil War for another illustration. Both Confederate and Union officers faced a stark choice at the outbreak of the Civil War. Which side would they fight for? Most officers chose to fight for the side where they owned land and were raising their families— General Robert E. Lee's decision, for example, was based on his loyalty to Virginia, where he lived as a citizen. In the same way, we can intellectually agree with Jesus about money, but our ultimate loyalty to either God or money is based on where our treasure is. Just as Lee could not serve both sides, neither can we serve God and money.

This is a much more basic consideration than whether or not the rich should give 10 percent of their income. Jesus bypasses behavioral formulas in order to address what we treasure. As we have seen, tithing was an Old Testament practice designed to teach the Israelites to fear and serve God. It was a healthy spiritual discipline in the age prior to the coming of the Spirit. While Jesus accepts the tithe of those who practice it and says that they should continue, he also reveals that strict tithers can be just as deluded about who they serve and what they love as people are who do not tithe at all.

By addressing the issue of what our hearts love (see Matt. 6:24), Jesus addresses the value that we place on money *per se*, from our first dollar to our last. The direction of our hearts shows up most clearly when it applies to funds that we "store up." When someone is struggling with the basic expenses of life and has no earthly treasure (net worth) or is in debt, he won't be thinking about what to do with accumulated wealth. This teaching is aimed in particular at the rich.

To rephrase Jesus's command: Rather than accumulating unneeded wealth, you should envision a different goal for your money. Because you love God, the goal of your financial plan should be to maximize what you can give to kingdom work—to God's people, his mission, and the needy. As you work and God blesses you with wealth, you will be blessed to give even more of it to the kingdom. As a byproduct of your love for God, you will become rich toward him and have a recession-proof investment in true riches that will be reserved in heaven for you.

This financial plan has no appeal for those whose hearts are set on money itself and on what it will buy in this life. Such investors do not put their hope (or funds) in a future city that God is building. Unlike Abraham, Moses, and David, they will not invest their current net worth in that future city. For people who serve money, investments need to provide a return during their lives, or perhaps the lives of their children.

Jesus calls his followers to lay up equity in God's ongoing, real-time kingdom. The Spirit has moved many to plan with this as their financial goal, but such investments are made only because God's kingdom is what their hearts treasure.

Most of us who are disciples of Jesus begin small in this area of generosity and grow from there. Growth in such love is possible because our investment in God's kingdom increases our hearts' attachment to that treasure. If our giving is motivated by a love for God, even a simple tithe can set off a cycle of growth in how much we treasure God and his kingdom.

The Inherent Deceitfulness of Coveting

Matthew 6:22–24 leads us to consider the implications of what we treasure.

> The eye is the lamp of the body. So, if your eye is healthy, your whole body will be full of light, but if your eye is bad, your whole body will be full of darkness. If then the light in you is darkness, how great is the darkness!

No one can serve two masters, for either he will hate the one and love the other, or he will be devoted to the one and despise the other. You cannot serve God and money.

Here Jesus uses another metaphor to illustrate the holistic claim that either God or money has on our souls. I believe he is referencing the tenth commandment: "You shall not covet your neighbor's house"—or wife, servant, and so on (Ex. 20:17). A coveting eye is a *bad* eye—it cannot see what is really there. It sees only darkness. Jesus is saying that the spiritually blind cannot see the reality of God's eternal kingdom. Wealth-induced blindness, he says, is the most intractable darkness. In Scripture, wealth and the desire for it are the most common sources of spiritual and moral blindness (see Matt. 13:22). Just as the blind man can only feel what is in front of him, so the one who serves money cannot see God's new kingdom.

Through the light shed by Christ, we can see, engage, and serve the values of God's coming new order. We can, like Abraham, look for a different city—one whose builder and maker is God. The Spirit gradually opens our blind eyes to the dazzling majesty of God's power and character, which is seen supremely in his Son and his redemptive purposes for the world.

Jesus extends the metaphor by pointing out that a good eye fills the entire body with light. A bad eye is just one organ, and yet it darkens everything. I remember the first time I visited a limestone cave in Tennessee. The highlight of the tour was the moment when we turned off all the lights and experienced total darkness. No adjustment to the dark did any good. It was still as completely black as soot. If those who are pursuing money are now in total darkness, how lost will they be when the true darkness comes?

The rich man who refused to give Lazarus the crumbs from his table was oblivious to the issues that Lazarus presented by being there at his doorway (see Luke 16:19–25). He was already blinded to the realities of life. There was Lazarus, needy and hungry, but the rich man ignored him in order to pursue his pleasures. When both men died, the tables were turned. The rich man was now needy. In agony he asked Abraham to send Lazarus to minister to him. With poetic reciprocal justice, the rich man's need was treated the same way that he had dealt with Lazarus. Lazarus would not come to him. The once rich man then begged Abraham to send Lazarus back to tell his brothers to love their neighbors, but Abraham informed him that they must listen to Moses—that that should be enough. Jesus states that even if someone rose from the dead to warn spiritually blind people, it would not convince them. That is the measure of their blindness.

Treasuring, knowing, and serving God are mutually exclusive with treasuring, knowing, and serving the blessings of the world. Each is a master that requires devotion. If we love and serve one, we will hate and repudiate the other. Jesus ends Matthew 6:24 with this startling summary: "You cannot serve God and money."

Jesus did much to demonstrate and authenticate the coming rule of God, but the Pharisees, the rich, the rulers, and the "wannabes" were blind to it. He granted forgiveness of sins, fed the hungry, turned water into wine, cast out demons, healed the sick, gave sight to the blind, restored the disabled, and raised at least three people from the dead. Some of the covetous heard Jesus and repented (such as Matthew and Zacchaeus), but most just ignored his claims. His claims didn't fit their life plan. Jesus's engagement with them drove them deeper into their spiritual blindness.

Finally he gave them the sign of Jonah—a sign so unassailably miraculous that any neutral investigator would have to grant it. Jesus was raised from the dead in a glorious body, thereby living under the laws of the new creation. He appeared to many as a means of assuring that he was indisputably the author and ruler of the new, everlasting kingdom. Before he left, he gave the gift of the Spirit to empower this good news to extend to the ends of the earth and to quench the deep darkness in our selfish hearts.

How Judaism "Eliminated the Middle Man"

N. T. Wright has masterfully documented why the religious establishment was enraged at Jesus.[5] When God arrived to rule and restore

5. See Wright, *Jesus and the Victory of God*, 383–439.

Israel, to bring back the exiles and the Gentiles, he threatened every institution that the establishment had co-opted for their purposes. They were quite willing to sacrifice others, the poor, and even Jesus in order to stay in control. Jesus announced the end of temple, city, and people unless they repented and joined his kingdom—but how great was their darkness!

The Babylonian captivity and the ministry of the prophets had purified Israel from active service to identified pagan gods. But without a change of heart within the worshipers, monotheism simply eliminated the middle man (the external idol) from the transaction. Now the Jews went directly to serving the acquisition of money, crops, cattle, and land. First-century Jews were blind to the idolatry of their quest to gain security in material things rather than in God. Wright comments, "Family and property were sustaining Jesus' contemporaries in an idolatrous pursuit, in a quest they could not hope to win."[6] Those who held property had invested the institutions of Judaism with a quasi-divine status, which they relied on for life.

Living to Have Money

In Matthew 6:19–24, Jesus identifies two characteristics of those who serve money or what it will buy. The first is that they seek and accumulate (lay up) treasures; the second is that they are anxious about losing them. Most of us are tempted by both. They are two sides of the same coin.

The first characteristic Jesus identifies is a controlling commitment to seek, acquire, or hold on to money. Those with this characteristic view wealth not as a by-product of their gifts, labor, or capital, but as the purpose itself. Having money takes over as their master. They have no interest in serving their neighbors through their labor or blessing others with their money. They are interested only in having money.

The Jews of Jesus's day had banished formal idolatry; but for them, money became Mammon—personalized as a god. Covetousness was a new, veiled idolatry. Jesus, as the Son of God, reinstated all

6. Wright, 405.

the warnings of the Old Testament prophets about seeking riches rather than God. But the Jews of that day, like their forebears, rejected Jesus's message and brought upon themselves the end of the temple in AD 70 and the destruction of Jerusalem.

Of course, this issue did not go away with Rome's destruction of Jerusalem. Jesus was addressing a fundamental issue for every human who has ever lived. We all ask, "Where will I find life?" As sinners, our default mode is not to trust God to provide life and not to know him as life. Our instinct is to rely on the resources of this world. Those who are well-positioned to achieve riches often decide that this is exactly what they will do.

Billions of dollars are made through showing folks how to get rich. The first book I read on real estate investment was entitled, *How to Make $1,000,000 in Real Estate in Three Years with No Cash Down.* There was no mention of the risks involved and nothing about how to provide good service for tenants or buyers. Hundreds of thousands of people have been suckered by this gospel, only to make the authors of the books and seminars rich.

Such schemes *are* a gospel. For some motivational speakers and writers, such as Napoleon Hill, the worship of Mammon is obvious. Through his now classic book, *Think and Grow Rich*, he popularized this attitude for rich wannabes. He wrote, "Every human being who reaches the age of understanding of the purpose of money wishes for it. Wishing will not bring riches. But desiring riches with a state of mind that becomes an obsession . . . and backing those plans with persistence which does not recognize failure will bring riches."[7] Hill then proceeded to construct a substitute religion complete with faith, daily devotions, and meditation—all in the service of the attainment of riches. His work is widely used even today in sales and motivational contexts to convince workers, franchisers, and salespeople that if they just believe, they can attain great riches. Nowhere is there any discussion about whether that is a worthy goal. It is assumed.

7. Napoleon Hill, *Think and Grow Rich* (N. Hollywood, CA: Wilshire Book Co., 1966), 35.

Perhaps Hill has done us a service by helping to expose the radical (heart) worship and religious character intrinsic to a commitment to become wealthy. He urges his disciples to serve their mental image of success in what they think, do, and believe. In this sense, he agrees with Jesus that one cannot serve God and money. He emphasizes that you must desire to become rich more than anything else, or you will most likely fail.

Such in-your-face greed blows away the fog of human ambivalence and reinforces the clear alternatives that Jesus presents. We cannot serve money and at the same time serve God. We will serve one and (by comparison) hate the other. What (or who) we choose to value as our source of meaning, worth, and security is our true god—regardless of our church attendance and religious profession.

A Sin for the Not-So-Rich

However, not all financial idolatry is related to a desire for riches. Jesus goes on to address another issue related to money: worry and anxiety. We worry about losing our money or about having enough for our survival.

Jesus says,

> Therefore I tell you, do not be anxious about your life, what you will eat or what you will drink, nor about your body, what you will put on. Is not life more than food, and the body more than clothing? Look at the birds of the air: they neither sow nor reap nor gather into barns, and yet your heavenly Father feeds them. Are you not of more value than they? And which of you by being anxious can add a single hour to his span of life? And why are you anxious about clothing? Consider the lilies of the field, how they grow: they neither toil nor spin, yet I tell you, even Solomon in all his glory was not arrayed like one of these. But if God so clothes the grass of the field, which today is alive and tomorrow is thrown into the oven, will he not much more clothe you, O you of little faith? Therefore do not be anxious, saying, "What shall we eat?" or "What shall we drink?" or "What shall we wear?" For the Gentiles seek after all these things,

and your heavenly Father knows that you need them all. But seek first the kingdom of God and his righteousness, and all these things will be added to you.

Therefore do not be anxious about tomorrow, for tomorrow will be anxious for itself. Sufficient for the day is its own trouble. (Matt. 6:25–34)

In Luke 12:15 Jesus says, in a similar vein, "One's life does not consist in the abundance of his possessions." The lesson is not only that we must trust the Father, who feeds the birds and brings forth the lilies, because he demonstrates his care to us, but also that our lives do not consist in material provisions anyway but in this very act of relationship with and trust in our Father.

According to Jesus, trust in the Father is not a means of obtaining food, children, or security. That was the unsuccessful (and idolatrous) bargain that people had with the pagan gods. Our lives, as believers, consist in enjoying relationship with God and his righteousness (his character being worked out in our lives). In him alone we find true life—a life that is higher and truer than food, adornments, and possessions can provide.

Yet this does not lead to asceticism or to a renunciation of the needs of the body. Jesus is quick to point out that the Father knows that our bodies need daily provisions. He invites us to ask him for daily bread and promises to supply us with enough—enough for us to fulfill his purposes for us and to find true and eternal life.

For some (such as most American evangelicals today), that will mean significant wealth. For others, it will mean suffering the hardship of having little in terms of food, clothes, or security. Though horrible losses may occur, our answer to anxiety about our earthly future is to trust in the Father himself and in his gracious, sovereign plan and promise to redeem us.

Jesus is not offering us a better way to get whatever earthly resources we want. This is not a "name it and claim it" program. He is offering us the option of living in relationship with him—which makes worry unnecessary, wrong, and destructive. It puts us at ease because we are in the hands of One who cares about us and will give us the resources that we need to make it home to him and the grace to bear whatever losses we experience.

Mammon for the Worrier

There is a connection between the two parts of Jesus's teaching in Matthew 6. Verses 19–24 require us to choose between God and Mammon in the face of our urge to accumulate assets for the future. Verses 28–34 require us to trust in God for daily provision in the face of our anxiety over lack of resources. Very often the two struggles exist within the same person.

Accumulating money and worrying about money both demonstrate a servitude to Mammon instead of to God. A poor person can hoard two coats and allow a family member to be cold. A rich person can spend all his waking hours worrying about the loss of his money.

Timothy Keller reflects on this idolatrous instinct when he writes, "Sin leads every person to reject God as our only source of meaning, security, and worth. If we reject God, our hearts must constantly manufacture *idols*—persons, relationships, objects, and conditions which we believe will give us fulfillment. We believe that these things, these conditions, will bring us the meaning, security, and worth we desire. The motivation, the drive toward these false goals is dreadfully strong. It is *worship!* We feel we must have these idols or we will die. These drives are called in the Bible the 'lusts of the flesh.'"[8]

An idolatrous relation with something often reveals itself when we think about losing that thing or are in the process of losing it. A deep anxiety, or even desperation, surfaces because we think we are losing our very lives. This often results in various forms of murder, deceit, betrayal, abandonment, and theft being carried out by those who feel so threatened. If we are better behaved than that, we just let the anxiety eat away at our insides, sapping the energy and perspective we need in order to address the problems that occasioned the anxiety.

We can see at this juncture that Jesus's teaching has a far-reaching

---

8. Timothy Keller, *Ministries of Mercy: The Call of the Jericho Road*, 3rd ed. (Phillipsburg, NJ: P&R Publishing, 2015), 49.

scope. It is not just the 5 percent of the US population whom we call "rich" that can be deceived. While the rich and the poor both have some special temptations and problems, we can all be deceived in one or more of the following ways:

SITUATION	TEMPTATION
We have very little money and long for more.	We dream about money and visualize having it.
We are poor and have given up any hope of legally obtaining money, and therefore do not consider ourselves truly alive.	We are tempted to "curse God and die." Others of us give up and consign ourselves and our children to intergenerational poverty. Efforts to climb out of poverty are easily overwhelmed; it is easier not to hope and just to exist.
We are poor or middle class and can't expect to be rich, but we still believe that life is found in what money buys.	We seek money illegally or foolishly, through crime, gambling, fraud, or inappropriate high-risk investments. We are those most often taken in by network marketing and Ponzi schemes that promise riches to anyone who pays the promoter. Some succumb to "name it and claim it" promotions and phone scams that offer 1,000 percent returns or free vacations.

We had money, but we lost it or it was taken away.	We are bitter and struggling. We still want the American Dream, but we have awakened from it to face the nightmare that we will never achieve it.
We used to be poor, but now we have achieved the upscale American Dream.	We are more terrified than ever that we may lose what we've gained and return to the suffering of our past.[9]
We are clutching what modest means we do possess.	We are anxious.
We are one of a few who have more money than can be spent in a lifetime.	We continue to accumulate money because of insecurity about losing it. We do not give proportionally

The rich, the poor, and the middle class alike—in other words, all of us—can be spiritually captured by money and by our desire for what it offers. We all need the challenges and promises that Jesus offers us in the area of money. He stands ready to disciple us in kingdom values and kingdom life.

9. I remember hearing an NBA player from a very poor, inner-city background comment that his fear of not having enough was easy to handle compared to the terror of losing the money that he now had.

Selling Possessions:
The Challenge for the Affluent

Having considered our heart attachment to our money and possessions, let's now look at how we use them.

Jesus says in Luke 12:32–33, "Fear not, little flock, for it is your Father's good pleasure to give you the kingdom. Sell your possessions, and give to the needy. Provide yourselves with moneybags that do not grow old, with a treasure in the heavens that does not fail." Here is more detail about how to be rich toward God and lay up treasures in heaven. In typical covenant fashion, Jesus precedes his command with a reminder that each of his people has received a kingdom that the Father is pleased to give them. There is a sense of the delight of a father who is giving a gift to his children. In view of that gift, Jesus exhorts his disciples to sell their possessions and give to the poor.

John the Baptist sent the first shot across the bow when he announced the nature of the coming kingdom. In Luke 3:8, when John introduced the coming Messiah, he told his listeners, "Bear fruits in keeping with repentance." When the people asked what they ought to do, he replied, "Whoever has two tunics is to share with him who has none, and whoever has food is to do likewise" (v. 11). This rather extreme wording highlighted how much more this command applied to those who had many tunics, abundant food, houses, fields, and accumulated wealth. Giving and sharing were the primary financial responses to the coming of the kingdom that John was announcing.

This is a direct command to all Christ-followers—first to evaluate what we do and do not need (in order to meet our own needs and those of our businesses), and then to understand that God's purpose in giving us extra assets is so that we might give them to others who are in need of relief or the gospel. The progressive giving formula "Give as God has prospered you" is retained by modern Christian teaching, but against a biblical background it has a much more challenging meaning than we tend to give it today. In a biblical context it means that anything that is not needed by you, your family, or your business has been given to you so you can give it to others in the right season and circumstances.

Unlike the legislation in the Old Testament (such as Leviticus 25 and Deuteronomy 15) we are not given a lot of detail as to how this giving should be done. That lack of detail is significant. Christ came to bring in a new order, in which giving would be done not because of old covenant legislation but because of the motivation of the Spirit of God. Those who would follow him and who had more assets than they needed for their own sustenance were to use those assets to help the needy. This, of course, required some planning and effort on the part of the wealthy donors. While Jesus presupposes that there is a means of distributing these funds strategically, he emphasizes the blessing to the donors more than to the beneficiaries.

There is no reason to believe that Jesus's disciples were not allowed to own clothing, farmland, herds, businesses, or homes. Jesus was clearly not commanding them here to take a vow of voluntary poverty or of communal ownership; he was commanding them to be generous. Vows of poverty or communal ownership are never commanded in Scripture. Monastic orders proliferated and accomplished much good in the history of the church—but there were some cases in which monks lived like kings in communally owned monasteries and businesses.

In biblical ethics, an abundance of resources is a providential blessing from God for the sake of those in need. "To whom much is given, much is required" (see Luke 12:48). So it was natural for John and Jesus to command those who were blessed to understand *why* they were so blessed and to share what they had, out of love for those around them who had specific needs.

While selling possessions was to be a universal Christian practice, leaving everything and following Jesus (in full-time vocational ministry) was not universal. The apostles were called that way, along with the rich young ruler of Matthew 19:16–22. This rich young man ignorantly thought he had kept all that God had commanded. We can presume that his life included consistent tithing. Jesus had compassion on this young man and called him to become one of his traveling disciples, but he required him to liquidate all his wealth and give it to the poor. The rich young man struggled and was deeply saddened. It was just too much to let go of. His love for his possessions caused him to turn his heart away from God, never to return. He treasured money more than God and what God was going to do through Jesus to save the world. Abraham, Moses, and David dedicated all that they had to the kingdom, but this young man could not.

Yet Jesus both allowed and commanded most of those whom he reached to go home. Zacchaeus repaid, four times over, all those he had extorted and gave half of his assets to the poor—but he kept the rest of his money and continued his business, without cheating people. Jesus did not challenge this but rejoiced that he had entered the kingdom of God. Jesus knew that Zacchaeus would continue to practice generosity with whatever resources exceeded his needs. The lesson here is that when your heart changes, generosity will follow, whether or not you enter ministry as a vocation.

The Christian practice of selling possessions is relevant to each of us, and we must apply it to our own situations. We will see this language again in Acts 2:45 and 4:34 as those who had wealth sold their assets as needs arose in their early church community.

Inheritance and Windfall Wealth

In Luke 12, a man asked Jesus to arbitrate a dispute over an inheritance—probably one involving land. He was so consumed with getting his share that he interrupted Jesus during the Sermon on the Mount! He wanted Jesus to enforce the terms of the inheritance; he was not looking for direction on how to respond to the situation in a godly way.

Jesus noted that he had not been appointed a judge between the man and his brother—but he had something much more important to tell them (and us). Luke writes,

> Someone in the crowd said to him, "Teacher, tell my brother to divide the inheritance with me." But he said to him, "Man, who made me a judge or arbitrator over you?" And he said to them, "Take care, and be on your guard against all covetousness, for one's life does not consist in the abundance of his possessions." And he told them a parable, saying, "The land of a rich man produced plentifully, and

he thought to himself, 'What shall I do, for I have nowhere to store my crops?' And he said, 'I will do this: I will tear down my barns and build larger ones, and there I will store all my grain and my goods. And I will say to my soul, "Soul, you have ample goods laid up for many years; relax, eat, drink, be merry."' But God said to him, 'Fool! This night your soul is required of you, and the things you have prepared, whose will they be?' So is the one who lays up treasure for himself and is not rich toward God." (Luke 12:13–21)

Jesus tells us that the man in the parable was already relatively well-to-do, when he suddenly harvested a bumper crop that was beyond his wildest dreams and did not have adequate space to store it. We overhear the conversation that the farmer had with himself at this financial crossroads. He was already wealthy; this crop would put him over the top. If he stored it to sell over a period of years in order to get the best price, it would support him for the rest of his life. There would be no need for him to work again.

So he asks himself, "What should I do?" Theoretically, he could have continued to work and used his profits to help the poor and improve his community. Or he could have taken an early retirement in order to serve God's people without pay for the rest of his life. Instead, he decided to build more barns, store the crops, and live the good life.

These kinds of conversations often take place in our inner thoughts. We do not share them, out of concern for appearances or perhaps out of fear that others' opinions will contradict our cherished plans. We want to do what we want, without interference.

The farmer may have considered whether he had any obligation to the poor under the Torah, but if he had always tithed and paid his temple taxes and offerings, then God had already gotten his share. Besides, he may have thought, he had employed hundreds of (low-wage) workers for many years. How could he be faulted for not helping the poor with his windfall funds?

He'd also earned it fair and square. He had no guilt over it. He had worked hard for years, and if anyone deserved it, he did! If he was ever to really live, he had better do it now.

So he made his fateful decision. Immediately God said to him,

"You fool! This very night your life will be required of you." He died, before he could build his barns, and was face-to-face with God. Jesus adds, "This is how it will be with anyone who stores up things for himself and is not rich toward God." The farmer died never knowing the purpose for the blessings that God had given him.

Jesus tells this story to warn *everyone* of covetousness. My guess is that the farmer coveted the rest, refinement, and leisure that his wealthy friends had. This was his chance to join them. This vision for the future possessed his soul and seduced him into a completely foolish decision.

The story concludes with the farmer's death, his loss of his worldly wealth, and his entry into eternal poverty in the next life. He would be joining the rich man from the story of Lazarus the beggar (see Luke 16:19–31). Jesus warns, "So is it with the one who lays up treasure for himself and is not rich toward God."

The sin here was apparently not a lack of tithing, or of external observation of the law, but rather a heart love for the good life and a commitment to use windfall funds to make it happen without regard for the greater, eternal good that could have been done with them in the kingdom of God. Many of us will face similar situations. Let me illustrate with two stories.

A Wise Man in Corporate America

I have a friend in his late fifties whose company offered him a very lucrative buyout of his upper management position. It was sufficient for him to retire and never work again. He was an active elder in his church and was committed to the Lord's work, so he had substantial ministry experience. Moreover, he was tired of the executive rat race and definitely enjoyed some hobbies, traveling, and hunting.

After he and his wife prayed about and discussed it, they decided to take the buyout, go to seminary, and devote the rest of their lives to ministry. God richly blessed that decision and has used my friend in critical roles in at least four ministries. He has lived modestly since that day, but he is rich toward his Father in heaven and rich for the many who will thank him for helping them into the kingdom.

There are thousands of wealthy, powerful, and famous people who have heard Jesus's warning and responded in faith. I have mentioned R. G. LeTourneau (LeTourneau Technologies), Art DeMoss (National Liberty Insurance Co.), Tony Rossi (Tropicana Orange Juice), and J. Howard Pew (Sunoco Oil Company), who made lots of money but sought first the kingdom of God. Even for those of us with only moderate wealth, our hearts' attitude toward money will be what shapes our economic planning.

The parable of the rich fool reminds me of a churchgoing, multi-millionaire investor who commented on his wife's enthusiasm for God. With a satisfied smile and a twinkle in his eye, he told a friend, "I am taking care of things in this life, and my wife is in charge of the next." He was trying to justify the fact that he largely ignored God, while also praising the success he'd had in making money. He was also commending his wife for staying out of his (hard, tough, down-to-earth) business and for keeping God "happy" for both of them. He had stored up millions but was a fool to think that his wife's godliness, or the sliver of wealth that he used to support her ministry activities, would offset his love of money. He figured that he had it covered both ways—in this life and the next. He has since died and, I fear, lost on both sides of the deal.

The tragedy of the rich man is not that he lost everything at the moment of death, but that he was not rich toward God. He is impoverished forever before the God who defines generosity, goodness, mercy, and compassion. He is in the state that was used to describe the church at Laodicea: "You say, I am rich, I have prospered, and I need nothing, not realizing that you are wretched, pitiable, poor, blind, and naked" (Rev. 3:17).

This poverty is the final poverty—separation from God. It is painful, unending, and irreversible, because it has to do with God, not just with money. The rich man in the parable did not seek God's will or wisdom during his years on earth, even though God granted him all that he needed and more. He rather attempted to use God's goodness to build his own kingdom. His final motivation was self. He ended eternally alone, apart from God, in a place for everyone who has lived looking out for themselves alone.

For the third time, Jesus hammers home the importance of not laying up treasures for ourselves. That means using them for something else. That "something else" is our neighbors—we are to bless our spouses, our children, our dependents, and the needy. While Jesus does not discourage tithing, he offers no talk of tithing being the key to the right use of money. The generosity of kingdom economics is rather controlled by the heart. Our hearts control our purpose for our first dollar earned and our last dollar saved.

I find my heart very hard to guard in this area. For me, it is like trying to hold on to a slimy, shaking fish. I am one who instinctively "keeps score," regarding my adequacy and value as a person, by my rate of increase of net worth or my lack thereof. I enjoy making money on a good deal in real estate or the stock market. But I have been tempted to let that distract me from the more important things that Christ is asking me to do. I so easily forget that I am God's son and a joint heir of the universe through my elder brother, Jesus. I forget that he is the one who will bring lasting fruit from my efforts to love others and serve him. Jesus's scorecard for me looks different from the one that the world system offers me. The poorest Christian in India is richer than those on the Forbes list of the richest 100 people—combined. Live to love with whatever God has granted you, and you will be richer toward God than you could ever imagine. You are part owner of God's own wealth, which was secured forever by Christ's finished work on the cross.

Questions for Review and Reflection

1. Why do you think there is so much teaching from Jesus on money-related matters?
2. Do you think that any of his teachings are no longer applicable today? Why or why not?
3. Which of his money-related teachings do you find to be the hardest to understand or fulfill?

6

Jesus, Money, and the Future

Sell your possessions and give to the poor. Provide purses
for yourselves that will not wear out, a treasure in heaven
that will not be exhausted. (Luke 12:33 NIV)

The gospel writers record many of Jesus's key teachings from the last few weeks of his life as he made his way to Jerusalem. A large percentage of these teachings had to do with money, as he prepared his disciples for his departure and, just as importantly, for the judgment of the last day.

Get Rich Quick or Get Rich Permanently

The parable of the dishonest manager jars us into taking an eternal perspective on how we use our money in this life.

[Jesus] also said to the disciples, "There was a rich man who had a manager, and charges were brought to him that this man was wasting his possessions. And he called him and said to him, 'What is this that I hear about you? Turn in the account of your management, for you can no longer be manager.' And the manager said to himself, 'What shall I do, since my master is taking the management away from me? I am not strong enough to dig, and I am ashamed to beg. I have decided what to do, so that when I am removed from management, people may receive me into their houses.' So, summoning his master's debtors one by one, he said to the first, 'How much do you owe my master?' He said, 'A hundred measures of oil.' He said to him, 'Take your bill, and sit down quickly and write fifty.' Then he said to another, 'And how much do you owe?' He said, 'A hundred measures of wheat.' He said to him, 'Take your bill, and write eighty.' The master commended the dishonest manager for his shrewdness. For the sons of this world are more shrewd in dealing with their own generation than the sons of light. And I tell you, make friends for yourselves by means of unrighteous wealth, so that when it fails they may receive you into the eternal dwellings.

"One who is faithful in a very little is also faithful in much, and one who is dishonest in a very little is also dishonest in much. If then you have not been faithful in the unrighteous wealth, who will entrust to you the true riches? And if you have not been faithful in that which is another's, who will give you that which is your own? No servant can serve two masters, for either he will hate the one and love the other, or he will be devoted to the one and despise the other. You cannot serve God and money." (Luke 16:1–13)

In this parable about money, or "unrighteous wealth," Jesus uses irony to drive home the point that if a dishonest manager is shrewd enough to forgive his master's business debts and create future obligations from his master's debtors, how much more should the sons of righteousness insure their future through a godly use of their worldly wealth? Jesus teaches us to make friends for ourselves (from those whom we help, forgive, or bless) by means of "unrighteous wealth" (our money), so that when it fails (when we die), they (the poor who are now exalted with God) may receive us into eternal dwellings (heaven). Our money will fail, he says—so don't be stupid. Quickly (before you die) create future obligations from God to you by lending and giving to the poor. This parable reflects the dynamics of Proverbs 19:17: "Whoever is generous to the poor lends to the LORD, and he will repay him for his deed."

Jesus continues to hammer away at the unique opportunities we have in this life to show mercy so that we will have a rich entrance into God's presence. Of course, Jesus presents the thinking of the dishonest manager as totally self-centered in order to jar his followers into realizing that even at the level of blatant self-interest, giving and lending to the poor is profoundly wise.

He contrasts the dishonest manager with his followers by essentially saying, "If you have not been trustworthy in handling worldly wealth (as a steward), who will trust you with true riches (or your own property)?" It is an ingenious way for Christ to remind us that all of our current money has been assigned to us by God, for his purposes— not ours. To be trustworthy with his property, we must give and lend to the poor and the needy according to the command of God, the owner. Then, when our management is found to be faithful, we will receive our own eternal property from him.

This is a profound and direct affirmation that all our wealth is assigned to us by God to be invested for the kingdom, within our specific circumstances and opportunities. This approach goes beyond giving a tenth or firstfruits. It causes us to recognize that in all our wealth we are stewards of someone else's property: God's. We are foolish to use it for our own purposes.

When we see the Lord, all believers will give account for what we have done with the wealth that he assigned us. We will either receive true riches or lose what we wasted of the worldly riches we were assigned. How Christ will work all this out is mostly a mystery. He chose not to reveal the details—probably for our good. But this should not cause us to tune out his clear teaching about our money. From the first dollar to the last, our money is assigned to us so we can carry out God's will by using it as a means to love others.

Luke followed up this key text on stewardship with the story of Lazarus and the rich man who used his worldly wealth selfishly, as we have seen. That rich man provides the perfect "how not to do it" picture.

The conversion of Zacchaeus is the final ministry event that Luke records in his account of Jesus's trip to Jerusalem (see Luke 19:1–10). It can be seen as the essential "how to do it" example for a rich man who finds salvation. Zacchaeus, a corrupt tax collector, wants to see Jesus. Jesus knows that and asks for hospitality at Zacchaeus's home. Zacchaeus confesses his sin publicly, commits to restore to each of his victims four times what he took from them, and donates half of his capital to the poor. Jesus tells him, "Today salvation has come to this house" (v. 9)—a public demonstration that even a wealthy man can find his way into the kingdom of God. Zacchaeus does not just tithe. He looks at his entire fortune and gives from it, keeping just enough to continue his business and other obligations.

Three Parables: How to Prepare for the Return of the King

Once Jesus arrives in Jerusalem, he engages in intensive teaching to prepare his followers for his departure and return. In Matthew 25 he relates three stories: the ten virgins, the ten talents, and the sheep and the goats. These stories dramatize how we should live with a view toward the final outcome of history when Christ will return. Not surprisingly, all three of them concern money.

The Ten Virgins (Matt. 25:1–13)

In Jesus's first parable, two sets of wedding attendants are awaiting the arrival of the groom, who is delayed. The wise attendants have extra oil so they can "go the distance" if his arrival takes a long time. The foolish attendants are not prepared and seek to borrow from the other five. They are rejected and have to go to purchase more. Before they return, the groom appears, and the five foolish attendants are locked out of the wedding feast.

The point of the parable is in verse 13: "Watch therefore, for you know neither the day nor the hour." With that strong warning, Jesus emphasizes that each of his disciples should live in a state of being prepared for his return. None of us can ride on another's coattails. We must be ready with our oil at any time.

Jesus does not identify exactly what the oil stands for. I believe it is the fruit (results) of the service that we offer during our lives. We are to be watchful about how we live, not lulled to sleep by the seeming uneventfulness and sameness of daily life. We can't forget why we are here. Those who are ready for his return look for the opportunities for good works that God provides, thereby making provision for themselves for when he arrives.

At some level, most of us can identify with those who took advantage of the groom's delay to get some sleep, because we too do not always seek out opportunities for love and service within our personal worlds, families, neighborhoods, and fellowships. We can easily turn the pages of our calendars without giving thought to preparing ourselves for the life to come or focusing on why we are here now.

Let me give an example of this in my own life. I became convicted that I was not watching out for opportunities to serve Christ and was just living out my busy schedule instead. I prayed about this, and God brought to mind an opportunity. I was able to initiate a relationship with a needy widower whom I knew from my job. It took some time out of my schedule for me to visit him, shop with him, and help to unscramble his situations. I was tempted to grumble about him, his attitudes, and *his* grumbling—but below it all was the comfort of knowing that I was doing Christ's will. I wish I could say that this was the rule in my life—but at least the Lord gave me one clear opportunity to prepare for the future by "buying some oil."

The Ten Talents (Matt. 25:14–30; Luke 19:11–27)

Jesus expands his point about how to prepare for his return by telling the parable of the talents in Matthew and the parable of the minas in Luke. He does so because his disciples were assuming that there would be no delay before the full kingdom of God arrived. To counter this, Jesus tells these stories. In both accounts, an ordinary man travels to a far county to receive a title allowing him to rule the kingdom in which he lives. Some citizens are not pleased, and they send a delegation to the great king opposing his appointment. Before he departs, the man calls three (or ten) servants and entrusts them with substantial capital of varying amounts, according to their ability. He instructs them to invest or do business for his benefit until he returns—even though there is resistance to his becoming king.

The man receives authority to rule and returns home as the lord and king of the realm. He asks his servants to account for their endeavors on his behalf. In both parables, the servants present the original money plus the money they have earned. Each one has earned it according to his allocated capital and ability. In both parables, however, one servant has neglected to invest or use his capital for the master's business. The servant lies about his reasons for this neglect—lies that are exposed by the lord. He takes the capital away from the lazy, self-serving servant and gives it to the one with the most. He then turns and judges those who sought to destroy his rule. This is a clear picture of an ascended Christ, who gives gifts and abilities to his servants and calls them to serve in a hostile environment during his absence. It also pictures him returning on clouds of glory to call everyone to account—both servants and enemies.

The bottom line is in verse 29: "For to everyone who has will more be given . . . but from the one who has not, even what he has will be taken away." This is parallel to the teaching of the parable of the ten virgins: Those who have something to offer (oil/profits) will be welcomed and rewarded in the kingdom. Those who have nothing to show because they lived for their own comfort, security, or ease will lose even what they have. The last servant is chided by the lord for not at least loaning the money to bankers, so that he would have something to offer the king.

This raises the question of what we are to invest for Christ until he comes. It presupposes that we are his servants and not his enemies. We are entrusted with his resources and asked to manage them for him in his absence; thus, this is not about how to *gain* a relationship with God but about how to *serve* him within that relationship.

Jesus is looking for something from each of us when he returns. What we have has come to us from him, and we use it for his purposes in order to produce an increase. In the parable, it is not the amount of the increase that is rewarded but the faithful diligence of the servant.

Our time, talents, and treasure are the best candidates for what we are to invest. Our Lord has granted each of us different amounts of these resources and asked us to invest them for him until he comes again. Do we see ourselves as servants/stewards of the time, talents, and treasure he has given us and as being responsible to use them for the Lord's service until he comes? Some have more resources and some have less, but all should be investing them for the King and his kingdom.

If you are a baptized follower of Christ, you are a steward of what has been granted to you for his purposes. The parable of the talents or minas is directly applicable to us. Our Lord will return, and we will be accountable for the use we have made of all that he has given us—including our money.

The Sheep and the Goats (Matt. 25:31–46)

Jesus's final teaching in Matthew 25 is more specific about what our service for him looks like. It answers the question "What does Christ want us to do with the time, talents, and treasure he has bestowed on us?" He answers that question in one of the most dramatic passages in Scripture.

When the Son of Man comes in his glory, and all the angels with him, then he will sit on his glorious throne. Before him will be gathered all the nations, and he will separate people one from another as a shepherd separates the sheep from the goats. And he will place the sheep on his right, but the goats on the left. Then the King will say to those on his right, "Come, you who are blessed by my Father, inherit the kingdom prepared for you from the foundation of the world. For I was hungry and you gave me food, I was thirsty and you gave me drink, I was a stranger and you welcomed me, I was naked and you clothed me, I was sick and you visited me, I was in prison and you came to me." Then the righteous will answer him, saying, "Lord, when did we see you hungry and feed you, or thirsty and give you drink? And when did we see you a stranger and welcome you, or naked and clothe you? And when did we see you sick or in prison and visit you?" And the King will answer them, "Truly, I say to you, as you did it to one of the least of these my brothers, you did it to me."

Then he will say to those on his left, "Depart from me, you cursed, into the eternal fire prepared for the devil and his angels. For I was hungry and you gave me no food, I was thirsty and you gave me no drink, I was a stranger and you did not welcome me, naked and you did not clothe me, sick and in prison and you did not visit me." Then they also will answer, saying, "Lord, when did we see you hungry or thirsty or a stranger or naked or sick or in prison, and did not minister to you?" Then he will answer them, saying, "Truly, I say to you, as you did not do it to one of the least of these, you did not do it to me." And these will go away into eternal punishment, but the righteous into eternal life.

From this we see wonderful examples of the work God left us to do on earth with the time, treasure, and talents he has granted to us. We minister to Christ when we feed the hungry, provide water for the thirsty, offer hospitality and welcome to the alien and immigrant, clothe and house those who lack protection against the elements, provide healing for the sick, and visit the prisoner and offer him companionship. These ministries are often carried out solo, as believers are active in loving their neighbors. This still applies to those of us who live in affluent, suburban communities where people have moved to escape the curses of poverty. Are we actively looking for ways to show the love of Christ in our homes, to our irritated or grumpy spouses, to our rebellious kids, to our gossiping relatives and coworkers, to the misfit neighbor who can't keep his house up to snuff, to the friend whose child can't read, to the coworker who is going through divorce or who has cancer but no spouse to help? Perhaps most of all, are we watching for opportunities to share the hope that we have in Christ with those who need it?

Modern media, print, and email help us to be watchful for good works we can do in our larger community and world. If "God so loved the world," it makes sense for us to join him in that. Such works often are carried out by small groups, churches, families, missions, and NGOs. Many millions of believers give to meet the needs of others who are far from where they live. In our differentiated global community, much of our financial service to Christ will be done through larger-scale, international expressions of the church and its mission. These entities become our hands and feet in building hospitals, rescuing the falsely imprisoned, releasing slaves, teaching literacy, providing economic opportunity for the poor, and ministering to those who are in recovery from the trauma of wars, substance abuse, sex work, sickness, and disability. These ministries are good examples of how we can fill our lamps with oil, prepare for the return of the King, and give our time, talents, and treasure for God's work and thereby end up ministering to Christ.

Pulling Back the Curtain on Reality

What is striking about all three of these accounts, as well as the four passages that we discussed in chapter 5, is that they all focus on a heart motivation to serve and obey Christ *in his absence*, resulting in a rich welcome into God's presence in the life to come.

Jesus clearly commands his disciples to sell their possessions and give, to be generous to the poor, to lend and share with the needy, to love others as he loved them. However, rather than emphasizing the "oughts" and the ethics, Jesus pulls back the curtain on the realities of the situation both now and in the future. Using excess wealth for oneself is not just wrong, it is foolish. Jesus meets those who are concerned with money on their own ground: How do we preserve, invest, and grow our wealth? We send it ahead, by doing God's will now. He will repay us many times over.

Jesus is helping us to look at the reality of life from the perspective of an eternity of kingdom life in a renewed creation. He gives us a dose of reality. Through parable, story, teaching, and example, he helps us to face the certainty of the end of life, the end of current history, his climactic return in judgment, and the establishment of the new world where God will dwell with his people.

Reality Is Ignored unless the Heart Is Renewed

Blinded, sinful humans need new hearts in order for any talk about being rich toward God to penetrate their understanding or be attractive to them. No amount of eternal investment will be "worth it" if, in our hearts, we are still serving the world's money now. Trusting in God's promise, and striving for the radical delayed gratification this involves, just will not work unless we have a new heart orientation and a belief in the God who makes the promises.

I consider myself a "hardened investor." That is another way of saying that I have made some bad investment decisions in my life. I now tend to look at future promises of return very skeptically—and that, unfortunately, is sometimes true with Christ's promises. It is almost a conditioned response for us to hear the promises but quietly decide not to act on them for fear that they will not pan out. They seem too nebulous, especially combined with the doubt we sometimes carry about whether we are even candidates for eternal life. That dynamic is probably part of the reason why Jesus drives this point home to the point of overkill. At least I know that I need it!

Jesus clearly does not ask the rich to become destitute and dependent and to take on the attendant curses of poverty. He commands them to divest themselves of *unneeded* wealth for the benefit of the poor and to become generous as their life financial strategy. Unless we have faith in Jesus, this command—even with the "carrot" of eternal life—has no pull. If we find life in our money or in the quest for it, we cannot give it away without feeling like we are giving away life itself. But if we find life in God, we feel compelled to become rich toward him, without fearing a "loss of life" now.

This will cause us to forgo legitimate peripheral pleasures, but in their place we will find a deeper joy by getting to know God. The Christian's home may be half the size that it would be otherwise, but God will be there. His car may be functional instead of being a monument to design, personal wealth, and extreme engineering, but his identity will be wrapped up in the living God. Her kids may not all be able to go to elite private schools (whether or not they need to), but those children will see God's kingdom and love demonstrated in their parents' service to the needy and lost.

Those who give generously and lay up treasures in heaven get to experience the very life of God, the great original Giver. Through their experience of *agape* love, they enter into the life of Jesus, who commanded us to love one another as we have been loved by him. Our giving from changed hearts connects us to Christ's life. Only he can work this in self-centered, fallen humans. He invites us all to lose our life for him so that we may truly gain it. He invites us to follow him because he is the Savior. He can draw, change, and disciple even the most addicted hoarders, manipulators, spenders, fearful savers, or money multipliers and save them from themselves and from the plot of Satan to claim them on the last day.

This brings us to a deeper dimension of Jesus's teaching about giving. It is the teaching that *we shall receive on the last day as we have given*. This has been implied by all we have studied thus far, but Jesus (and the apostles) directly teach that this dynamic will play out on judgment day.

Giving and the Day of Judgment

While it may be surprising, the Bible seems to teach that the attitudes and behavior that are associated with our generosity (or lack thereof) will be front and center when we stand before Christ on the last day. In order for us to understand this properly, it will be helpful for us to remind ourselves of some biblical teaching that is not often the topic of the preaching and teaching we hear around us—namely, the teaching that we will be judged by the mercy or judgment that we have dispensed to others during our lives. The judgment that will be administered on the last day to the believer and the unbeliever will have a reciprocal quality to it. Jesus teaches that those who have been given much will receive much.

Let's first look at some passages about the nature of the last judgment in general. Most speak about the day of judgment as a judgment that will involve good or bad deeds. We have reviewed Jesus's teaching to this effect in Matthew 25. He also makes this truth more than clear in John 5:28–29.

> Do not marvel at this, for an hour is coming when all who are in the tombs will hear his voice and come out, those who have done good to the resurrection of life, and those who have done evil to the resurrection of judgment.

In the judgment, God does not seem to "cut a break" to believers but judges all without partiality. Every human being will stand before him in one judgment, as we see in these passages:

> For if you forgive others their trespasses, your heavenly Father will also forgive you, but if you do not forgive others their trespasses, neither will your Father forgive your trespasses. (Matt. 6:14–15)

Judge not, that you be not judged. For with the judgment you pro-
nounce you will be judged, and with the measure you use it will be
measured to you. (Matt. 7:1–2)

Judge not, and you will not be judged; condemn not, and you will
not be condemned; forgive, and you will be forgiven; give, and it
will be given to you. Good measure, pressed down, shaken together,
running over, will be put into your lap. For with the measure you
use it will be measured back to you. (Luke 6:37–38)

The clearest passage on this might be Romans 2:1–5. Paul begins
the chapter by addressing those who do not have the Bible—the pagan
Gentiles. He shows them that they have a keen moral sense when
they are wronged and that they know substantial right from wrong.
He teaches that they will be judged, because they have judged (and
punished) others for doing the very same things that they do themselves. Paul warns them that they will have no excuse on the day of
judgment, because God will judge them with the standard and punishment they have used on others. Paul then reveals to them their dire
situation before God. He says, drawing from Psalm 62:12,

[God] will render to each one according to his works: to those who
by patience in well-doing seek for glory and honor and immortality,
he will give eternal life; but for those who are self-seeking and do
not obey the truth, but obey unrighteousness, there will be wrath
and fury. There will be tribulation and distress for every human
being who does evil, the Jew first and also the Greek, but glory and
honor and peace for everyone who does good, the Jew first and also
the Greek. For God shows no partiality. (Rom. 2:6–11).

God is not setting up the "last day" judgment to decide whether
anyone can stand up to the perfection of his holiness. We need perfect righteousness and holiness in order to be in a justified sonship
relationship with God. That is available now only through Christ and
through faith in his finished work. But on the last day he will judge
humans by their own standards, behaviors, and judgments. In that

way, every mouth will be silenced. This judgment will be in truth and will involve the fierce, penetrating knowledge of what was thought in secret and done in the dark, when no one knew or could know. It will "out" the hidden things and confront our deepest motives for our dealings, thoughts, desires, and fantasies. Paul warns both pagans and Jews that they will be judged without partiality and condemned by their own mouths and behaviors. With the measure that they measured to others, it will be meted out to them.

Justification before God versus Vindication before the Accuser

Yet for the believer, God guarantees that on the last day he will confirm the justification we have received in this life. He promises that he will defend us all so that we survive this terrible day of the Lord. The Father appoints his Son to be both judge and defense attorney against our enemy and accuser, Satan. Satan's role in the judgment is not extensively discussed in Scripture. However, from his interactions with God in the book of Job, his temptation of Jesus, and his efforts to defeat Christians, it seems pretty certain that he will be there to try to claim our souls for himself. He will make good on his name—the Accuser—by bringing charges against us to show that we are his property, not God's redeemed people. He wants to prove that God's salvation had no effect and did not work. Perhaps most pointedly, he wants to show that if God condemns Satan to hell, he will have to condemn his precious elect as well.

But Christ will be there to counter all this. Jesus will publicly demonstrate a vindication that is sufficient to shut the mouth of the Accuser and will gloriously confirm his mercy to each of his elect children. We can count on that. If God justifies us, who can condemn us? We see a preview of that scene in Matthew 25, with the story of the sheep and the goats. God will show that his chosen people, though sinful, forgave those who sinned against them, and therefore deserve to be forgiven themselves. He will show that they loved their enemies and the helpless and that therefore, even if the elect were once enemies of God, it is just for him to love and forgive them. He will show that they gave to those who did not have enough, and therefore he will demonstrate his justice by meeting their need as they met the needs of others. He will show that they visited and comforted those who were condemned in prison, and so it is eminently just for God to comfort them in their bondage. With that, and many other demonstrations, Christ will shut Satan's mouth and silence the complaints of the condemned using the words and actions of his saints while also condemning the wicked with their own words and actions.

As we return to Luke 6:38, a passage we quoted earlier, we make the important observation that it includes giving. Jesus says, "Give, and it will be given to you." This maps onto his extensive teaching about the difference between laying up treasure for ourselves and giving to the needy. Those who give generously will find that God gives to them. They lay up a foundation (an account) for an everlasting life of abundance with God. They are not only vindicated on the last day but are shown to have vast credit with God, which he will "repay" in eternity.

This makes generosity, doing good works, and forgiving our enemies much more than good, obedient things we should do in this life. They are part of God's plan to demonstrate his righteousness and glory in us and to prepare us to be revealed as victors on the day of judgment. Moreover, they are the means of our rich entry into a new world where we will enjoy the fruits of our love to others—and all to the glory of Christ.

This also accounts for the way in which there will be grades of reward among God's people in heaven, while every person in hell will essentially design their own condemnation, based on their thoughts, motives, and treatment of others. (See the parable of Lazarus and the rich man in Luke 16:19–31.)

This personalized destiny will account for all of the complex factors in a person's life: nature, nurture, and circumstance. To whom much is given, much will be required; to whom little is given, less will be required. It will be brilliantly and unassailably just for all. It will right every wrong and bring history's justice, injustice, oppression, cruelty, compassion, loyalty, betrayal, deceit, and truth to a final and definitive resolution. All creation will offer praise to the Lamb, who is worthy to reign, to judge, and to redeem and renew all things in justice and grace. The saints of God will rest in their souls, despite all past evil. Evil will be resolved so that there will be no need to remember it anymore.

Our final accountability to Christ is often used by biblical writers to remind us to obey our Lord now—to continually repent, seek new obedience, and buy up our God-appointed opportunities to show forgiveness, compassion, mercy, and love, thereby reflecting our Lord.

This is actually a much bigger deal than we are inclined to recognize. Our tendency is to want our "salvation admission card" and then to just drift toward judgment day with the knowledge that we are safe (eternally secure). When we recognize this attitude in ourselves, we should repent of it and pursue the life of love and good works that Christ commands. Grace is never grounds for just drifting through our lives as disciples of Christ—much less for direct disobedience.

This is the big picture of what is at stake in our learning to give. It makes arguments about whether we tithe on our gross or net income seem silly. Giving to kingdom needs is much more than paying our "fair share" of church or mission expenses. It is part of designing our future in God's renewed earth. It is how we reflect the love and character of our Lord—the great Giver in creation and the greatest Giver in redemption. It is part of becoming like him, preparing to be with him, and being vindicated from the Accuser of the brethren on the last day.

Our thesis has been that the purpose of money for believers is to be a resource for giving. Jesus taught this and lived it. He accomplished our redemption so that we could enter into that purpose.

So how did Jesus do at turning people's hearts away from having a primary focus on survival, security, wealth, and accumulation for themselves? A revolution took place in the economics of God's people. The ram's horn of Jubilee began to sound—not just in Jerusalem but in Judea, Samaria, and the uttermost parts of the world. The world has never duplicated what took place next, as the kingdom of God was unveiled in Acts. Let's turn there now.

Questions for Review and Reflection

1. Based on the parables of the virgins, the talents, and the sheep and goats, what fruit will Jesus be looking for in our lives?
2. Does it seem practical or realistic for Jesus to teach that the supreme earthly calling or purpose of our lives is to do good works (i.e., to love our neighbors)?
3. How could Jesus both teach that on the last day we will receive as we have given and still be consistent with the teaching that salvation comes by grace alone through belief in him?

7

Money in the
Jerusalem Church

There was not a needy person among them. (Acts 4:34)

Luke suggests that the Acts of the Apostles records the ongoing works of Jesus Christ (see Acts 1:1), as he pours out his Spirit on mankind, establishes his renewed people, and witnesses to the world. Certainly the apostles thought that their task was to witness, to teach, and to apply the teachings of Christ to the church. The Great Commission recorded in Matthew 28:19–20 makes this abundantly clear.

> Go therefore and make disciples of all nations, baptizing them in the name of the Father and of the Son and of the Holy Spirit, *teaching them to observe all that I have commanded you.* And behold, I am with you always, to the end of the age.

Believers in the church after Pentecost embodied the work, ministry, and teachings of Christ. He guaranteed them that his presence would empower and guide them throughout the entire church age.

Acts seems to be structured around this commission to evangelize and disciple the world, first in Jerusalem (Acts 1–7), then in Judea (Acts 8:1–3) and Samaria (Acts 8:1–25), and finally in all nations— reaching all the way to the seat of world power in Rome (Acts 8:26– 28:31). Acts is organized to provide an account of what Christ did to establish his church under the new covenant as well as what we need to know in order to understand how his work is applied to this last stage of human history.

The teachings of Christ on issues related to money are prominent in the Gospels. In Acts, we see the outworking of his teachings. The life we see the believers living in their renewed community continues to be a guide to the church to this day. Luke says that the early disciples

> devoted themselves to the apostles' teaching and the fellowship, to the breaking of bread and the prayers. And awe came upon every soul, and many wonders and signs were being done through the apostles. And all who believed were together and had all things in common. And they were selling their possessions and belongings and distributing the proceeds to all, as any had need. (Acts 2:42–45)

As part of their fellowship, the believers practiced what theology calls "the communion of the saints."[1] The root of the Greek word for this phrase (*koinonia*) means "common." The believers held all their gifts, graces, and material possessions as being common to all, and many of them voluntarily sold possessions in order to give to those in need.

It is not surprising that Luke highlights this. It is a direct fulfillment of Jesus's teaching in the Gospels. In Luke 12:33 Jesus commanded his followers to "sell your possessions, and give to the needy." Those who had stored up possessions began to distribute them, gaining the attention and favor of the people of Jerusalem, which led to more church growth.

In Acts 4:32, 34–35, Luke gives a fuller description of this phenomenon.

> Now the full number of those who believed were of one heart and soul, and no one said that any of the things that belonged to him was his own, but they had everything in common. . . . There was not a needy person among them, for as many as were owners of lands or houses sold them and brought the proceeds of what was

---

1. Westminster Confession of Faith, chapter 26.

sold and laid it at the apostles' feet, and it was distributed to each as any had need.

Luke's use of language connects this account to the promise of Deuteronomy, where Moses described a similar condition that would prevail if God's people obeyed him. He said that if Israel would only obey, "There will be no poor among you" (Deut. 15:4). Just as God promised that he would end poverty if his people obeyed, so Luke now declares that that time has arrived. Moses had commanded those with possessions to put them to use among the needy: "You shall not harden your heart or shut your hand against your poor brother, but you shall open your hand to him and lend him sufficient for this need, whatever it may be" (Deut. 15:7–8). This describes the practical generosity and compassion that was exercised in the Jerusalem church.

Ironically, God knew that in the age of Deuteronomy there would be disobedience, so in the same chapter Moses says, "There will never cease to be poor in the land. *Therefore* I command you, 'You shall open wide your hand to your brother, to the needy and to the poor, in your land'" (v. 11).

In Jerusalem, after Pentecost, God's people finally obeyed. For the first time in biblical history, the promise of Deuteronomy 15 was substantially fulfilled, at least for a portion of the church. It was a witness to the fact that Messiah and the kingdom had come and that God was ruling his people again.

Not only was this a dramatic fulfillment of Deuteronomy 15 and other Jubilee passages, but it represented a stark reversal of every world culture—including Roman Palestine. According to recent studies of post-exilic Palestinian culture, stratification became more systematic as Persian rule gave way to Greek, Hasmonaean, and finally Roman rule.[2] Tracy Lemos concludes that in Roman Palestine, there was a clear, increasing drive toward the concentration of ownership of wealth, land, and palaces. Most of the land was controlled by a small

---

2. See T. M. Lemos, *Marriage Gifts and Social Change in Ancient Palestine: 1200 BCE to 200 CE* (New York: Cambridge University Press, 2010), 224–25.

number of families, which greatly expanded the numbers of landless peasants, tenant farmers, and professional bandits.

Lemos recounts the economic plight of non-slave, landless workers. They typically earned about one denarius for a day's wage. That is significant, because a daily portion of wheat for one person would be one-twelfth of a denarius. For a family with four children, that comes to 180 denarii a year just for wheat. On top of that, they needed vegetables, fruits, and occasional meat. On this basis there was no money for clothing or housing. It becomes easy to see why these folks could never get enough money to rent land, much less buy a small plot on which to raise crops.[3]

This turnaround among the believers in Jerusalem was a countercultural revolution, which attested to the reality of the new messianic rule over God's people. The Messiah had made atonement for sin and brought in the Day of Jubilee. Most remarkably, this renewal for the poor was not the result of a new set of laws or sanctions imposed upon the people; it was the result of the power of the Word and the Holy Spirit, which stirred up God's people to live out their love for one another as they had been taught by Moses and Jesus.

It fulfilled all the Old Testament principles of economic justice and mercy without any of the detailed institutions of the law, such as the return of land, cancelling of debts, release of slaves, gleanings, and tithes for the poor. This great change was accomplished through offerings of money, which was paralleled in the Old Testament only in the people's joyous freewill offerings for the construction of the tabernacle and the temple—signs of God's coming to dwell with them.

How God Protected Grace-Based Giving

Acts 5 jumps right into more financial issues that resulted from these new patterns of generosity. A couple named Ananias and Sapphira had sold some land and decided to use it for the needs of the poor. However, they secretly decided to keep some of the proceeds for themselves while telling the apostles that they were giving them

3. See Lemos, 225–26.

all of it. They were struck dead by God for lying to the Holy Spirit. In his rebuke of Ananias, Peter said something significant about the economics of their gifts: "While it remained unsold, did it not remain your own? And after it was sold, was it not at your disposal? Why is it that you have contrived this deed in your heart? You have not lied to man but to God" (Acts 5:4).

The backdrop for this sin is at the end of Acts 4. A believer named Barnabas came forward and sold a large amount of property, and folks were probably in awe of his love and generosity. As we all know, example is often the most powerful teacher and motivator. Many others followed Barnabas, and Christ was greatly honored and the poor uplifted.

Ananias wanted some of the money from his sale, but he also wanted the approval and favor of the people. He did not want to be seen as selfish compared to Barnabas. He figured that giving some of the proceeds was a price worth paying for the approbation. It was a transaction of value for him. But in order to get the approval he coveted, he had to lie. Neither he nor his wife calculated the Holy Spirit's role into the transaction—the role of guarding the church from falling into a subtle "transaction-based" giving model.[4] No doubt this episode was recorded by Luke in order to help believers guard against temptations and abuses of this kind down through the ages.

As the passage makes clear, the transformation that occurred in the believers' giving to the poor was not because they were asked to turn over their possessions to the church, as is practiced in some cults and spiritual orders. Peter emphasized that Ananias and Sapphira owned their land and had the right to refrain from gifting it to the church. It could not be clearer that they could have brought a portion of the proceeds and kept the remainder. But, desiring the approval of man, Ananias lied in order to appear more righteous and spiritual in the eyes of others.

---

4. A transaction-based giving approach is one in which a gift is given for the calculated benefit that will result for the donor in this life. Many fundraising professionals use this approach by offering to provide donors with recognition and status in exchange for a large gift.

Whatever objections might be raised to this model of sharing, it has nothing to do with socialism, through which assets are owned by the community or state. The Holy Spirit went out of his way to clarify this and brought dramatic discipline to Ananias and Sapphira in order to make the point once and for all.

Many of us feel threatened or experience deep unease at the example of the Jerusalem church. We are tempted to write the practice off as an ill-advised experiment in socialism. Some have suggested that it was only because everyone had spent their capital in a moment of "irrational exuberance" (in the memorable words of Alan Greenspan) that they ended up starving during the famine that fell on the land a few years later. It is, however, twisting the clear intent of the Scripture to suggest that the apostles perpetrated an unwise notion of sharing and giving. Under that view, Ananias would have been the only smart one in the bunch! The culture-transforming giving that took place was done voluntarily, out of loving obedience to the commands of Christ. It was a fulfillment of biblical love and obedience, not a departure from it.

The holding of lands, farms, and other assets was seen as a matter of Christian liberty for the believers. There was no law or guideline enacted by the apostles saying that it was wrong to have capital or more than a particular *amount* of capital. Ownership of land or wealth was not prohibited. It was considered a blessing—part of the economics of opportunity in Mosaic law that were applied under Joshua. Through these, each tribe and family received, at no charge, their portion of land from God, to be held in perpetuity and divided among their children for an everlasting inheritance. This pointed clearly to the heavenly kingdom that Messiah would bring.

However, in the 800 years before the apostles, land ownership had become grossly restricted because of Israel's failure to observe the day of Jubilee. Now it was beginning to be reversed. Those who had lands sold them out of love for those who did not have the opportunity to earn a living and provide for themselves. This created new economic opportunity for the poor. Such new opportunity was not the church's message or primary purpose, but this by-product was a powerful witness to the reality of Jesus being the Son of God.

Now, instead of following the Mosaic law that demanded the Jubilee release of land, debts, and slaves, the church in Jerusalem applied that same principle but in a totally voluntary way, as they were motivated by the love of Christ. It was a kind of spiritually motivated Jubilee that finally did, by grace, what the Mosaic law was powerless to do. Since it was motivated by the love, faith, and wisdom of these early saints, it was nothing that the law could ever demand. It was truly what Jesus meant when he said that love is the fulfillment of the law.

Let me explain this important distinction a bit more. The things that the Bible prohibits us from doing are not conditional upon our situations or circumstances. But its great positive commands (such as "Love your neighbor"), though morally absolute, are intensely situational in terms of how they are applied.[5] For example, I am forbidden to steal from my neighbor under any and all conditions. The positive side of that command is that I am to be generous and bless my neighbor. What that might look like depends radically on the situation. Perhaps you see him shoveling twenty-four inches of snow, and you realize that he would be blessed by borrowing your snowblower. That kind of positive love cannot be laid out in specifics or policies. It must be recognized as the situation arises, under the leading of the Spirit.

To take this principle a bit further, any lack of positive love for a neighbor is a sin of omission, though it is normally not subject to church discipline. Failing to loan him a snowblower is not a violation of a specific prohibition, the way stealing *his* snowblower would be. More to the point, expressing or practicing enmity, hurt, insult, or ill

5. See James C. Petty, *Step by Step: Divine Guidance for Ordinary Christians* (Phillipsburg, NJ: P&R Publishing, 1999). Beginning on page 95 is an extensive discussion of the difference between prohibitions and positive commandments. The positive commands for us to express love are just as much a matter of obedience as the prohibitions are, but they involve a freedom of expression and situation that is not part of the prohibitions. For instance, the Bible clearly forbids theft in all forms and all situations, but the positive side of that command is that we are to share and give to others. What that looks like for each individual will depend on the situation. So-called "situational ethics" does not apply to biblical prohibitions, but it could be seen to apply to positive commands.

will is sin and does make one subject to the discipline of the church. In the same way, possessing unneeded capital is not prohibited in the Old or New Testaments. Only positive, obedient love expresses generosity with those resources. This generosity can never be achieved through prohibitions and does not constitute grounds for church discipline, censure, or seizure (as with communism).

This change that the church brought, as it now emphasized the work of positive love, introduced a huge area of freedom in which love can operate. The church is open to the rich, the middle class, and the poor to come as they are and bow the knee to Jesus. The church depends on the work of the Spirit to direct and motivate its members to be generous as a reflection of Christ's love for them. As it turns out, that is enough motivation, because the law of God is now written onto hearts of flesh by the Holy Spirit. Cases like Zacchaeus (see Luke 19:1–10) and the Macedonian Christians (see 2 Cor. 8:1–15) are examples of believers' Spirit-directed giving in response to God's grace.

Yet, as we've noted, many people feel uncomfortable with (and even threatened by) this practice of the early church and have sought to restrict or at least discourage such practices today. Many of us who have this mindset can identify with Ananias's plight. We think that we want to serve Christ, but giving so much capital as a normal Christian practice seems out of reach for our faith—as it did for Ananias.

Consider some of the solutions that have been proposed to eliminate the relevance of the early church's example. As noted, some people have proposed that it was a well-intentioned mistake—one that led to a need for famine relief, since the rich did not have savings anymore. Others have seen it as an almost miraculous sign that we could never command or reproduce today. Others have said that it may be a great example or ideal but that it's impractical for our consumer-driven, expensive lifestyle, and so it can be ignored. Others say that Jesus's commands to the rich to sell lands and give to the poor apply to his final establishment of "kingdom rule," not to our era.

I find no warrant in Scripture for the church's neglect of this feature of fellowship it articulates so clearly. I propose that it presents sharing not as a ministry of the apostles but as something that "all believers" did (see Acts 2:44), in the same vein as their fellowship from house to house. Sharing was basic to church life, not an add-on. It implemented the clear commands of Christ regarding generosity to the poor. It solved the intractable problems of the loss of economic opportunity that the Old Testament Jubilee and release laws had addressed, and it did so without returning believers to circumcision, Old Testament laws, or new economic laws handed down by the apostles. It was a substantial "down payment" on Christ's ministry of preaching good news to the poor. It was a historical expression of God's release for the poor, to be completely fulfilled in the new heavens and earth, where final justice will reign. It witnessed powerfully to the watching world of the love that believers had for each other and, as a result, witnessed that Jesus was truly the Son of God (see John 13:35).

It is ironic that, while Christ's kingdom is not "of this world," his rule would show itself among these early believers in a most nitty-gritty way: in their hearts, lives, and money. He ruled in such a powerful way that it would forever change the culture of the emerging church, the Roman Empire, and the church's ability to be salt and light in the international community.

Widowgate

The commitments of the believers in Acts 2 and Act 4 were (and are) challenging to maintain over the long term. In the providence of God, a serious administrative problem sprang up regarding the equality of relief funding for widows in Jerusalem (see Acts 6:1–7). Jewish widows from Gentile lands would often return to the safety and protection of Jewish law and culture, and its attending benefits, in their later years. Widows had few economic options for supporting themselves, and this was particularly difficult in Gentile cultures. Poverty in that day had a female face to it—as it does today.

The influx of widows into Jerusalem from around the world who needed to be fed was probably not looked upon very kindly by the locals, who had hung in there in Judea and not defected to the Gentile world. There would be some resentment over these "half-hearted Jews" now returning to feed off of the generosity of the local Jewish community, which was struggling to feed its own widows. Within the church, widows who were native to Jerusalem were enrolled and getting food from the new Christian community, but widows who were not relationally connected to the local leaders were being neglected in the distribution of food.

With the large growth rate of the church, this situation had developed to the point that it was creating ill will in the church. In Acts 6, the apostles recognized this watershed problem and appointed men "full of faith and of the Holy Spirit" (v. 5) to deal with it. These were converted Jewish men who were also from Gentile lands. They were given authority to straighten out the mess and to ensure that relief would be properly administered in the future. This relieved the apostles so that they could be faithful to teach and lead worship, which Christ had called them to do.

God empowered that ministry by filling these men with the Spirit, enabling them to give powerful testimony of why they were following Christ. It is quite possible that the work of the early deacons in Acts 6 was more threatening to the established order than the preaching of the apostles. At any rate, when one of them, Stephen, was put on trial, his face shone "like the face of an angel" (v. 15) and he was stoned to death.

The equal status afforded to Grecian widows may have been an affront to the Jewish establishment, but this solution to the challenge represented a tremendous victory for the young church. It resulted in another wave of encouragement, conversions (particularly of priests), and favor with the people of Jerusalem (see v. 7).

It is clear that those in the early church saw their personal resources not as ultimately being there for themselves but as assets for the Lord's work, and particularly for the redemption of poor brothers and sisters (see Acts 4:32). Yet this value was pursued not by law but by gracious, voluntary sharing. The early church restructured itself to deal effectively with the demands of the new ministry, which included lots of funds coming in and going out. I am sure that the poor in the church understood Christ's words more clearly—that he came to preach the gospel to the poor and proclaim the first fruits of Jubilee. They were living its reality.

In summary we can say the following: The way that the apostles applied Jesus's teaching makes it clear that they saw the purpose of money (after it was used to supply its owner's needs) as being made available for loving others. They gave themselves to God and to each other. This is the new covenant model of mutual ownership between God and his people and between his people and each other. This showed immediately in their conduct and behavior—not via a new rule, tax, or law, but by appeal to the commands Christ had given them to love one another as he had loved them.

Questions for Review and Reflection

1. What Old Testament principles and promises were being fulfilled in the passage of Acts that reveals that there was "not a needy person among" the believers in the church after Pentecost?

2. Was the elimination of poverty among the early Jerusalem church primarily a miracle (like Peter's healing of the lame beggar was), or was it also an example of the church applying Christ's commands and values to its fellowship?

3. What is your best guess at how much money it would generally take each year to "eliminate" poverty in your local congregation so that it could be said that there is "no needy person among" you? Are these needy believers in the local church the extent of the poor people for whom Christians have a primary responsibility?

8

"Remembering the Poor" in the Gentile Church

Only, they asked us to remember the poor, the very thing I was eager to do. (Gal. 2:10)

From Jerusalem, the church was scattered by persecution; yet God used this to bring the gospel to many Gentile nations. The remainder of Acts describes this Gentile missionary effort, but we will focus here on the apostles' teaching about money and giving as found in their letters from this stage of church life. It all began with a meeting in Jerusalem. Galatians 2:7–10 allows us to listen in.

> On the contrary, when they saw that I had been entrusted with the gospel to the uncircumcised, just as Peter had been entrusted with the gospel to the circumcised (for he who worked through Peter for his apostolic ministry to the circumcised worked also through me for mine to the Gentiles), and when James and Cephas and John, who seemed to be pillars, perceived the grace that was given to me, they gave the right hand of fellowship to Barnabas and me, that we should go to the Gentiles and they to the circumcised. Only, they asked us to remember the poor, the very thing I was eager to do.

This key passage helps us to understand the nature of Paul's missionary ministry. Let's focus on three features of Paul's reported transactions with the apostles.

The Strategy: Preach Grace and
Teach Gentiles about Generosity

What exactly did the men in these verses ask of Paul? First, they agreed to commission him to *teach* the Gentiles the gospel. The passage publicly recognizes the division of labor they had agreed on for their missionary endeavors. They were in agreement on all points of the gospel and discussed the challenge of working together with the stark divisions of culture and background between the Jews and the non-Jews. But of all the points that were discussed, the only item that was important enough to be added to Paul's commission was that he remember the poor. This makes it a lot more than a suggestion. It was a priority at this particular time in the discipling of the Gentiles.

It might be a bit like a coach during a timeout in a basketball game. If he says, "Guys, we have to pass the basketball," it doesn't mean that they shouldn't dribble or shoot; it just means that passing is the strategic key to the game at that point.

In a similar way, Peter exhorts Paul here to teach the Gentiles to remember the poor. Obviously this does not mean that he or the Gentiles should neglect worship, Bible study, or fellowship in homes, but that he should make sure that this feature of Christian life is actively practiced. Paul has already been taught this from Christ, has observed the generosity of the early Jerusalem Christians, and is zealously leading the church in it through his example and teaching.

Helping the Poor: A Permanent Ministry

Peter tells Paul to *continue* to remember the poor. The Greek verb tense makes it clear that this remembering is an ongoing and continuing action, not a response to a particular situation, such as a natural disaster (like Hurricane Sandy). It was not a onetime emotional reaction to a revival. It was not a response to a lack of a free market economy, because Rome had its version of a free market. It was situational only in that poverty was widespread, entrenched, and intergenerational among all the peoples where Paul would travel.

Peter tells Paul to *continue* doing this, because it was critical for what happened in Jerusalem to continue in the Gentile world. That was no easy task. What happened in Jerusalem in Acts 4:32–35 was miraculous by world standards.

Peter and the other apostles certainly implemented this in Jerusalem. The office of deacon has its origins in the determination "not to forget." The early church restructured itself so as not to neglect those who had no voice or position of power. They did this by dividing responsibility into word ministry and deed ministry. The deacons were to double down on ministry to the widows, the orphans, the aliens, and the sick, thereby relieving the apostles and elders to concentrate on word ministry.

Yet the idea of launching a similar ministry to the needy in the Gentile church was a daunting prospect. Gentile decision-makers believed that poverty was just payment for misdeeds. Showing mercy was a miscarriage of justice. Contrary to Moses's teaching, philanthropy was usually restricted to "the deserving" (e.g., the rich, the honorable, the powerful, and the successful). Philanthropy was understood as a reciprocal transaction between such folk, with kudos all around. Substantial relief and development for the "losers" in a society was about as countercultural a value as one could come up with.

To make matters more difficult, there were untold millions of Gentiles to be discipled, according to Christ's commission in Acts 1:8. Reaching the Jewish community was a small task in comparison. That these new Gentile believers should be charged with eliminating poverty in their midst was as hard to fathom then as it is now.

Despite these obstacles, Paul accepted this challenge, because he believed that selfish, materialistic Gentiles could learn to love as they had been loved. At heart they were no different from Jews— they were fallen sinners who had been renewed by Christ. So Paul accepted the challenge of "continuing" to teach the churches to remember the poor across the known world. He made good on that in a big way by leading the Gentiles' collection for the starving saints in Judea.

The Motive of Love

The third key to this passage is the word *remember*. Why was Paul told to "remember"? Because we have a tendency to forget. Why do we forget things? Because we have no vested interest in them.

When I go to the grocery store, I have no problem remembering to buy the foods that I like. So my wife tells me to remember the things that I will surely forget, like the canned onion rings. I have no idea why she wants them, and I know I will forget.

Peter uses the word *remember* because we are prone to forget to care for the poor. There are obvious reasons for this. We do not have a short-term vested interest in their welfare, even if they are believers. We do not know them, and they cannot repay us or our church. We forget because they have no access to us. They can't and won't get in our face, beg, or otherwise petition us, much less make us feel guilty or uncomfortable as punishment for not helping. The poor are restricted to despairing or causing riots, and are usually far removed from those with money. In fact, it is usually the con artists who come knocking on our church doors. You probably won't hear from the real poor at the church office. We also forget because we just get caught up in or distracted by our priorities—making it in a dog-eat-dog world where it takes $60,000 just to survive as a family. Our financial and work commitments are so high that we don't go looking for new ways to give away our funds or to help others who have large needs. We are relieved just to get through the day.

But I believe there is a deeper reason for Peter's use of the word *remember*. It has a deep and long biblical history. To *remember* is to act in love. God *remembered* his people in Egypt and delivered them. We are to *remember* his redemption from Egypt and his death on our behalf. We *remember* the poor because we ourselves were *remembered* when we were lost and undone. *Remembering* the poor has to do with grace, not law—with God's grace toward us. Not only is Jesus's work the example and definition of love, but the risen Christ has invaded our hearts and compels us to love as he loved us. We receive the Lord's Supper "in remembrance" of him (Luke 22:19).

Each Christian's very identity is as one who receives God's mercy and reflects it to others. This is how all will know that God sent his Son. The fact that fallen, self-centered humans would show compassion on their enemies and on those who can't repay them is a miracle surpassed only by the forgiveness of sin itself. As Francis Schaeffer loved to say, "Love is the final apologetic."

If Paul (or Peter) were here today to give our church a commission, I believe he would tell us to preach the gospel, teach, and disciple, but also to be particularly careful to remember the poor. We still have a large "Gentile" population to evangelize, as well as many poor. What the apostles did in Jerusalem is still the biblical example of how the gospel impacts both rich and poor people in a community or region.

The Battle for Mercy in the Gentile Church

As we have noted, the apostles knew that the renewed concern for the poor that was being seen in Jerusalem was not part of the Gentiles' culture, history, or archetypal values. This unique renewal of concern and obedience would surely be diluted or overwhelmed by the sheer numbers of Gentile converts unless a clear effort was put forth to disciple Gentile converts in this area. Let's examine how Paul and the apostles worked this out in the exploding, multicultural apostolic church.

Second Corinthians 8 and 9 are the gold standard of teaching on the critical theological and moral issues of giving in the Gentile church. The truths that these chapters contain appear elsewhere, but here Paul sets them in order and explores them at length, for our benefit, as nowhere else in Scripture.

Corinth was a wealthy commercial and trading center—a bit like Los Angeles is to the United States. In 1 Corinthians 16:1–3, Paul introduces them to the famine offering. He writes,

> Now concerning the collection for the saints: as I directed the churches of Galatia, so you also are to do. On the first day of every week, each of you is to put something aside and store it up, as he may prosper, so that there will be no collecting when I come. And when I arrive, I will send those whom you accredit by letter to carry your gift to Jerusalem.

This offering was evidently taken by the Corinthians but failed to measure up to God's grace to them or to their relative wealth. They asked for more time to save up for a second installment. Second Corinthians 8 and 9 prepare the Corinthian church for this second effort, as Paul reminds them of what they are doing, why they are doing it, its significance, and the blessings that will flow from it. He presents eight overriding principles and values in this passage to help non-Jewish Christians understand biblical giving and generosity.

1. Give Yourself First

Paul shows that Christian giving begins with *giving ourselves to God and to one another*. He begins by enthusiastically reporting the wonderful contribution to the relief offering that had been provided by the churches of Macedonia.

> We want you to know, brothers, about the grace of God that has been given among the churches of Macedonia, for in a severe test of affliction, their abundance of joy and their extreme poverty have overflowed in a wealth of generosity on their part. For they gave according to their means, as I can testify, and beyond their means, of their own accord, begging us earnestly for the favor of taking part in the relief of the saints—and this, not as we expected, but they gave themselves first to the Lord and then by the will of God to us. (2 Cor. 8:1–5)

These believers had consecrated all that they were and all that they had to God. Paul even admits that he protested the amount of their generosity, and they responded by pleading for the privilege of participating in the offering. Paul accepted their gift with amazement and used their example to inspire the Corinthians' love and to stimulate them to complete their gift.

2. Recognize Covenantal Ownership

This devoting of ourselves to God and to one another has *covenantal roots*. In classic covenantal bonds, the parties give themselves to each other. Paul is speaking against the background of the covenantal love that God promised to Abraham: "I will establish my covenant between me and you . . . to be God to you and to your offspring after you . . . and I will be their God" (Gen. 17:7–8). In that covenant, God and Abraham each became owners of the other.

At Sinai, God announced to his people that they would be "my treasured possession among all peoples, for all the earth is mine; and you shall be to me a kingdom of priests and a holy nation" (Ex. 19:5–6). These themes were summarized in the mutual ownership of the covenant formula: "I will be *your* God, and you shall be *my* people" (Jer. 7:23; see also Ex. 6:7; Lev. 26:12; Jer. 11:4).

This theme is expanded as redemptive history unfolds in the new covenant. God literally gives himself to his people as "their God," as he gave his only Son (see John 3:16), and he literally "buys" or redeems them from bondage to sin in order to make them his people. We are his—bought and paid for.

It is that relationship of mutual giving that finally forms our eternal destiny. John writes, "And I heard a loud voice from the throne saying, 'Behold, the dwelling place of God is with man. He will dwell with them, and they will be his people, and God himself will be with them as their God'" (Rev. 21:3). This signals the total fulfillment of God's promise to reestablish his fellowship with man. Once disrupted by Adam and Eve, this fellowship is now restored through a permanent relationship of mutual possession.

We see covenant union illustrated in marriage. Moses writes that "a man shall leave his father and his mother and hold fast to his wife, and they shall become one flesh" (Gen. 2:24; cf. Mal. 2:13–16). This union is likened to the covenantal love relationship between Christ and the church in Ephesians 5:22–33. A husband and a wife possess each other through a mutual giving of themselves. Paul even applies this mutual possession to the moral issue of each partner providing sexual fulfillment to the other, since each one "has authority" over the body of the other (see 1 Cor. 7:3–5).

The biblical concept of fellowship (*koinonia*) is therefore covenantal, going way beyond social relationship. Coming from the Greek word for "common," it refers most properly to that which we hold in common or in which we have a common interest. Fellowship with God is mutual ownership based on love.

The same covenantal love is part of the fellowship between believers. The Macedonians reflected that covenantal love by giving (devoting) themselves to the Lord, saying, "Lord, we are yours." What we give is not just time on Sunday, not just 10 percent of our income, not just Christian service—but all of who we are and what we have.

In giving themselves to the Lord, the Macedonians gave themselves to God's people. Their fellowship, communion, and union with God drove their fellowship, communion, and union with one another. Thus everything that they had was available for the needs of God's people, and it was Paul's mission to meet these needs.

When God gives himself to us, it is not a presence alone that he gives us. It comes with all his wealth and glory to meet our needs. When we inherit God as "our God," he brings with him a relationship of love and communication as well as all the richness, righteousness, and life that he possesses. His righteousness is imputed to us, and our sin is imputed to him. His life is given to us, and our death is absorbed by his Son. This mutual ownership comes to final fulfillment in the new heavens, the new earth, the new city, the new civilization, and the reality of joy and everlasting life (see Rev. 21–22). We will get to live where God lives. It is our city, because it is his.

In a parallel way, when we give ourselves to the Lord, we devote all that we are and have to him. This transforms us from being owners of ourselves and our resources to being trustees of the wealth, gifts, life, and resources God has given us. Our time, talents, and treasure are "devoted" to God.

The church in Macedonia recognized the common ownership that all Christians had in the Lord and in one another. Out of that understanding of oneness, they gave to assist the saints in Jerusalem. This vision of their oneness with God and with other Christians explained the dramatic amount that they gave in response to the need. They asked, "How much can I give?" For them, it was not a question of "What should I give?" or "What is required of me?" This helped the Corinthians see their superficial commitment to the covenantal ownership that they had in one another.

Covenant fellowship helps to explain why the purpose of money is giving. There is a sense in which we look at all our money as being "not ours" but held in common for the needs of other believers and for God's purposes in the world. John Frame sums it up well: "Fellowship is also giving. I mentioned earlier the radical sharing of the church in Acts 4–5. This giving, as Paul says, is first a giving of oneself, then of one's wealth (2 Cor. 8:5). After all, if you have given yourself away to the Lord and to your brothers and sisters, it shouldn't be too much to give your wealth."[1]

3. Believe in the Communion of the Saints

This leads us to the neglected doctrine of *the communion of the saints*. The bread and wine are signs and seals of our union not only with Christ but also with one another, as members of his body. This union is not only spiritual, in the sense of being ethereal, invisible, and private. Rather, the communion of the saints involves us in the real-world communication of gifts and graces through the visible body of Christ—the church.

This is such a key point in biblical fellowship that it is worth an extensive quote from the Westminster Confession of Faith. Written in 1643, it gives eloquent expression to this reality and to its attendant obligations.

> All saints, that are united to Jesus Christ their Head, by his Spirit, and by faith, have fellowship with him in his graces, sufferings, death, resurrection, and glory: and, being united to one another in love, they have communion in each other's gifts and graces, and are obliged to the performance of such duties, public and private, as do conduce to their mutual good, both in the inward and outward man.
>
> Saints by profession are bound to maintain an holy fellowship and communion in the worship of God, and in performing such other spiritual services as tend to their mutual edification; as also in relieving each other in outward things, according to their several abilities and necessities. . . .

1. John M. Frame, *Systematic Theology: An Introduction to Christian Belief* (Phillipsburg, NJ: P&R Publishing, 2013), 1051.

> . . . Nor doth their communion one with another, as saints, take away, or infringe the title or propriety which each man hath in his goods and possessions.[2]

This doctrine, and particularly its dimension of economic sharing, was not an invention of the English Puritans. John Calvin, the French theologian of the Reformation, reflected on the destiny of the goods that God gives to the believer: "There cannot be a surer rule, nor a stronger exhortation to the observance of it, than when we are taught that all the endowments which we possess are divine deposits entrusted to us for the very purpose of being distributed for the good of our neighbor."[3]

Most of us in our culture are so focused on protecting our private property against the claims of state ownership or taxation that we fail to realize that the kingdom of God claims a higher level of mutual ownership. We bring the private-property mentality to the discussion of giving, and so we focus only on whatever "taxing" (i.e., tithing) authority God might exercise in the new covenant era. We end up talking only about whether or not we should tithe 10 percent.

But the remarkable generosity that we see in the Macedonians was not confined to some romantic, early version of Christianity. The Spirit's work continued powerfully into the post-apostolic period. During the first four centuries, the church community made great progress toward ending the curse of poverty in its ranks, despite explosive growth that included many poor members.

Since those days, many individuals, churches, spiritual orders, and communities have laid significant resources at the feet of the Lord and his people. Great impact and glory for God have resulted. These will be the cherished stories of the kingdom and will be told forever, both because of their vast number and because they witness to everything that is worthy about Christ's work in his people. Some of these stories are known now, such as the widow and her offering (see Luke 21:2),

2. Westminster Confession of Faith, chapter 26.
3. John Calvin, *Institutes of the Christian Religion*, trans. Henry Beveridge (Peabody, MA: Hendrickson Publishers, 2008), 3.7.5.

Barnabas (see Acts 4:36–37), and Count Ludwig Von Zinzendorf, who in 1722 took in hundreds of persecuted immigrant believers, founded the Moravian movement, and became the father of modern missions. Most of the stories are lost to church history—but not to the church's Lord.

4. Respond with the Grace You Have Been Given

Now to the fourth great principle. In 2 Corinthians 8, Paul attributes the Macedonians' wonderful offering to the "the grace of God that has been given" (v. 1). He is referring not to the grace of earthly riches but to these churches' experience of forgiveness, new life, and the presence of the Holy Spirit. It was not Paul's fundraising abilities that produced such an outpouring; it was *the power of the gospel* in the givers' lives. Paul reflects on this grace.

> I say this not as a command, but to prove by the earnestness of others that your love also is genuine. For you know the grace of our Lord Jesus Christ, that though he was rich, yet for your sake became poor, so that you by his poverty might become rich. (2 Cor. 8:8–9)

Paul is not afraid to put the Corinthians' sincerity to the test by comparing it to the sincerity of the Macedonians, since they both know and trust in the same Lord Jesus. Their motive for giving is being able to respond to the grace that was given to them in Christ. For Paul, financial generosity to the needy is a sure by-product of believing the gospel and following Christ. The greater our knowledge of Christ's love for us, the more we will desire to offer ourselves and our resources to the needy.

People of Protestant denominations have historically emphasized the gospel of salvation by grace alone. Luther articulated the doctrine of justification theologically for the first time in church history. Calvin followed by more clearly formulating the teachings of Scripture that support salvation by grace alone. These biblical teachings became known as the Five Points of Calvinism:

- We are helpless to save ourselves (total depravity).

- Our salvation is a result of God's sovereign choice (unconditional election).
- Christ's love is very personally directed toward saving those whom he died for, prior to any act on their part (limited, or directed, atonement).
- Once God has chosen a sinner, his grace is irresistible and finally results in salvation (irresistible grace).
- All saints shall and must persevere to the end in their faith, and so are all saved (perseverance of the saints).

These doctrines powerfully reinforce the message of 2 Corinthians 8:8–10 and have become known as the "doctrines of grace." As we are discipled in the magnitude of grace, we should be more motivated to serve and love others. Sadly, many Reformed churches have been taken over by what is called the "social gospel," which denies all five of these points and reduces Christianity to a free-floating commandment for us to love one another. These churches have largely lost their power to proclaim or practice the compassion of God.

However, rediscoveries of the gospel have been concurrent with great outpourings of compassion toward others through evangelism, revival, missions, and relief for the needy. This was true especially during the Puritan movement, the first and second Great Awakenings in the English-speaking world, and the Pietist movement in Germany under Zinzendorf. Today, a resurgent Calvinism and evangelicalism, of Pentecostal and non-Pentecostal varieties, are again driving an expansion of mercy and missions.

5. Excel in Giving

In Paul's fifth point, he makes it clear that giving is an "act of grace" that *can be cultivated.* We can grow into it and excel in it: "But as you excel in everything—in faith, in speech, in knowledge, in all earnestness, and in our love for you—see that you excel in this act of grace also" (2 Cor. 8:7).

The Corinthian believers were very zealous for "power" Christianity. They sought, to a point of imbalance, the more dramatic gifts of the Spirit (tongues without interpretation, prophecies without discernment, knowledge of spirits, miracles, and so on). Paul acknowledges their charismatic excellence but points them to the greater gift of love (see 1 Cor. 13).

In 2 Corinthians 8, he reminds the believers to cultivate the grace of giving with a zeal that is equal to or greater than their cultivation of these other gifts. As a wealthy, impressive, and knowledgeable church, they had perhaps assumed that they would be able to "hit it out of the park" on the famine offering. Instead, they fell so short of their goal that Paul called them to renew their efforts and bring genuine generosity to bear on behalf of the starving saints in Jerusalem. They had loudly proclaimed their zeal for these saints but had given little. Their desire to help needed to be matched by their actual doing of it, according to their means.

We have already identified consecration and gospel motivation as key ingredients in 2 Corinthians 8:1–8. There are others in this passage, but the point is that giving is not a necessary evil for running a ministry; it is a divine grace to be cultivated, and one in which we should excel, to the benefit of God's kingdom and our own lives.

Therefore, churches need to pursue the sanctification of their members in this area as much as in the areas of loving spouses, rearing children, witnessing to neighbors, praying, and understanding Scripture. Intense spiritual battles are fought in this area, and we dare not delegate it to professional fundraisers or consultants. Paul did not let the Corinthians enter it alone, and neither should today's pastors and leaders.

6. Avoid "Too Much" and "Too Little"

Second Corinthians 8 concludes with a sixth great principle: sharing is the key to avoiding both the curse of having too little and the trap of having too much (see v. 15). Paul begins by discussing the pressure of meeting dire human need. He assures the Corinthians that if they are ready to do so and they express this by giving in accordance with what they have, they will please God and accomplish their part in meeting the full need.

He does not want the rather rich Corinthians to feel a compulsion to meet the full need themselves, but rather to give in remembrance of

Christ's mercy to them and to trust God to provide the goal. If they give themselves to the Lord and then give according to their means, the need will be met by God. Paul wants to be crystal clear that he is not asking them to assume a burden that others have created by failing to give because they prefer to keep their wealth.

He proves this from Scripture by referring to the way God provided manna to his people in the wilderness. We saw in chapter 3 that each Israelite, whether he collected a lot or a little, had enough but not too much. Those who hoarded it discovered that their excess rotted. This self-adjusting provision seems to be what Paul is talking about.

He applies this by saying that the present wealth of the Corinthians (assuming that they gave according to their means and from a gospel motive) would meet the needs of the saints who otherwise would have "too little." This would also meet the wealthy's own need not to have "too much." He also reminds the Corinthians that Israel's abundance will supply their need, in that it was these Jewish believers who brought them the gospel itself. All this is orchestrated by God and, when exchanged, produces "fairness."

Through this process of giving, God establishes a biblical kind of equality. There will be substantial differences of income and wealth, but there will not be too much for the prosperous or too little for the poor (see 2 Cor. 8:13–15). Paul pictured the people of God as one people who shared an international but corporate unity that called for this model of economic sharing.

Giving to the poor, with these goals in mind, was built into the ethos and culture of the early church. I do not see how we can avoid the clear conviction that giving to the poor, so that each one has enough but not too much, is still valid in God's kingdom. If that is true, it is most challenging for the Western church.

Therefore, this teaching is as challenging and important to believers today as it was in AD 56. Today, in God's providence, we have a very uneven distribution of wealth within the body of Christ. The Corinthians, as Americans do today, sat on a large part of that wealth. Paul let them know that God had blessed them with this wealth so that it could be shared to meet the famine need at that time.

7. Trust God to Provide for All Your Giving

This hints at the next great principle in this passage. Second Corinthians 9:6–11 is one of the most remarkable passages in the Scriptures because of the way it deals with the issue of resources for giving and rewards for giving. These are still hot-button issues today. Paul writes,

> The point is this: whoever sows sparingly will also reap sparingly, and whoever sows bountifully will also reap bountifully. Each one must give as he has decided in his heart, not reluctantly or under compulsion, for God loves a cheerful giver. And God is able to make all grace abound to you, so that having all sufficiency in all things at all times, you may abound in every good work. As it is written,
>
> > "He has distributed freely, he has given to the poor;
> > his righteousness endures forever."
>
> He who supplies seed to the sower and bread for food will supply and multiply your seed for sowing and increase the harvest of your righteousness. You will be enriched in every way to be generous in every way, which through us will produce thanksgiving to God. (2 Cor. 9:6–11)

This passage explains how such expansive giving is accomplished and how all God's kingdom causes can be funded. Paul begins by quoting a proverb that reflects a two-thousand-year-old train of thought in biblical ethics: "Whoever sows sparingly will also reap sparingly, and whoever sows generously will also reap generously." Here, to give is to sow. And just as an agricultural harvest is proportional to its sowing, so it is with giving. *The more generously one gives, the more generously one will reap at harvest.*

Sowing involves not the amount of funds that are contributed but the heart condition of the giver. As Philip Hughes rightly points out,

> The source of giving is not the purse, but the heart, as the next verse makes clear. The poor widow who gave two common mites, the least of all gifts in quantity, none the less, because she gave her whole living, gave more than all the others together who, out of

their superfluity, gave silver and gold at no cost to themselves (Mk. 12:41ff.). It was she who gave, and sowed, bountifully, not they. . . . The sphere of giving, then, presents no exception to the inexorable rule, valid in the moral no less than in the agricultural realm, that a man reaps according the manner of his sowing, which Paul enunciates in Gal. 6:7ff.[4]

There are no laws or formulas in this area of decision making about giving, except that God has set it up so that we determine our own future reaping by our personal, free decisions about sowing. Our love models God's in that it is freely offered—not under compulsion or law.

So what does it mean to reap? Paul encourages the people to give (sow) generously because God "is able to make all grace abound to you, so that having all sufficiency in all things at all times, you may abound in every good work" (2 Cor. 9:8). Whatever that means, I cannot imagine a stronger way of saying that God will be able to meet both your true needs and the needs of his kingdom. As Miroslav Volf aptly remarks, "For the Apostle, wealth is not primarily a matter of 'having' but of 'being.'"[5]

The very God who created seed and supplies it to earthly sowers (i.e., farmers) will also supply enough for you to be rich in every way, so that you can increase your generosity on every occasion, enlarge the harvest of your righteousness, meet your needs in this life, and expand the perimeter of the good work that is done in his name.

But God, through Paul, is saying something even more countercultural and radical. He is saying that, as his people give generously, God can be counted on to increase their supply of resources so that every good work can be accomplished to his glory. This is the revolutionary principle that God will always provide sufficiently for his own kingdom's work and will do it through the generosity of his own people.

God is committed to investing his resources in Christians so that no good work will lack the funds it needs if they sow generously. In

4. Philip E. Hughes, *The Second Epistle to the Corinthians*, The New International Commentary on the New Testament (Grand Rapids: Eerdmans, 1962), 329.

5. Miroslav Volf, *Free of Charge: Giving and Forgiving in a Culture Stripped of Grace* (Grand Rapids: Zondervan, 2005), 109.

short, everything that God wants us to do is provided for through the accounts and purses of his people. I challenged myself to find one instance in the Old Testament when God's people lacked the resources to fulfill his commands. I could not find one. They came up short only when they drew back from a task or sought resources from false gods.

There is also a progressive aspect to this, since these resources can actually grow. As Miroslav Volf said so well, "If you give what you were given to give, more will be given to you."[6] As Christians sow generously, God enhances their motivation and ability to give more, increasing the giving, which again increases the provision of God. This surprising, beneficent cycle takes place progressively in the lives of God's people and the work of his kingdom. The cycle will finally be fulfilled in the eternal rewards given in the age to come.

Paul experienced this cycle as he appealed to the Galatians for help and their gift spurred on the Corinthians, who spurred on the Macedonians, whose gift then ignited the Corinthians' second effort to give more. Of course, it is hard to predict the amplifying work of the Spirit of God, but the dynamic is clearly affirmed by Paul.

This is a kind of kingdom prosperity for Christian givers, which is designed to amplify their giving and the impact of their good works, now and into eternity. It comes to those who give out of thanksgiving to God for the gift of his Son instead of being motivated by earthly riches, power, or advantage. Earthly advantage or reward is not sufficient to motivate the consecrated selflessness of true Christian giving.

This stands in stark contrast to the culture of the Roman Empire. Offering sacrifices to obtain the favor of the gods and better the circumstances of this life was (and is) the root of all pagan worship. Our God promises to give us a better life in his unseen but revealed kingdom. It is manifest now but will be fully revealed only on the last day. For now, he reassures his people that he will provide enough money and resources for them to accomplish his will for them in this life. He will care for them in exquisite detail and attention, that they might not only be saved but also complete the works that he ordained for them before the foundation of the world (see Eph. 2:10).

6. Volf, 79.

Sadly, but not surprisingly, a twisted version of this promise of kingdom prosperity exists in religious circles today. It has been called the "health and wealth" theology. It is best characterized not as a theology but as a resurrected paganism. It is taught particularly by TV and radio preachers who are dependent on the media because of the money it raises for them and their lifestyle. They both indirectly and directly communicate that giving money to their ministry is an act of "seed faith" that will unleash financial and health blessings on the donor. This is a direct twisting of the teaching of Paul in 2 Corinthians 9:10.

This quote from one preacher is typical: "If you have been at a low-level harvest for a long time, then it's time to release your prosperity with higher seed-level giving and a greater expectation of an unprecedented harvest. It's time to move into high gear and release the prosperity anointing over yourself and your loved ones! Today I am asking you to move up to a higher level. I believe strongly that I am supposed to ask God's people right now to prayerfully consider giving a sacrificial gift of $1,000."[7]

Shamans from all cultures, pagan gods, and health and wealth preachers claim the power to reverse poverty and sickness—connected, of course, to financial gifts being given to them and to certain ancestors or gods that they collect for. The purchased magic napkin or bracelet, the "seed faith" cash gift, or even the secret technique of "positive faith thinking" will let the downtrodden regain success in their lives. The best modern survey of this prosperity teaching has been recently published by Kate Bowler.[8]

---

7. See Justin Peters, *Clouds without Water* (Justin Peters Ministries, 2 CD set, 2010). Information at justinpeters.org. He has studied these ministries in depth and believes that he is called to offer a biblical perspective about them. Unfortunately, specific critiques of these preachers are often met with lawsuits rather than with financial disclosure, which confirms that they are peddling the gospel for their own benefit. Generous religious liberty laws in the United States protect anyone who claims to be a church from financial disclosure. As it happened in some of the monasteries of Europe in the Middle Ages, religious workers can take a vow of religious vocation and live lives that are fit for a king, so long as they stay in the "monastery" and are part of its fundraising machine.

8. See Kate Bowler, *Blessed: A History of the American Prosperity Gospel* (Oxford: Oxford University Press, 2013).

As believers give money to self-proclaimed "anointed ones" in order to get health and wealth for themselves, they are reinforcing an incentive that will actually reduce their motivation and capacity for true giving in the future. God does not employ a "pay to play" scheme for the sick. The sick should call for the elders of the church to pray for them. The poor should not send money to strangers who offer them riches in return. Rather, if they lack the necessities of life, they should seek the help of their church. Beyond that, they should live in contentment with what they have, put away worry, and trust their heavenly Father for their daily bread as they seek labor that will pay a living wage.

"Pay to play" pagan giving schemes are also deadly for churches' compassion toward their own poor. If poverty is caused by lack of faith, then churches are relieved of any practical obligation to or compassion for the needy—except to exhort them to "claim God's blessing" in faith. In fact, from a pagan perspective, it is bad to help the needy, because you are reinforcing their lack of faith. In contrast to all this is Luke's report in Acts 4 that there were "no poor among them" because of the saints' generosity (see v. 34). This "miracle" did not come about because the poor discovered some secret knowledge of positive faith (such as "name it and claim it") or made offerings to the apostles in order to "unleash" prosperity.

In poor communities, pastors have an important responsibility to engender a proper hope in those who have been stuck in the stress of poverty—sometimes for generations. Such people's temptation is to give up all hope and protect themselves from further hurt and disappointment. It is a valid and important ministry to exhort these believers to ask their Father in heaven for their daily bread. The church should join them in that prayer and should partner with them in offering these people appropriate assistance. This includes teaching them to admit that they do not have enough, to offer believing prayer to God, and to exercise faith by continuing to seek ways to provide for themselves. God can work employment and economic miracles for his people. However, James 4:13–17 says that we cannot "claim it" in advance; it will happen only "if the Lord wills." Tell God what you want him to do. Faith is believing that God hears us and is *able* to answer our prayer. That is the only faith that Jesus required of those whom he healed.

Some pastors in poor communities take this biblical approach but are then pressured by competing "prosperity churches" to add an unbiblical overlay of false teaching that promises people that they will become wealthy. When this does not work, it discourages people from offering believing prayers and pursuing better work. Biblical churches should speak with one voice to counter this heresy and move our leaders back to "remembering the poor," as Paul and the apostles did, so they can help people with work adjustment, work skill issues, and access to appropriate resources.

To return to Paul's main message here, Christian giving is a means by which God gives his own children the resources, motivation, and opportunities to be better off in the life of his kingdom. He progressively enhances his children's resources, opportunities, and motivations for generous giving and good works, helping them to lay up for themselves kingdom treasure that they can never lose. In the process, he equips and funds his church for every good work.

The implication of this is almost disturbing: We should never say that any good work, commission, or command of God is impossible due to a lack of funding. There may be a process required to obtain the resources, but 2 Corinthians 9 holds out the promise that God himself will be involved with that process. He will provide the resources and relationships that can meet the need.

Remember the humorous story of the preacher who told his congregation that he had good news about the building campaign? He was delighted to announce that there were enough funds in the church to complete the entire building project. The only bad news was that those funds were still in the wallets of the church members. The story is a bit lame, but it illustrates a sad truth: when we come up short in funding the kingdom of God, it is not God who has failed to provide the resources. It is we, his people, who have failed to offer them to his service.

This is a particularly important truth for us to remember as we look at the massive needs around the world or even just the needs of Christians and those whom they live among. Can we meaningfully engage world missions, hunger, and poverty with a sober sense that the resources will be there as we sow generously according to God's will? The answer is yes. We will explain this in chapter 12.

8. Give Proportionally

Finally, Paul states the eighth principle: that giving should be *universal and proportional*. Like the divine institutions of labor, marriage, and the Sabbath, the offering of firstfruits to God is rooted in the earliest times, even before Abraham. Paul affirms the Old Testament guideline of proportional and universal giving in 2 Corinthians 8:12: "For if the readiness is there, it is acceptable according to what a person has, not according to what he does not have" (see also 1 Cor. 16:1–3).

The basic, proportional discipline that God commanded of Old Testament landowners was that a tenth of all their crops was to be given to him. The Levites were in turn to tithe these tithes for the temple staff. Paul here does not institute or refer to any obligation to tithing, but he does strongly command that everyone give as God has blessed him. There is no minimum or maximum.

In Paul's teaching, part of the liberty that Christ purchased for us is the freedom from the detailed prescriptions of the Mosaic law, including the tithe laws. These laws were quite specific as to how, when, and where the tithe was to be given, and they were different every third year. They were important for God's people in the age of their spiritual childhood and tutelage, but Paul does not appeal to them as binding now.

However, given that 10 percent was required of all landowners and even of the Levites (see Num. 18:25–27), this says a lot about the baseline level of giving that we should consider today. I like how Randy Alcorn characterizes the tithe as the "training wheels of giving."[9] When Jesus confronted the Pharisees, it is significant that he did not condemn their tithing of garden herbs but convicted them for forgetting the greater provision of the law against stealing (by devouring widows' houses, etc.).

9. Randy Alcorn, *Money, Possessions, and Eternity*, rev. and updated ed. (Carol Stream, IL: Tyndale House, 2003), 173.

How do we compare to those in Malachi who were suffering under severe economic depression and persecution and yet were told by God to bring their tithes into his storehouse so that he would bless them and care for them in ways they could not imagine? Considering the blessing we have received in the Spirit and the full knowledge we have of the love God showed us in Christ, how can we even discuss whether or not to give less than 10 percent? How would we compare if we did as Paul suggested and tested the sincerity of our love by comparing it with that of believers in the Old Testament (see 2 Cor. 8:8)? Or with the giving of the Macedonians?

We live in the richest culture in history, so even thinking about giving "just 10 percent" seems ludicrous—even though, for many of us, giving at that base is very hard at first. Yet if we step out and learn to give at this basic level, we have a foundation on which we can build greater giving, as we grow in faith and love for Christ and his kingdom.

In Paul's core teaching, we have come face-to-face with the extraordinary vision that is embodied in his mission to the Gentiles. He has been discipling them to

- give themselves to the Lord, which included their wealth, and then give themselves to one another, as Christ gave himself for them.
- give as a response to the giving of God in the gospel and to the mercy that was poured out on us by Christ.
- seek to excel in the grace of giving.
- believe that God adequately funds all his kingdom enterprises through the giving of pre-positioned resources that come to believers from him.
- give proportionally instead of with a cap of 10 percent.

We are now ready to look at how these principles were applied to the New Testament church in the rest of the Epistles.

Questions for Review and Reflection

1. How did biblical and pagan Gentile philanthropy differ?
2. Why do you think the apostle Peter exhorted Paul to teach the Gentiles to "remember the poor"?
3. How does Paul's promise of God's abundant blessing on those who are generous differ from the "prosperity gospel" that we hear about today?

9

Money and Giving
in the Epistles

In all things I have shown you that by working hard in this way we must help the weak and remember the words of the Lord Jesus, how he himself said, "It is more blessed to give than to receive." (Acts 20:35)

Second Corinthians 8 and 9 set out the key principles that governed the theology and practice of giving in the New Testament era. A number of passages in the other Epistles help to apply these principles, focusing more explicitly on God's purpose for work and the money that he grants us.

Many passages imply that the biblical purpose for our money is that we might love God and others with it. This understanding of money is explicitly taught in a passage from Paul's letter to the Ephesians (see Eph. 4:28) and in Paul's speech to the Ephesian elders (see Acts 20:33–34). Let's look at these two crux passages before examining other supporting passages in the New Testament Epistles.

Work to Help the Needy (Eph. 4:28)

This passage occurs in Paul's discourse on how Christians should "walk," or live, in the world. He exhorts the Ephesians to imitate him as he imitates Christ, putting off the identities and behaviors of the Gentiles and putting on the new life as well as conduct that reflects Christ. He covers how this applies to many areas of life, and in the midst of this he writes, "Let the thief no longer steal, but rather let him labor, doing honest work with his own hands, so that he may have something to share with anyone in need." This has the put-off/put-on dynamic that is so familiar to Paul's readers (see Eph. 4:17–5:21). He commands thieves in the Ephesian church to get rid of all forms of theft and to replace it with its opposite: generosity.

Theft was a major issue in Roman culture. The rich often stole from their slaves, debtors, and day laborers. Slaves often stole from their masters. Tax collectors stole from everyone. Soldiers got part of their pay through extorting people. Religious authorities stole from worshippers and widows. Merchants stole from customers with false weights and measures. And the poor often robbed others in order to live, since a day's wage would not feed a family of four.

This reminds me of the billions of dollars that are taken through fraud and theft on Wall Street (such as the savings and loan scam in 1989 and the subprime mortgage scam in 2007). And of course billions of dollars are stolen through tax cheating, Social Security disability and Medicare fraud, and the sale of defective products, from airbags to fake products from overseas. While more money is stolen through white-collar crime, there is also the other end of the business, as illiterate young men roam the streets of the world without any positive options and are sucked into criminal enterprises. Many see it as their only choice. Thankfully, thousands of these men end up being reached and remaking a life for themselves in Christ. Paul's words cover all kinds of theft and can be used to bring about the redemption of both high- and low-end swindlers and thieves.

Look closely at the reason why thieves should seek a living through legitimate work, even in the dismal job market of that day. Paul's surprising answer is so that they may *have something to give to the one in need.* In other words, their rehab efforts should have the long-term goal of giving to others in need, not just of self-support.

Paul is not suggesting that earning money for one's own sustenance is wrong. In fact, self-support is required in Ephesians 4:28, because one must meet one's own needs in order to have funds to share with others. In 1 Thessalonians 4:11–12 he says, "Work with your hands . . . so that you may . . . be dependent on no one." In

1 Timothy 5:8, he teaches that providing for the needs of one's family is a morally nonnegotiable form of love. He commands families to care for their own older relatives and widows rather than let them become dependent on the church. Brethren who are idle are to be disciplined and considered more morally compromised than an unbeliever.

Paul commands all these thieves not only to stop stealing but to work with their hands at honest labor (literally, at "that which is good"). It takes great faith to leave a profitable but illegal enterprise for a legal one that pays less and from which you could be fired. Former thieves were to trust God and in that sense "take their chances" on the job market and on God's provision.

What is different and challenging about this command is its point that generosity to the needy is the deeper reason for work. It is not just for the self-sufficiency of those who work and their family dependents. Its final purpose and meaning is to express love for one's needy neighbor, the sick, the orphan, the slave, the depressed, the ignorant, and the spiritually lost.

It is not correct to conclude that Paul is saying that former thieves (or Christians in general) are only to give to the poor and not to support their churches, pastors, or missionaries. Paul mentions giving to the poor for two reasons. First, most of the giving in the early church was for the relief of the poor, so it was a general way to speak of all giving. Second, giving to the needy most vividly illustrated the new dynamic of converted thieves giving *to* people instead of taking from them.

A New View of Work

Ephesians 4:28 reflects the broader, very countercultural view of work that is attached to the gospel message. Let's briefly summarize its main points.

The Dignity of Work

Paul affirms the dignity of work, and especially of manual labor ("with his hands"). This was as countercultural as were Paul's views on husbands having to live and even sacrifice for the happiness of their wives. Paul endorses manual labor as being pleasing to God (see Eph.

6:5–9) and was himself most likely a professional leatherworker. His teaching about the dignity of work should remind the church that the goal of any short-term assistance we provide to the needy is to see them become givers themselves through finding viable work. Our aid should never remove someone's motivation to seek paid work to support his or her family.

The Place of Work

In Paul's culture, manual work was seen as a curse that was exacted on those of lower character and intelligence. The Greek (and pagan) perspective was that earthly wealth or poverty was the outworking of the good or evil of the individual. Those who were good spent their time in contemplation and conversation and at the city gates doing the business of the town—not slaving in the fields for just enough to survive. If something bad happened to someone who was thought to be good, it meant that he or she must have been hiding their evil or failures. (See Job's three friends.) This is the default thinking of pagan ethics the world over, as in the doctrine of karma in Hinduism.

Labor itself was considered to be part of a lower form of "animal" life. The Greek ideal was to be wealthy enough to own slaves and avoid all labor[1] and to instead pursue the mind and spirit, which alone were related to the divine part of man. The idea of divine dignity in ordinary work was unknown.

The notion that one worked in order to give money to the needy was even more absurd. To be sure, there was philanthropy in Paul's day, but only to "worthy people of noble character." Since poverty was seen as an indicator of moral deficiency, this severely limited prospects for charity.[2] The poor were relegated to their suffering, and the rich underwrote cultural and public work projects for those who could reciprocate.

This Greek view of philanthropy has entered into classic Western thinking about giving, especially in terms of its focus on giving only

---

1. See Lee Hardy, *The Fabric of This World* (Grand Rapids: Eerdmans, 1990), 6–10.
2. See Thomas H. Jeavons and Rebekah Burch Basinger, *Growing Givers' Hearts: Treating Fundraising as Ministry* (San Francisco: Jossey-Bass, 2000), 47–48.

to the "deserving poor." This suggests that we are to avoid helping those whose sin shows, such as those who are seeking escape from a life of theft, prostitution, swindling, addictions, gambling, and organized crime. While this view does not hold much sway in consciously Christian missionary circles, it is still quite powerful in the philanthropic thinking of some established foundations.

The Place of Charity

Charity to the poor was largely a Jewish idea being injected into a Gentile culture. As we've seen in Galatians, Paul promised Peter and the other apostles that he would remember the poor and teach the Gentiles to do the same. It was a new way of relating to the needy.

The Call for Character

Paul (on Christ's behalf) aimed for character transformation, not just for conduct that avoided evil. Jay Adams, one of the founders of the biblical counseling movement, used to ask his students (of which I was one), "When is a thief not a thief?" The answer is not "When he stops stealing." If a thief is arrested, he will stop stealing, but this does not change his character. The answer that Adams looked for was "When he becomes generous and begins to give his money away." At that point he has "put on" the opposite of theft and has become a giver. This put-off/put-on mentality is the path to a change of identity, not just the cessation of bad behavior. An eastern religion would require only a cessation of theft. Christ points us to the commands of positive love as they are worked out in each area of the commandments.

All the commandments of God have two parts. They have *prohibitions* (such as "You shall not steal") as well as containing (sometimes by implication) *positive commands* (such as "Give generously to the needs of your neighbor"). They have "put-offs" and "put-ons." Much of the gospel's transforming power comes when we replace put-offs with put-ons. Many thieves had doubtless experienced the curses of poverty and saw thievery as the only way out. Now they were to work to help provide a better way out for other thieves, prostitutes, orphans, widows, and poor who were coming to hear the claims of Christ.

God aims to sanctify us at three levels: in our hearts, in our character (our moral habits), and in our conduct. If you have received the new birth in the Spirit, cried, "Be merciful to me, a sinner," and followed Christ as his disciple, then he is working to create a giver's heart in you. That heart encompasses every dollar and resource you have. The question becomes "How much can I give?"—not "How much do I have to give?"

How Paul Walked the Talk (Acts 20:33–34)

What would this look like in real life? We read a description in Paul's farewell speech to the Ephesian elders in Acts 20:25–38. At the climax of the speech (vv. 33–34), he says to them,

> I coveted no one's silver or gold or apparel. You yourselves know that these hands ministered to my necessities and to those who were with me. In all things I have shown you that by working hard in this way we must help the weak and remember the words of the Lord Jesus, how he himself said, "It is more blessed to give than to receive."

Paul sets an example of hard work, making it clear that his work proceeds out of a desire not to accumulate wealth but to meet his needs and the needs of those with him, so that they will not be a burden on the church. He also desires to give to the weak (i.e., the needy).

He then quotes a saying of Jesus that is not recorded in the Gospels: "It is more blessed to give than to receive." Paul's language emphasizes that he is working to demonstrate that all Christians work out of a desire to help the needy. Paul's vision for work was to have something to give. Like Abraham and all those in the covenant line, he accepted blessing so that he could be a blessing.

Paul is not saying that inheriting or obtaining money through investments and businesses is wrong. In fact, earning or inheriting lots of money would be a great help in the application of his command. Paul's concern is that, whether we are rich or poor, we are content and generous—not storing up beyond our projected needs or those of our families.

This passage confirms that the Ephesians 4:28 passage was to be the example for all—including for the elders of the church. Paul is firm on the point that everyone should work hard so that they can become active givers. Making his lesson more powerful was the fact that he had the right as an apostle to ask for payment for his services. But in order to avoid potential misunderstandings regarding his motives and to better teach the believers in Ephesus about money, he refrained from asking for funds. Instead he contributed to the needs of the saints there, highlighting for the Gentiles that their new identity in Christ was one of loving one another, which involved a complete change of their attitude toward work.

Loving Means Giving

To teach that we work and earn money in order to give it to others is an application of the more general command for us to love and give in all areas of life. God demonstrated love by *giving* his Son so that whoever believes in him shall have everlasting life. Christ laid aside his crown and position in order to *give* his life as a ransom for all. He *gave* us the gift of the Holy Spirit at great cost to himself. In Ephesians and elsewhere, husbands are commanded to give themselves to their wives, and wives are to give respect to their husbands for the Lord's sake. Slaves are commanded to give heart obedience to their owners for the Lord's sake, and owners are commanded to give workers fair wages. We contribute our service and giftedness to the church. Giving is at the heart of love.

In God's kingdom, money is a means of expressing the heart's response to God's grace. The heart that seeks to love receives blessing so that it can be a blessing.

In summary, I suggest that the Bible teaches the following:

- From a monetary point of view, it might be said that the Christian lives to give.
- Generous giving should be the final goal of our saving, investing, and financial planning, and it should control our financial dreams.

How then do we implement this in our lives, our budgets, and our church communities?

Instructions for the "Haves"

In 1 Timothy 6:17–19, Paul charges the rich not to be proud and not to set their hopes on accumulated assets, but on God, who delights in giving us all things to enjoy. In doing so, he affirms the blessing of material wealth but warns us not to serve it. To those whom God has blessed with riches, he says,

> They are to do good, to be rich in good works, to be generous and ready to share, thus storing up treasure for themselves as a good foundation for the future, so that they may take hold of that which is truly life. (vv. 18–19)

We know that these verses cannot be interpreted to mean that we are justified (saved) by our "good works." Ephesians 2:8–10 parses that distinction—we are saved by grace, through faith, *apart* from works, but are saved *for* good works. Good works will necessarily mark the life of a Christian.

So what does Paul mean when he says, "So that they may take hold of that which is truly life"? The Bible teaches that generosity has a special application to the rich. As they store up treasure in heaven, they are more and more personally protected from the deceitfulness and peril of riches that are outlined in 1 Timothy 6:8–10. As Paul mentions there, wealth and its pursuit have caused many to stray from the faith, fall into a snare, and pierce themselves through with many sorrows. The love of money is the root of many evils.

Just as Jesus was, Paul is especially concerned with helping the rich to handle wealth within the kingdom of God. His emphasis is not so much on stewardship but on generous giving. The rich who are generous are helped to persevere in their faith and will have a joyful entrance to a future life, where they are rich toward God.

Wealth and Recognizing the Lord's Body

First Corinthians 11:17–34 is another remarkable passage on wealth and poverty, though we usually consider it on the basis of its instructions for the Lord's Supper. While it does offer that, it also references our need for self-examination so that we can "discern the Lord's body" (see v. 29). What is Paul referring to here?

During the believers' meals together in Corinth, it seems that each family was to bring their own food. Some poor families could not bring food to the communion meal and went hungry. Others would bring large quantities of food for themselves and would enjoy their meal without concern for those who had little or nothing. They would even become drunk in their presence.

Paul rebukes them, suggesting that if they are just coming to feed themselves, they should do so at home. He warns them that "whoever, therefore, eats the bread or drinks the cup of the Lord in an unworthy manner will be guilty concerning the body and blood of the Lord" (v. 27). Instead, each one should examine himself, because

> anyone who eats and drinks without discerning the body eats and drinks judgment on himself. That is why many of you are weak and ill, and some have died. But if we judged ourselves truly, we would not be judged. But when we are judged by the Lord, we are disciplined so that we may not be condemned along with the world. (1 Cor. 11:29–32)

Paul rebukes some at Corinth for the division between those who had much and those who had nothing. He is disturbed that this disunity was taking place at the very time when the church was affirming their union in the Lord's Supper. For Paul, it was like a fistfight at a wedding. He indicates that the Lord himself was angry and had brought discipline on the church for tolerating such division.

The church is the spiritual body of Christ, but that does not mean that we have no *earthly* interest in our brothers and sisters. Paul contradicts the false belief that each believer is free to pursue his earthly wealth, appetites, and kingdom and then to shift into worship, fellowship, and communion without regard to the issues of material life.

Paul exhorts the rich to wait until they are sure that their brothers and sisters have sufficient food. A violation of this is seen not as a lack of courtesy but as a fundamental breach of the very meaning of Christ's one body being broken for all. This kind of behavior during communion is not a lack of decorum or of appropriate symbolism; it is a fundamental breakdown of the communion of saints when the needs of the poor are not considered to be "part of the fellowship."

While today the bread and wine for communion are supplied by the church, many congregations meet without recognizing the needs of members who are hungry or lacking the basics of life. These can be easily overlooked—especially because of how regional our churches often are. More wealthy churches often meet in the suburbs, while poorer and immigrant churches meet in urban areas. The urban churches often bear the suffering of great human need without recognition or visible sharing from wealthier Christians. Because we are geographically separated, we often don't know how or where to start to help, and we soon stop trying. Both wealthier and poorer Christians are discouraged by bad experiences from prior attempts. Rather than seeking God's wisdom together to help us resolve the issue (as in Acts 6), we have given up. In my view, this is one reason for the spiritual weakness of our suburban churches and the ongoing poverty of many urban Christian families.

When we celebrate the Lord's Supper, we should recognize the nature of Christ's body and actively share the necessities of life with our poorer brothers and sisters—in both our immediate congregation and our regional network.

Generosity and Compassion: The Mark of a Christian

There is a clear connection between salvation and generosity and compassion. This fruit of repentance is not optional but is an intrinsic part of a believer's new life. It marks believers as Christ's to the watching world and strengthens their assurance of salvation. It is not another "ought" but a statement of reality.

This makes sense, because if every person loves either God or money at the heart level, this will show in every area of their lives. We will be either givers or takers in everything that we do. This holds true for the poor, the middle class, and the wannabe rich as well as the truly rich. In the Bible, a person's attitude toward God or money often indicates his love (or lack thereof) for others.

Biblically, someone who is lacking in love, compassion for the poor, or generosity does not show the signs of having been saved. Such a person should consider whether or not he has truly bowed the knee to Christ as his Savior and Lord. On the day of judgment, the saved will be identified by the lives they have lived.

John says the same things in different language in 1 John.

> By this we know love, that he laid down his life for us, and we ought to lay down our lives for the brothers. But if anyone has the world's goods and sees his brother in need, yet closes his heart against him, how does God's love abide in him? Little children, let us not love in word or talk but in deed and in truth. (1 John 3:16–18)

This need for Christians to show compassion is prominent in John's writings. We saw in John 5:25–29 that Jesus predicted that the righteous and the wicked will be raised together at the judgment and then separated according to their works. None of this should be construed to contradict John's clear teaching that, in order to be saved and to inherit everlasting life, the sinner must receive and rest on Christ as his Lord and Savior. But, as we saw in Matthew 25, believers are identified by their works—the fruits of their repentance.

The passages that we have studied make clear that generosity and compassion are the marks of all Christians. Everyone whose life is found in God will find ways to show love and generosity.

The Book of James

James, the brother of Jesus, wrote to support Jewish communities around the Roman Empire and to explain the new Christian ethic to them. He warned about six sins related to money that faced Jewish

Christians who were living in a prosperous Gentile trading economy. These warnings update and reinforce wisdom from Proverbs, from Jesus's teaching, and from Paul's.

Don't Be Deluded by Riches (James 1:10–11)

James urges Christians to remember that the rich believer is really poor because of all the honor and wealth he will lose at death. On the other hand, the poor believer is really rich because of the high position and eternal blessings he has gained in Christ.

Without an awareness of the coming judgment and the eternal state, materialists are right that man can only eat, drink, and be merry in this life. The poor are doubly cursed within this materialist worldview, and few poor people adopt such a brutal outlook. Christians are to remember the big picture and keep God's grace to them, the judgment, and their eternal state very much in view.

Don't Favor the Rich (James 2:1–12)

The rich can bring money, connection, and honor to the local church, but despite that, Christians are to show equal honor to the poor. After all, God chose them to be the dominant population in his kingdom and will raise them to be first in that kingdom. It seems that the churches James was writing to wanted more of the rich to join them. They were probably tempted to believe that they had too many poor already.

Warn Hypocrites Who Have Money (James 2:14–15)

Beware of those who talk graciously and pray for God's provision for the poor but do not obey his command to love and assist the needy. Such professing believers are not showing signs that they trust in Jesus. James is countering a false interpretation of Paul's teaching that says that salvation is by a faith that is *alone* (that is, without works of faith). He shows that faith always results in works of faith.

Repent of Coveting and Loving the World (James 4:1–6)

Conflicts, fights, and abuse arise from hearts that demand life from the resources of this world and at the expense of others. Such lovers of the world cannot be friends with God. Being in love with the world constitutes spiritual adultery. God should be our first love and loyalty.

Entrepreneurs Should Stay Humble (James 4:13–16)

James commands believers who have hope of making money to submit their business plans to God for his revision. They should say, "If the Lord wills, we will live and do this or that" (v. 15). Believers should bring a sober judgment to business affairs—one that is rooted in their knowledge of the fall and the reality of death and corruption. Business planners should not set their hearts on the money that they hope to make. This continues the biblical theme that, while some plans may make us money, our lives are much more than our money.

Those Who Are Rich Should Repent While There Is Time (James 5:1–8)

James addresses the unrepentant Jewish rich with the sternest warnings in the New Testament. He echoes Jeremiah, Amos, and Jesus in his warnings to them to repent while there is still time, and he points out the particularly harsh punishment awaiting them because of the way they have used their power and wealth to exploit, cheat, and oppress others. He evokes a picture (from an eternal perspective) of their hoarded wealth having rotted and moths having consumed their garments. This ruined wealth will testify against them on the day of judgment, when God himself will accuse them. Evidently, most of the Jewish wealthy had not converted to Christ, so he just calls them the "rich people." A few were making inquiries about Christ, and, in his second warning above, he instructed the church on how to treat them.

James does not comment theologically on the purpose of our work or money, but he makes it clear that there are two heart attitudes we can have. One trusts in, covets, and honors wealth. The other lives with eternity in view and causes us to use our wealth to assist the needy, hold it with an open hand, and flee temptations to use the power of wealth to manipulate others and gain more for ourselves.

Revelation in Brief

In addition to the Epistles, Revelation also has some powerful money-related themes. We will hint at them now and return in more detail later. Revelation describes the rise of an international merchant trading system that becomes complicit with the forces of the Antichrist (see Rev. 18). Through this great wealth machine, the forces of Sodom, Canaan, Babylon, Rome, Tyre, and Sidon are all resurrected in a new Super-Babylon. When Christ comes to destroy the Antichrist, this great city and its oppressive system are laid waste. This elicits mourning from all the merchants of the earth, as smoke from the city rises for all to see. Exploring this dynamic is beyond the purview of this book. However, the letter to the church at Laodicea (see Rev. 3:14–22) is particularly relevant to our situation in the wealthy West, and we will explore it in detail in chapter 13.

In summary, the Epistles assume that Christians are required to work in order to support themselves and their dependents so that they will avoid becoming a burden on others. Work finds its kingdom fulfillment in making us able to give to others. It moves us from the ranks of the taker to the ranks of the giver. We do not earn money so that we can provide ourselves a life of affluence or mitigate all possible risks. The Bible's perspective is overwhelmingly that the extent to which we have been blessed is a means for us to help the needy and to support good works of mercy and missions.

Questions for Review and Reflection

1. What was the new view of work that the apostle Paul introduced to the Gentiles?
2. According to Paul, what is the final economic goal of work?
3. Why did Paul confront the Corinthians about the sin of allowing some to go hungry at their communion dinners? What are the implications of his rebuke for us today?

10

The Theology of Money:
Live to Give

*As we have opportunity, let us do good to everyone, and especially
to those who are of the household of faith. (Gal. 6:10)*

In our biblical survey, we have highlighted the teaching that all our
money is granted to us by God so that we can love others. In short, the
purpose for money is giving. We might even say that we live to give.
That overarching belief is, I suggest, connected to four corollary beliefs
that give it definition and application, as when light is separated into
colors upon shining through a prism. Now that we have completed
this biblical survey, we can explore the way these four ideas coalesce
into the basic elements of a theology of wealth and giving. We'll begin
with a sharper definition of the main thesis and then lay out the four
truths connected to it.

The Thesis: Our Money Is a
Means for Us to Love Others

We are blessed so that we might be a blessing. Specifically, the
money that we have comes to us with God's purpose attached to it:
that it be used to provide for us and then for others. We can illustrate
this with an analogy from the world of not-for-profit accounting. The
funds that come to believers from God are similar to what accoun-
tants call "restricted funds." They can be used only for the purpose

designated by the donor. For example, if someone gives to support a particular missionary, those funds can't be used for general operations at the mission or for some other missionary. They are restricted to the donor's intention. As Christians, we should view *all* our funds as restricted by God to caring for ourselves (and our dependents) and then giving to others. The funds are not ours outright but are given to us so that we can build up the body of Christ, relieve the poor, and disciple the nations.

In this way, we function as "trustees" for God. We have been granted specific funds to use in the particular manner and for the particular purpose that has been set out by the giver, who is God. We cannot use them in whatever way we like. They come with the mandate that we are to use them for God's purposes. So those who have money should see themselves as servants, stewards, or trustees of that money for God.

However, there is another view that many of us hold by default: the belief that, though our funds are given to us by God, he does not attach any particular meaning or purpose to most of it. We *can* use it as we see fit—minus the tithe that is due back to God. This view usually acknowledges God's provision and thanks him for it, but then simply offers a token back to him in appreciation.

This default view usually recognizes the familiar biblical mandate that we are to support ourselves and our dependents (see 1 Thess. 4:11–12), and so it sees most of our money as falling vaguely under the heading of "self-support." The order of priority becomes:

1. Thankfully recognizing the fact that our funds come from God and that we are stewards of those funds.
2. Giving a tithe or portion of the funds back to God.
3. Using the balance wisely to provide for ourselves and our families.
4. Seeing funds in excess of this as being unrestricted in God's view and available for our use in any way we choose.

Given the high cost of living in the West, self-support is usually how most of our funds are used. This is especially true for younger workers, people with children, lower- and middle-income earners, and people without much accumulated wealth (i.e., with a low net worth). Such people have a lot less discretionary income, because their fixed costs take a higher percentage of what they earn.

But biblically, self-support is meant to be a means to another end: generosity. This generosity is not limited to a traditional 10 percent tithe but extends to all our funds. Under this scheme, we might chart our priorities for our money this way:

1. All our funds are assigned to us from God, so we are stewards and trustees of all of it for kingdom purposes.
2. We must first use our money to meet our needs and to love our dependents, so that they will not be a burden or need the help of others but will be equipped to serve to the full extent of their strengths and gifts.
3. The balance is to be given to love others, as guided by the commands and commissions of Christ.

We saw how this principle was taught in Ephesians 4:28 and especially in Acts 20:34–35, where Paul set an example by working to keep his team from being a burden and so that he could give to the needs of others.

When we bow the knee to Christ, we become stewards of God's wealth for his goals. Our time, treasures, and talents are his—bought with a price and dedicated to the works of his kingdom. We acknowledge that all that we have is really owned by God and (most crucially) entrusted to us to be invested for his purposes. The parable of the talents and similar teachings embody this view (see Matt. 25:14–30; Luke 19:11–26).

Acknowledging God's ownership of our resources is only the first part of stewardship. An equally important part is then investing those resources for the Master's benefit. In fact, acknowledging his ownership of resources without investing them is the reason why the steward with one talent was cast out and condemned in Matthew 25:30. He took it and sat on it. Better not to take it than to take it and do nothing!

The situation is not unlike that of a migrant worker who comes to the United States to do farm labor and sends his earnings back to his needy family at home. Before his arrival in the United States, his wife, children, and parents had all slowly been starving to death. With no hope of seeing any change, the father left home and headed for the States. Of course, he must feed and clothe himself, but that is not why he works. He is in the States in order to send money home to his hungry family.

Because he loves them, he does not ask himself, "How much am I obligated to send?" His question is rather "How much can I send from this pay period?" He has to keep enough to care for his health and nutrition so that he can keep working. But it is his love for his family that motivates his self-care. He does not know whether he will make it back home to see them, and it is too risky for him to try to get them to the United States. So he sends his money where he cannot go, in hopes that his family will prosper at a better level while he is away.

In a similar way, Christians should analyze every dollar they have to see whether it can be used for the kingdom. This illustration cannot be pressed too far, but it does highlight the mentality that Christians should have as we plan how to use our money. We too are like aliens (migrants) in this world culture. Though we live in this world, our King, kingdom, culture, and life are not of this world. We are sending money into *that* kingdom. It goes to life-and-death issues—to preaching forgiveness and hope to the nations, to building up the saints into the life of God, to relieving their suffering and need, and to equipping them to become self-sufficient. Such remittances to our future country evoke God's pleasure, and he delights to reward his sons and daughters who have invested in the needs and opportunities of his kingdom. The words of Jim Elliot are relevant here: "He is no fool who gives what he cannot keep to gain what he cannot lose."

In sum: we work in order to have something to give.

The great revivalist John Wesley understood this. The third part of his famous formula expresses it well: "Gain all you can . . . Save all you can . . . Give all you can."[1] Wesley was correct that there is no limit

---

1. John Wesley, "The Use of Money," in *The Works of John Wesley*, vol. 6, ed. Thomas Jackson (London, 1872), available online at https://www.whdl.org/use-money-sermon-50.

on what a Christian may earn (although seeking wealth is wrong). "Top-line" income is not constrained. Instead, Christians focus on a bottom-line goal: to give all we can.

With that foundation, here are some of the principles and practices that can guide us in how we should use our money as God's trustees. You will recognize that these more theological corollaries are largely drawn from the eight principles of 2 Corinthians 8 and 9.

Corollary 1: God's Call Comes with God's Provision

The Lord of heaven and earth does not send his people on a fool's errand. He provides for the support of his kingdom by granting his people all the time, gifts, and treasure they need in order to complete his intended work. God provides for the fulfillment of his commands and commissions. In this view, our money is God's investment in his own kingdom. He has endowed and positioned each individual Christian with the unique spiritual gifts and specific monies that are needed so that, when they are combined with those of other believers, the church can carry out all that he has commanded it to do at every period in history. As they say in African-American churches, "If it is God's will, it is God's bill."

We have seen how this was illustrated in each age of redemptive history—from supplies that were gathered for Noah's ark, to the multiplication of Abraham's herds, to Joseph's provision of grain during the famine, to the Israelites' donation of their "plunder" from Egypt to the building of the tabernacle, to God's provision of water, manna, and meat during the wilderness wanderings, to the land that was given to every Israelite family, to the wealth that David gave to the temple, to the women's provision for Jesus and his disciples, to the growing church's full support for the poor in Jerusalem, to the Gentile Christians' gift of money to the hungry Jewish Christians in Palestine.

We know that God gives people the spiritual gifts that they need for the particular ministries he would have them fulfill, and in the same way he provides resources that are tailored to the particular challenges of each church's ministry callings. Just as each person has to exercise the gifts he has been given in order for them to be a blessing, so each person is called to contribute the particular amounts of wealth and resources that he can provide in the situations in which he finds himself. He (and his resources) were placed in that church, mission, village, community, and nation by God for a specific reason—a reason that is often made visible only when his gifts and monies are offered and used. As Paul teaches the Ephesians, "Grace was given to each one of us according to the measure of Christ's gift . . . from whom the whole body, joined and held together by every joint with which it is equipped, when each part is working properly, makes the body grow so that it builds itself up in love" (Eph. 4:7, 16).

If this is true, we can expect that the worldwide church is fully equipped for the task of church planting, building up the church, mission, and mercy. Financially, that means that we can be confident that there is enough money within the worldwide body to carry out God's kingdom program across the globe.

So how much do Christians have? The total wealth of the world-wide Christian community is not known. However, the 35 million "hard-core" US evangelicals alone control roughly $1.75 trillion of net worth and $1 trillion of annual income currently.[2] While 35 million is probably a low estimate of the total number of evangelicals overall, this illustrates the point that God has endowed his people with sub-stantial resources for the tasks that he has assigned us.

By God's plan, today's Western church is the richest church in human history. Since the Industrial Revolution and the mass conver-sions during the two Great Awakenings in the United States, God has deposited a large share of wealth with us as a resource for the discipling of the nations and the showing of his mercy. As business, wealth, and higher income spreads to Asian churches, we can expect to see new streams of resource arise for the kingdom. This is already happening to a great extent in South Korea. And this dynamic will spread to other areas where both economic growth and evangelism

2. To obtain these numbers, I multiplied the average US household income and net worth by 35 million.

are strong: Malaysia, China, and even Africa—where national GDPs (gross domestic products) are growing at a very high rate. India remains a challenge, but prayer and continued investment in missions there could yet bring change. Currently, most Christians there (except in the Kerala province) are very poor and in the low castes.

A word of caution is needed here. The Bible does *not* teach that a lack of money or giftedness in a particular Christian mission or church means that the enterprise is illegitimate or not in God's will. Many missions and church enterprises are short on funds or personnel. This corollary states that such a shortage is not because God failed to provide the wealth necessary to carry it out. It is not God's fault! If the mission or church is doing God's will, then somewhere within the body of Christ, God has provided the resources that are needed for it to succeed. These resources or gifts may not be offered by those who possess them, but they are there. The fault lies with those who have withheld the resources or been unwilling to offer themselves and their gifts to the church.

Christ has been exalted to heaven, where he gives gifts to men (see Eph. 4:8) and distributes to the poor (see 2 Cor. 9:9). He gives these gifts to the body for the common good, and so the body can perform its work fully only if every part contributes what God has given it.

This is the reason that the Great Commission has not yet been fulfilled. While the roots of this are spiritual, lack of money is the practical reason why there are communities with no churches and why poor believers are still suffering around the world. Granted, a substantial amount was accomplished in the twentieth century in the areas of both evangelism and mercy ministry, but that progress (which has been funded by the minority) also shows what could still be done if the full provision for mercy and mission were offered by God's people.

Corollary #2: Biblical Generosity Is Motivated by God's Grace

Generosity of biblical proportions can be motivated only by the working of God's grace in the human heart. That grace is revealed to those who trust in Jesus's finished work on the cross. Praying "God, be merciful to me, a sinner" is a transaction of grace. We were blind, lost, and enemies of God when Christ died for us, sought us, and called us to share his righteousness, sonship, access to the Father, indwelling of the Holy Spirit, and everlasting life. All this was given to us by pure grace and received by faith alone, apart from any merit we might muster.

In 2 Corinthians 8:8–10, we saw that Paul sees our motive for giving as being rooted in our response to that grace. The greater our knowledge of Christ's love for us, the more we will desire to offer ourselves and our resources for the blessing of others.

Christian generosity has distinct characteristics that are rooted in grace.

The Believer Becomes Like Christ and So Gives as Christ Gave

Christ's grace is at work in the believer, and so our giving mirrors his in response. Jesus did not just tithe his glory to us. He laid it all aside in order to take upon himself our humanity, in all its sin. Now we are empowered to imitate Christ in our lives (see Eph. 5:1) and to walk in love. As his followers, we should not clutch riches, comfort, or honor to ourselves but, like him, should give freely out of love and compassion in order to meet the need of others. This is giving that is driven by our experience of God's forgiveness and sacrifice. It is loving as we have been loved.

In my conversations with mature Christian donors over the years, I have noticed the following traits in them that confirmed that their basic motivation for giving was a response to God's grace. Tithing was rarely mentioned as an important factor for them, nor was any "standard" that they believed God expected. Their giving was not related to the effectiveness of an appeal or the greatness of a need. Most often, thankfulness for God's grace and goodness was a prime motivating factor for them. These givers demonstrate an evident love for God's purposes in the world and a sense of joy and privilege at being able to be a part of those purposes. They all talk about wanting to give more and reveal a delight in giving. They give despite lousy appeals, lack of teaching on giving in their churches, and the abuse of giving that is rampant among certain TV preachers. Many think about ways to increase their giving. Some make private "plans" with God for future earnings to be dedicated to his kingdom. Many times (but not all), God seems to take these folks up on the "deals," and they are able to hand large profits over to the kingdom with joy. Their giving comes from deep within their own motivation. They have changed from being those who live to get to being those who live to give.

Biblical Generosity Is Always Freely Offered

Grace-based giving is not "extracted" by compulsion, formula, or pressure. Paul says in 2 Corinthians 9:7 that God loves a cheerful giver—one who gives as he has decided in his heart, not under compulsion or reluctantly. Biblical generosity is truly wholehearted. It can be so when a heart is set upon God as its source of life. The giver does not serve a desire for money but serves God, who did not cling to his position but gave himself a ransom for all.

As we saw earlier, pagan worship is built around reciprocal transactions. Offerings are brought to appease gods and curry their favor in the hope that rain, fertility, military victory, and good fortune will result. Pagan gods were not nearly as concerned about sin; they were believed to respond to offerings of value that were given in exchange for earthly blessings. Among the Canaanites, the execution and offering of one's own children was considered the best way to obtain a favorable response from the Baals or other gods.

Old Testament saints were taught that offerings were given to cover sin but that forgiveness was a result of God's lovingkindness and grace in response to their faith. In due season, God would provide the only sacrifice that can take away sins.

Giving Is Always Proportional to Wealth

Giving in proportion to what one has, and giving on the Lord's Day, are the only specific guidelines for giving in the New Testament (see 1 Cor. 16:1–2). Tithing is not commanded in the New Testament because, as we have seen, tithing was tied to the Old Testament structure of "rent" being owed to God for land, of temple worship, of Levitical support, and of the offering of firstfruits and firstborn animals. When the Mosaic ceremonial law was superseded by the new covenant, those provisions were fulfilled and transformed in Christ. The Acts of the Apostles illustrates the new, Spirit-led transformation of the people's giving.

Jesus did not rebuke or discourage the giving of tithes. What he condemned was a legalistic tithing of herbs and spices as a cover for theft and oppression. As we saw in chapter 4, tithing was a teaching tool used in the Old Testament to disciple God's people in giving. It functioned as training wheels for teaching generosity to selfish sinners, and it can still help us to compare the sincerity of our love for God with that of believers from before the full grace of God was revealed.

Just as importantly, God does not look at the specific dollar amount of our gifts. He looks at the amount of the gift in proportion to our wealth. In the story of the widow and the two coins (see Luke 21:1–4), Jesus saw the widow's gift as being greater than the gifts of all the wealthy. They gave from their excess, but she gave all that she had. The wealthy received adulation at the temple but little credit with God. God's rewards in heaven will reflect Jesus's teaching here.

Though our giving should normally be no less than that of the Old Testament saints, there is no upper limit to giving in our environment of grace. God accepts much more than 10 percent if it is given out of love. This is consistent with God's strategy for us to shift our giving to a matter of our gratefulness for his grace, which also has no upper limit. How could biblical generosity be anything but proportional?

Corollary #3: Biblical Generosity Reflects the Mind-set of the Communion of the Saints

In the Apostles' Creed, we confess that we believe in the "communion of saints." By this we confess that the church is one in Christ and that we share with all other Christians the gifts, graces, and treasure with which Christ has blessed us. Earlier, we saw how this was practiced in Acts. Acts 4:32 says, "Now the full number of those who believed were of one heart and soul, and no one said that any of the things that belonged to him was his own, but they had everything in common." This dramatic change of mind-set brought about a new Jubilee and ended poverty in the early church. It was the material out-working of their unity of heart and soul. We saw how that mind-set was dramatically reaffirmed by Paul in 2 Corinthians 8 and 9, where he explained that giving starts with our giving ourselves to Christ and to his people.

Of course, this mind-set is not new. From the beginning of God's covenant with Abraham, God and his people entered into a relation-ship of mutual ownership and sharing. I Am would be their God, and they would be his people—their fates forever tied together. Christ ratified this covenant by giving himself in order to purchase us back for God. As his redeemed people, we consecrate ourselves to Christ and his body (see Rom. 12:1–2)—to loving one another and fulfilling his commissions.

This means that all believers should see their wealth, abilities, and time not as their own but as being available to the entire communion of believers. We saw how this principle guided Paul's response to the famine in Palestine (see 2 Cor. 8:14). He taught that God's provision for the church as a whole was intended to create a communion of resources so that those who had much would not have too much and those who had little would not have too little.

Jesus predicted this common life in the new community that he would build. In Mark 10:29–30 he says, "Truly, I say to you, there is no one who has left house or brothers or sisters or mother or father or children or lands, for my sake and for the gospel, who will not receive a hundredfold now in this time, houses and brothers and sisters and mothers and children and lands, with persecutions, and in the age to come eternal life." This saying is hyperbolic and is meant to grab his listeners' attention, but it conveys a profound truth about the rela-tionship between believers in the new kingdom community that Jesus was going to build. It hints at the communion of the saints that the Apostles' Creed so aptly highlights.

How would this mind-set apply today? If we consider the distribu-tion of resources among Christians today, believers have an abundant supply of income and wealth, particularly in the West. But, as in the famine in Palestine in AD 40, this wealth is not always local to the need. It is the communion that saints maintain with one another that enables us to know about and address the needs of another part of the body.

To illustrate, most of us who are in affluent neighborhoods know about needs in our local congregations. Using my former congregation as an example, something like 5 percent of total church giving (0.5 percent of household income) could end the curses of poverty among our own members. It would require real work on the part of the deacons and their helpers, but it happens. In the case of that church, however, it helps that the average household income came close to $90,000 in 2015.

Urban congregations, on the other hand, have huge needs and little income or capital wealth distributed among their families. The average household income in Philadelphia, for example, is $35,000. During my fifteen years running an educational mission in Philadelphia, I saw the great needs in the K–12 education of the children of some 40,000 poor urban believers. Neighborhood public schools were and are still largely destructive to education. Many of these covenant children cannot read and are convinced that they cannot learn. To enable these 40,000 children to attend better, private, Christian schools, the Christian community in Philadelphia would need to give $200 million a year for their education.

That large number seems like the very reason that we do not talk about the communion of the saints at this level. Yet stop and think: 2.3 million households in the Philadelphia metro region give $4.9 billion to all charitable causes, which represents 2.5 percent of their income.[3] About 32 percent of that (or $1.6 billion) goes to religious organizations.[4] Since most religious giving is Christian giving,

3. See "Regional Spotlight: Greater Philadelphia—Philanthropic Landscape," CCS Fundraising, 2017, available online at https://ccsfundraising.com/wp-content/uploads/2018/04/CCS_Regional-Landscape-Philadelphia_FINAL.pdf, p. 5. This is at least a good estimate of the potential giving of Christians in this area—and, if we assume that giving is Philadelphia is typical of giving in most major cities, it makes a point about potential giving in general.

4. See Alex Daniels, "Religious Americans Give More, New Study Finds," *The Chronicle of Philanthropy*, November 25, 2013, https://www.philanthropy.com/article/Religious-Americans-Give-More/153973. The study that he discusses looked

increasing this 2.5 percent to a full tithe would produce 3.3 billion additional dollars. With that, Christians could easily cover the $200 million it would cost to educate and disciple most of these low-income urban children, changing their lives and the face of Philadelphia forever. Sadly, these funds are neither offered nor asked for, and so many of these children are lost to illiteracy, unemployment, incarceration, and addictions—often missing the gospel itself.

The same dynamics hold true on the international scene: of the 800 million folks who are caught in the destructive downward cycle of poverty, about 180 million are believers in Christ. If American "hard-core" evangelicals tithed their income, they could provide a $500 microloan to each one of these brothers and sisters *every year*. Tithing our estates after death would double that amount.

I am not advocating helping only church members or ignoring unbelievers. I am simply illustrating the power of the wealth God has assigned to those in his church, should the communion of the saints ever be exercised in full. I hope these numbers help us to envision the communion of the saints in its full biblical power.

Corollary #4: On the Last Day We Shall Receive as We Gave

We reviewed Jesus's remarkable teaching about the special kind of poetic justice that will be administered on the last day, when every person (believer and unbeliever; those with the Bible and those without) will be judged according to what they have done and said in the flesh. Luke 6:37–38 says,

---

at how much money goes not only to congregations but also to charities that have religious identities but secular missions. It showed that religious giving is sweeping: 41 percent of all charitable gifts from households in the year that it studied went to congregations, while 32 percent went to other nonprofits that have a religious identity and 27 percent went to secular charities. The results of the study had an 8 percent margin of error. See also David P. King and Thad Austin, "Religious Giving Holds Steady," Lilly Family School of Philanthropy, Indiana University–Purdue University Indianapolis, June 13, 2017, https://philanthropy.iupui.edu /news-events/insights-newsletter/2017-issues/june-2017-issue1.html.

Judge not, and you will not be judged; condemn not, and you will not be condemned; forgive, and you will be forgiven; give, and it will be given to you. Good measure, pressed down, shaken together, running over, will be put into your lap. For with the measure you use it will be measured back to you.

This judgment will be based on the extent of people's generosity in giving. It will also be based on the extent to which they showed mercy, visited prisoners, fed the thirsty and hungry, and clothed the naked. These are the works of love. On the final day of the Lord, all these deeds, or the lack thereof, will

- identify God's true people, separating the sheep from the goats (see Matt. 25:31–46).
- vindicate his people from Satan's charges that they are not truly righteous (see Job 1–2) and that it is unfair for God to condemn some and acquit his elect. Satan, of course, wants to take everyone to hell with him.
- condemn the unrepentant out of their own mouths and assign them to experience the evil that they prescribed for others.
- reward the righteous with recognition and reward of their treatment of others in everlasting life on a renewed earth.

This topic is far greater than we can deal with in this book, but it is sufficient to note that the Bible makes it clear that there will be a personalized process to the final judgment—one that will lead us to everlasting life or everlasting condemnation based on our deeds. It will be the opposite of an administrative process in which saints just flash their "decision card" and pass through to heaven while those without the "decision" paperwork are left to be lost. It will be a justice so profound and unassailable that every mouth will be stopped and every knee will bow (or be forced to bow) and confess that Jesus is Lord. This will be especially true for those who hate him and have ridiculed his justice.

Amazingly, God's impartiality on the judgment day (see Rom.

2:6–11) does *not* mean that our present enjoyment of justification by faith alone is compromised in any way.[5] In fact, the judgment will vindicate our justification in Christ by grace through faith (see Rom. 8:33–34).

In the same vein, Paul writes,

> Since we have been justified by faith, we have peace with God through our Lord Jesus Christ. (Rom. 5:1)

> For by grace you have been saved through faith. And this is not your own doing; it is the gift of God, not a result of works, so that no one may boast. For we are his workmanship, created in Christ Jesus for good works, which God prepared beforehand, that we should walk in them. (Eph. 2:8–10)

We are justified because the "active and passive" righteousness of Christ is applied to us when we believe.[6] Neither does this last-day teaching set aside the truth that God chose us for salvation before the foundation of the world. He did not choose us because of any righteousness that he found in us.

Our inability to fathom the depths of these profound truths nevertheless allows us to see that God is both deeply, personally loving and yet totally, unassailably impartial in judgment. Paul breaks out

---

5. The message of the gospel is clear that salvation is not something that we earn; it is all a result of grace that is freely given to us in Christ through faith (not works). In the Christian life, we never get to a place where our good works atone for our past sins or provide enough merit to save us. In fact, sanctification involves seeing more deeply the sin of our hearts and our need for God's grace in Christ each moment.

6. A full discussion of this point can be found in the Committee on Christian Education's "Report on Justification" that was presented to the seventy-third general assembly of the Orthodox Presbyterian Church and is available online at https://www.opc.org/GA/justification.pdf. This report was written to answer the challenges to the Reformation interpretation of justification coming from the "New Perspective on Paul" (especially in N. T. Wright's works) and the Federal Vision theology coming from the Auburn Avenue Presbyterian Church network. Numerous scholarly works address this issue, but the OPC report does so in a way that informed church members can follow. It references the primary scholarly works up until the time of its publication in 2006.

in praise while contemplating this dynamic (see Rom. 11:33–34). He stands in awe of the wisdom and glory of God.

God's commands require obedience, because he is God. They are not there so we can establish our justification before God based on our works or our obedience. God's commands help to conform us to his Son's character and to progressively transform us into his image (see Rom. 8:28). Turning from sin to new obedience will be a lifelong, fruitful endeavor for Christians—one that will mark us off as his saints and prepare us for the great day of vindication.

That new life changes us from being those who take to being those who give. God does this in such a way that on the last day he will give to us *as* we gave to others (see Luke 6:38). Generosity, as a character quality and a practice, is a significant part of our sanctification and our preparation for meeting the Lord. It is a non-negotiable in our discipleship—equal in importance to being forgiven (as we forgive) and being accepted (as we refrain from judgment on others).

For such reasons, cultivating excellence in the grace of giving should take on profound significance in the teaching and discipling ministry of the church. Paul's exhortation to the Corinthians to do just that means that such teaching and ministry should be more than an apologetic sermon on stewardship when the budget is not met. It should be an essential ingredient of the church's vision for its members and for their preparation for seeing God.

Now that we have reviewed the Bible's theology of money and giving, we are ready to embark on the most daunting part of the book: how do we practice these truths and realities? Even more challenging: how do we break out of the pattern of a few evangelicals giving a lot and most of them giving at levels that do not reflect the grace of God?

Questions for Review and Reflection

1. Why does the author argue that acknowledging God's ownership of all that we have is only the first step of biblical stewardship?

2. In what sense can Christians affirm that God has provided for all that his kingdom will need in order to do his work and fulfill his commands?

3. Why do you think tithing is not commanded in the New Testament and yet proportional giving is?

Part 2

LIVING OUT THE PURPOSE OF MONEY

11

Money and Giving in the Western Church

On the first day of every week, each of you is to put
something aside and store it up, as he may prosper, so that
there will be no collecting when I come. (1 Cor. 16:2)

Many of the values and practices of the apostolic church continued into the post–New Testament era. The church fathers continued the apostles' tradition by "remembering the poor" (see Gal. 2:10) and discipling the new mission fields of Asia Minor and Europe to do the same. Their values are reflected in this passage from Tertullian, a church father from about AD 200, as he describes their "Piety Deposit Fund."

There is no buying and selling of any sort in the things of God. Though we have our treasure-chest, it is not made up of purchase-money, as of a religion that has its price. On the monthly day, if he likes, each puts in a small donation; but only if it be his pleasure, and only if he be able: for there is no compulsion; all is voluntary. These gifts are, as it were, piety's deposit fund. For they are not taken thence and spent on feasts, and drinking-bouts, and eating-houses, but to support and bury poor people, to supply the wants of boys and girls destitute of means and parents, and of old persons confined now to the house; such, too, as have suffered shipwreck; and if there happen to be any in the mines, or banished to the islands, or shut up in the prisons, for nothing but their fidelity to the cause of God's Church, they become the nurslings of that confession.[1]

The early church was also a major initiator of literacy and of the developments that flow from it. New converts, both male and female, were catechized and baptized and often learned to read the Bible as part of that training. Augustine wryly noted in the fourth century that the women of the church were better educated than the pagan philosophers of the time.[2] As this educational dynamic matured, the catechetical schools became regional cathedral schools, which eventually grew into some of the great universities of Europe.

Andy Crouch, through his book *Culture Making*, pointed me to the research of Dr. Rodney Stark, which is summarized in *The Rise of Christianity*. Stark studied the dynamic of the rapid growth of early Christianity in the Roman Empire.[3] He highlighted the fact that two major epidemics swept through the Roman Empire at a time when Christianity was growing but was not a majority. These epidemics claimed about a third of the population of the empire. As Crouch summarizes it, "In the face of terrible conditions, pagan elites and their priests simply fled the cities. The only functioning social network left behind was the church, which provided basic nursing care to Christians and non-Christians alike, along with a hope that transcended death. . . . The church had no magic or medicine to cure the plague, but it turns out that survival even of a terrible disease has a lot to do with one's access to the most basic elements of life."[4]

1. Tertullian, "Apology," trans. S. Thelwall, in *The Ante-Nicene Fathers: Translations of the Writings of the Fathers down to A.D. 325*, ed. Alexander Roberts and James Donaldson, vol. 3, *Latin Christianity: Its Founder, Tertullian* (repr., New York: Charles Scribner's Sons, 1903), 46. Thanks to Rev. Rob Hamilton, who alerted me to this quote.

2. See Alvin J. Schmidt, *How Christianity Changed the World* (Grand Rapids: Zondervan, 2004), 171–72.

3. See Andy Crouch, *Culture Making: Recovering Our Creative Calling* (Downers Grove, IL: IVP, 2009), 156–58. Crouch refers to the seminal work of Dr. Rodney Stark of Baylor University and to his chapter on "Epidemics, Networks, and Conversion" in *The Rise of Christianity: A Sociologist Reconsiders History* (Princeton: Princeton University Press, 1996), 73–94.

4. Crouch, 156–57.

Stark reported that Christians, by simply providing "conscientious nursing without any medications could cut the mortality rate by two-thirds or even more."[5] He documented the way this pattern was repeated in the areas of ethnic tension, oppression of women, and infanticide. In each case, as Crouch highlights, the church mounted culturally creative and public efforts that resulted in an ingathering of pagans—family by family and network by network. There were few mass conversions.

By the time of the Roman emperor Julian (AD 360–62), there was an extensive Christian system of caring for the poor. Because Julian wanted to restore pagan worship as Rome's official religion, he ordered that hospices be established in each town for the poor's relief. He said, "It is disgraceful that . . . while the impious Galileans [Christians] support both their own poor and ours as well, all men see that our people lack aid from us!"[6] Third-century Christians had shamed the Roman authorities into having to begin a government-sponsored welfare system if they had any hope of restoring paganism to Rome.

However, Julian's effort did little to blunt the spread of the Christian faith, and Christianity became the civil religion of the Roman Empire even as the empire was collapsing culturally, economically, and militarily. Augustine was its great theologian, philosopher, and architect. He separated the civil government from the Christian church as distinct institutions. While we may fault Augustine for laying the foundation for the state church, he thus spared Europe from the temporal rule of a caliph, a Roman-style god-king, or a messianic prophet/priest/king. And, while the rise of the popes in Europe weakened the kings, the two offices were never merged. This planted the seeds from which the separation of church and state would emerge 1,400 years later in the American republic.

Reading about the attitude and practices of the church in the Roman Empire made me wonder what kind of change would be

---

5. Crouch, 157.

6. Quoted in G. W. H. Lampe, *"Diakonia in the Early Church,"* in *Service in Christ*, ed. J. I. McCord (Grand Rapids: Eerdmans, 1960), 50, quoted in Timothy Keller, *Ministries of Mercy: The Call of the Jericho Road*, 3rd ed. (Phillipsburg, NJ: P&R Publishing, 2015), 95.

required for today's church to take on the scourges of our culture: inner-city poverty and crime, the spiraling growth of organized street gangs recruiting our city youth, opioid addiction, children being thrust into foster homes through a dysfunctional social service system, sex and slave-labor trafficking here and abroad, and the lack of rule of law and access to property ownership for serfs around the world. Given the resources of the church today and its vast numbers, I believe that these challenges would be on the same scale as those in the Roman Empire. While Christians do move to the front lines during epidemics, we are not as comfortable taking on the other issues that the post-apostolic church addressed.

The Early and Medieval Church: AD 400 to AD 1500

The establishment of Roman Christianity meant the end of the "evangelical" or "free church" era of the Christian movement and the beginning of a profound and ultimately destructive development for the church and her giving practices. As Christianity became the official religion, bishops and their staffs were increasingly paid by the state. The political influence of the Roman empire gave way to the spiritual reign and primacy of Roman bishops. Yet the bishop in Rome became (almost inevitably) the one to confirm and bless national monarchs so that, by the Middle Ages, he functioned as the central authority over vast stretches of Europe. That included the national resources of each of these converted sovereign states.

The Eastern Orthodox and Slavic churches fell away from Roman influence. They eventually balked at the political and spiritual domination of Rome and, in 1054, separated from the rule of the Roman bishop in order to form the Orthodox churches. They did, however, retain the Augustinian model of the Christian state protecting and supporting the Christian church. In the same way, the Christian church spiritually protected the state.

From AD 400 onward, the spiritual vitality of Christianity seemed to be largely channeled into the monastic movement. Spiritual orders carried out most of the missionary effort, scholarly study, and mercy ministry. What had originally been carried out by enrolled widows,[7] deacons, and educated lay leaders was now carried out by monks and nuns.

On December 25, 800, Pope Leo crowned Charlemagne as the new emperor of a revived assembly of central European nations that eventually became known as the Holy Roman Empire. Trends toward national established churches were set in stone, and citizenship and church membership became largely a packaged deal.

Ordinary laymen and women were generally not taught to read the Bible or other books any longer, since the church, the Pope, and its theologians would interpret Scripture for them. Scriptures were not translated into native tongues. Mass was said in non-native, standard Latin. The emphasis of the church shifted from understanding (requiring catechesis and confession) to participation in (attendance at) the sacraments. Sacraments became the primary means by which salvation was bestowed. Illiteracy became the norm for the masses, except for princes, doctors, lawyers, church rulers, and theologians.

Despite this destructive development, it is hard to overestimate the power and influence of the monastic movements that continued to spread the Christian faith to new areas. Monasteries also became centers of mercy ministry, culture, service, and spiritual support for their communities. They became social, cultural, and economic powers in their own right. Yet this siphoned off those with spiritual ambition from lay, secular callings or parish priestly work. That dynamic should remind Protestant leaders of our current parachurch missions that do so much of the heavy lifting in ministry today.

While there are numerous exceptions, I believe that the impact of

7. Paul refers to the status of widows in the church in 1 Timothy 5:3–16. Widows who were "enrolled" were at least sixty years old, had no family to support them, and had a track record of godliness in their relationships and good works. They received financial support from the church and were committed not to marry (in order to obtain financial support). It seems that Paul implies that these women were supported and freed up to do works of mercy and service on Christ's behalf. They would have formed a sizable force of Christian "social workers" who were engaged in ministry to the sick, the infirm, prisoners, and infants left to die. Such a view helps to explain why the church was able to respond to the curses of Roman life, such as infanticide and plague, with such power.

state-sponsored churches has, on balance, been negative for the progress of the gospel, the work of the church, and the practice of giving.
These churches did promote a kind of Christian civilization for Europe
and the Slavic lands. It can fairly be said that the church created the
states of Europe from the chaos of the fall of Rome, thereby building
in church support from the beginning. The national churches were
protected, financed, and cared for by the civil authorities, but they
often ended up as dead vessels holding the cultural core of the nation.

Regeneration and salvation were no longer viewed as being related
to hearing, understanding, and believing the gospel. Salvation was
thought to be accomplished largely through the administration of the
sacraments, and Christian theology and ethics were enforced by the
sword of the civil magistrate and the resources of the state. What
voluntary giving there was on the part of the laity was often tied to
pew rentals, building improvements, indulgences, and other spiritual benefits in what became an almost commercial arrangement. Art
objects, relics, and crafts were donated in exchange for eternal merit
in heaven. The Vatican raised $6 billion in gold ducats to build St.
Peter's Basilica, but such fund-raising often involved abusive practices
such as the sale of indulgences and other church privileges or positions.

Reform and Disestablishment: 1500–1784

This proved deadly to the spiritual vitality of the people in both
the Orthodox and Roman Catholic churches. By the time of Martin
Luther (1483–1546), the system went from being spiritually dead-
ening to being corrupt and abusive. These corruptions fueled the
Reformation, which sought to reform the church by moving its practices and theology back to the time of Augustine. Luther and Calvin
both retained the Augustinian model of church and state being separate but Christian institutions that were each accountable to God.

Their reforms sought to restore the teaching and practices of the
gospel to the people. However, this also led to a new type of state
church and gave it the power to tax for church expenses. Protestant
churches became more intensely national: the Swiss Reformed
Church, the German Lutheran Church, the Dutch Reformed Church,

the Church of England, and so on. All of them were arrayed against the Catholic churches in their regions. Conflicts between churches became conflicts between countries, cultures, and economies, and vice versa. This led to bloody religious wars like the Thirty Years War (1618–1648).

Others in the "Radical Reformation" (the Anabaptist movement that included Mennonites, Quakers, Amish, and so on) wanted to abandon the Augustinian model and have a completely non-political church and a non-ecclesiastical government. Yet that movement was suppressed by the Reformed and Lutheran state churches, which resulted in mass migration to the United States. Some visceral distrust lingers even today among Anabaptists.

With the "help" of the Deists, the Unitarians, and every other brand of faith, the United States was eventually forced to recognize that religious freedom was impossible to maintain under the Augustinian model. The US Constitution ended the tenure of state churches in New England and in all the other colonies.

England traveled an analogous but different path. Only as a result of the persecutions of the Puritans, Baptists, and Presbyterians in England, and the disaster under Cromwell, did that nation realize the need for embracing religious freedom. However, like Europe, England could not bring itself to divest itself of an official state church culture. Still, the revivals under John Wesley and George Whitefield brought a great uprising of charitable giving and volunteering for the poor, even within nominally supported state churches.

Wesley was forced to begin a "free church" (the Methodist Church) to pursue a godly church life that discipled its members in Christian living, including godly giving and stewardship. Wesley also set a strong personal example of generosity. Through publishing, he made about 1,400 British pounds a year (a fortune at the time) but died with nothing in his estate, as he had planned. George Mueller followed his example and gave away $180,000, dying with $850 in his estate.[8]

---

8. See Basil Miller, *George Mueller: The Man of Faith* (Grand Rapids: Zondervan, 1941), 126–27, cited in Keller, *Ministries of Mercy*, 73.

In 1780, during the first Great Awakening and the Methodist revivals, Robert Raines began the Sunday school movement in order to educate slum kids in newly industrialized English cities. This movement evangelized and discipled four generations of urban workers. Within 150 years, 1.25 million children were in Sunday schools. In 1887, the British aristocracy was shamed into providing public schools for all children.

Only in the United States and nations that have been more recently evangelized (such as China, Korea, India, and some African countries) was the entire church freed from the yoke of official state-based cultural Christianity. It turns out that these are the nations of greatest and most vital church growth. The Pentecostal movement in Latin America has challenged the official status of the Catholic Church there. These nations have kept a token state church that fewer and fewer people attend, while large numbers of them convert to regional Pentecostal churches.

I believe it is safe to assert that the vitality of Christian faith has often been directly proportional to the extent to which the state church has withered, died, or been disestablished. Such freedom seems to be a necessary—but not always sufficient—condition for the church's spiritual vitality. So, as we look at the progress of Christian giving, it is best for us to discuss a culture that has largely been free from the interference of ecclesiastical taxation and state church support—namely, the United States after 1784.

The American Church: 1784 to WWII

To what extent has the American church since 1784[9] practiced biblical stewardship and giving? Ignoring the coercive practices of some sects, evangelicals in the United States are now the most generous givers, giving between 3 and 4 percent of their household income to charitable purposes. The United States is already far and away the most generous developed nation, in terms of both the 2.5 percent of

9. That is the date of the ratification of the US Constitution, which, together with the Bill of Rights, formally ended state churches in the United States.

personal income and the 2 percent of GDP (gross domestic product) it contributes. It also leads the world in fixed dollar giving ($390 billion in 2017). Because of the two Great Awakenings, a foundation of strong, biblically-based churches, and a very prosperous economy, I believe that giving has become much more self-conscious and developed in the United States than elsewhere in the West, especially since the American Civil War.

The Industrial Revolution in the 1800s (which lasted through the Gilded Age) created more wealth than in all the previous years of world history. This revolution made America unlike any previous kingdoms (Egypt, Babylon, or Rome), because its wealth has been *distributed* to millions of people, creating the first large middle class and a prosperous working class.

That revolution is still picking up speed as it spreads across Asia, Latin America, Africa, and Russia, lifting millions of people from subsistence living, despite new problems that are created by industrialization and globalized market economies. While the number of people in extreme poverty (800 million) has decreased only a little since 1820, the *percentage* of the world population that is poor has decreased from 90 percent in 1820 to 10 percent today.[10] This is largely the product of emerging market economies in Asia.

The response of the American church to the phenomenal wealth that was produced by the Industrial Revolution was to embrace the market economy.[11] The church came to see the new industrialization as a blessing that would allow the godly to prosper. In this emerging nineteenth- and twentieth-century economy, financial provision

10. See Stephen Pinker, *Enlightenment Now: The Case for Reason, Science, Humanism, and Progress* (New York: Viking Press, 2018), 87–88. Pinker's book is the best up-to-date survey of world social, economic, and political conditions—though he uses his findings to argue that science, rationality, and humanism can continue world progress and solve our world problems, without reference to transcendent morals or the God of Christianity.

11. See Mark A. Noll, ed., *God and Mammon: Protestants, Money, and the Market, 1790–1860* (New York: Oxford University Press, 2001). Noll has edited a wonderful collection of historical studies on money and giving during this period in American history. It is unusual to find quality historical studies on money and religion, but this is one.

was not assumed to depend on one's ancestry, class, family trade, or inherited capital but rather on one's exercising the virtues of industry, thrift, frugality, sobriety, honesty, and generosity.

Preaching during this era contrasted these qualities with qualities of idleness, intemperance, prodigality, sloth, and extravagance, which would lead to economic ruin and poverty. It was thought that surely morality would improve under a free market, even without the oversight of the church or the aristocracy. The free market's discipline was self-administered and self-reinforcing.[12]

Causing tension with this, particularly for Calvinists like the Philadelphia Presbyterians, was the awareness that God still determined both riches and poverty by providentially providing the health, opportunity, and economy in which work could be financially rewarding.[13] Therefore, thanks was still due to him for every blessing.

As Mark Noll points out, the church addressed the morality of economic success by teaching two qualities that were held in tension. "To envy and covet the wealth of others was idolatrous and an implicit denial of God's authority over worldly affairs. On the other hand, laypersons were told that contentment did not mean inactivity or passive acceptance of the status quo. Rather, they must try to improve their social and economic circumstances even while accepting their current condition graciously. The task set before them, then, was to exhibit economic ambition and economic satisfaction simultaneously."[14]

In this urbanized market economy that continued to emerge (despite at least three financial panics/recessions), an exploding class of mechanics, workers, and clerks was developing from Old World subsistence into somewhat dependable urban working class prosperity. Business owners were proliferating, as well, owing to the legalization and spread of the legal entities known as corporations[15] after the Civil

12. See Noll, 176.
13. See Noll, 177.
14. Noll, 181.
15. Corporations were opposed by Thomas Jefferson but supported by the New England establishment and promoted by Daniel Webster. Webster won. The corporation model allowed a business entity to act like a person but not be a person. A corporation was controlled by a board of people who could be replaced as needed.

War. This business entity had far fewer restrictions on it than the old "state-chartered corporations."[16]

In the 1800s, population, membership, and giving increased significantly in church denominations, which began to manage themselves using corporate management techniques. Pew rentals, glebes (small farms that were given to ministers), book sales, and missionary society offerings were forsaken in favor of comprehensive stewardship campaigns, which sent the message that all of our possessions are given to us in trust so we will use them for God's purposes.[17] According to Victor Claar, it was after the Civil War that pastors "dusted off" the concept of the tithe as a baseline for giving in the American free church environment.[18] For the first time in post-apostolic church history, tithing became the default giving standard, at least for Protestants.

Yet church leaders, both liberal and evangelical, largely accepted the new commercial advertising that induced members to buy better clothes, appliances, cars, wares, and furnishings. This was pioneered through the department-store model begun by John Wanamaker (a prominent Presbyterian layman). Wanamaker's department-store concept was wildly successful. Professional marketers then began to sell products by connecting them to lifestyle, happiness, satisfaction, peace, and fulfillment.

Gary Scott Smith refers to this period: "For many, self-realization became more important than self-control and the values of self-gratification and indulgence—crucial to high levels of consumption—replaced those of self-denial and frugality." Advertisers sought to liberate the middle class "from the tyranny of Puritanism, parsimoniousness and material asceticism and to convince Americans that

---

They could continue over generations (unlike a person) and therefore accumulate massive wealth and influence.

16. Robin Klay and John Lunn, "American Evangelicalism and the National Economy, 1870–1997," in Larry Eskridge and Mark A. Noll, eds., *More Money, More Ministry: Money and Evangelicals in Recent North American History* (Grand Rapids: Eerdmans, 2000), 19.

17. See Charles Hambrick-Stowe, "'Sanctified Business': Historical Perspectives on Financing Revivals of Religion," in Eskridge and Noll, 89.

18. Victor V. Claar and Robin J. Klay, *Economics in Christian Perspective: Theory, Policy and Life Choices* (Downers Grove, IL: InterVarsity Press, 2007), 86.

desiring, purchasing and enjoying material goods were salutary rather than sinful."[19]

There was some protest about this among evangelical leaders, but it was drowned out by the sheer magnitude and success of the products being sold. Advertisers directly assaulted the Puritan ethic of frugality and thrift and, in its place, offered customers installment payments and the hope of having everything they really wanted.[20] US manufacturing embarked on such a path of growth that the factories would have vastly overproduced their goods if there had not been corresponding, huge increases in consumer buying. Advertising sought to create a desire for these products, and it was successful. Today's consumer-driven economy is, of course, the result of this drive.

In the early 1900s, the practice of giving was taught as an important way for people to develop character, not just to raise money.[21] Despite that, church leaders largely accepted the idea that a desire to better oneself financially in this world's goods would be better for both the economy and the family. It was thought that if the worker continued having a strong relationship with Christ and avoided luxuries, he would not be spiritually harmed. Bettering himself financially would certainly enable the worker to give more to the church and to the needy. Yet there was little effort to equip workers and their managers with a theology that would guide them in how to use this prosperity beyond just to improve their lifestyle and would help them to understand what "luxuries" were. Workers typically decided this for themselves, with little help from their churches.

By 1916, church income was $316 million in today's dollars—half as much as the amount that the federal government brought in through its own efforts. Since that high, it has now dropped to only

19. Otis Pease, *The Responsibilities of American Advertising: Private Control and Public Influence, 1920–1940* (New Haven, CT: Yale University Press, 1958), 41, quoted in Gary Scott Smith, "Evangelicals Confront Corporate Capitalism: Advertising, Consumerism, Stewardship, and Spirituality, 1880–1930," in Eskridge and Noll, 40–41.

20. See Smith, "Evangelicals Confront Corporate Capitalism," in Eskridge and Noll, 75.

21. See Smith, "Evangelicals Confront Corporate Capitalism," in Eskridge and Noll, 61.

4 percent of the amount that the government brings in. In the early twentieth century, 50 percent of evangelicals tithed their income, and most had a much more positive view of stewardship campaigns than today's evangelicals do.[22]

It is interesting that the percent of people's income that they gave to the church peaked, in the United States, during the depths of the Depression in 1933—while their amount of total giving did crash during this period, it did not crash in proportion to how much their overall *income* crashed.[23] Perhaps believers during the Great Depression did not want to cut back too much on their giving during the hard times. They had awakened from the American Dream in the midst of a collapse of the world economic system and were focused, as people are in many emergencies, on helping one another. Sometimes a crisis can bring out the best in people—including Christians.

The early 1900s brought forth theological liberalism, which was largely imported from Germany. This in turn engendered the fundamentalist/modernist controversy in most major denominations. This was especially true in the North. Modernists denied miracles, substitutionary atonement, and the infallible authority of Scripture, and in its place they rolled out the "social gospel," which taught that the key task of the church must be relief and development for the needy. Preaching the traditional gospel was not considered relevant anymore in view of the values that were implicit in Darwin, Freud, industrialization, and Marx.

Conservatives (the fundamentalists) largely left the mainline institutions and founded Bible colleges to train their ministry leaders and missionaries. They strongly rejected the social gospel—to such an extent that they eschewed all social involvement and taught the church to stick to the spiritual welfare of its members and community. This dynamic was sinfully co-opted in the South to keep the church from speaking out against the treatment of African-Americans and

22. See See Smith, "Evangelicals Confront Corporate Capitalism," in Eskridge and Noll, 75.

23. See Christian Smith and Michael O. Emerson with Patricia Snell, *Passing the Plate: Why American Christians Don't Give Away More Money* (New York: Oxford University Press, 2008), 49.

from helping them to achieve civil rights. Additionally, thousands of missionaries and ministers launched into ministry without getting graduate divinity degrees.

Modernism began after the Civil War, but the defeat of the fundamentalists took almost a hundred years to complete. By the early 1950s, this defeat was largely complete in the North and almost complete in the metro centers of the New South. Unfortunately, the mainline churches did not create the revolution in generosity or in relief for the poor that their theology called for. The social gospel made for visionary and compassionate sermons but for few sustainable movements in relief or development. Giving was static, and attendance was down. Many seminaries began living off their endowments as interest in traditional pastoral ministry eroded.

On the other hand, the fundamentalists began to realize in the late 1940s that they did need educated clergy and that God did call them to minister to the poor here and around the world. They began to emerge from their self-made bunker. From this came the evangelical revolution led by Carl F. H. Henry, Billy Graham, Charles Fuller, Bob Pierce, and others. Evangelical graduate-level seminaries were founded, magazines were launched, and significant relief agencies were founded to join The Salvation Army and Mennonite Central Committee in ministering to the poor: World Vision, Compassion International, Bread for the World, Samaritan's Purse, Prison Fellowship, and, more recently, International Justice Mission.

The resurrection of evangelicalism was stunning. In 2016, the ten largest Protestant seminaries were all evangelical. Even Princeton Seminary dropped off the list.[24] Most biblical scholars are now orthodox in theology and adhere to a strong view of the authority of Scripture. However, theological liberalism still holds supreme in the prestigious university divinity schools that can support academic research and PhD programs.

The giving that had become flat in the mainline churches was

24. Chelsen Vicari reports this list, which is based on data from the Association of Theological Schools, in Chelsen Vicari, "What Are America's Largest Seminaries?" *Juicy Ecumenism* (blog), The Institute on Religion & Democracy, August 1, 2016, https://juicyecumenism.com/2016/08/01/americas-largest-seminaries/.

outdone by the evangelical churches, which gave 3–4 percent of their household income while the mainline and Catholic churches came in at about 2.5 percent. This positioned the evangelical churches to take the lead in pastoral formation, missions, and relief of the poor around the world. They were the dark horse running on the inside lane, stretching for the leadership of the American church. Few took them seriously at that time, and many are still adjusting to their rise.

Questions for Review and Reflection

1. How did Christians respond to the two great plagues that ravaged Roman cities during the postapostolic period? How do you think you would respond in a similar situation?
2. How did Christians shame the Roman emperor into attempting a public welfare system?
3. What happened during the medieval period to end the high level of generosity that church members had previously shown?

12

Giving in the Post–World War II Era

I have learned in whatever situation I am to be content.
I know how to be brought low, and I know how to abound.
In any and every circumstance, I have learned the secret of
facing plenty and hunger, abundance and need. I can do all
things through him who strengthens me. (Phil. 4:11–13)

The real test of the church's response to wealth was yet to come. From the "chicken in every pot" mentality after World War II, we moved to the mentality of "a luxury car in every driveway." From 1945 to 1968, a tsunami of wealth broke over the United States that was unlike any seen in history. As white Americans emerged from the Great War and the Great Depression, they realized that they could join a well-funded middle class and have all their needs, and many wants and efficiencies, available for purchase.

For a hundred years, immigrants (who were mostly Catholic) came here from Europe for a better life. Their aspirations were to earn a decent living where work was rewarded and not stolen. They sought to get away from the oppression and poverty of the Old World and to earn a viable living—that was it. Many achieved that in the first half of the twentieth century. But now, with the economy exploding, they and many others could set their sights higher. They could enjoy the following:

- free-standing, 2,000-square-foot homes in Levittown that had bedrooms for everyone
- new homogeneous communities in the suburbs, away from urban crime
- private automobiles—even ones designed with beautiful fins and chrome
- quality clothes, and foods from every cuisine
- low-cost health care
- guaranteed company pensions and hope for a retirement in Florida at age sixty-five
- two or more weeks of annual vacation (with enough money from the rest of the year to have fun on that vacation)
- enough savings to buy appreciating assets like second homes and securities, which would provide them with significant amounts of future capital, leading to even greater financial security

The effect of this on our nation was electric—we were launched into the suburban "utopia" of the 1950s and 60s by an economy that was built primarily on manufacturing and domestic consumption, not on exports.

Products, services, and lifestyle upgrades were launched monthly. GM, Ford, and Chrysler unveiled new cars each year, and many folks bought them annually. Every dollar that was earned could be efficiently translated into an upgrade in affluence. Most stuff was cheap compared to what even the rich had paid for such goods in the previous century. (Of course, the dream was downgraded from Rolls Royces to Ford station wagons and from country estates to four-bedroom split-level homes in the Levittowns.) Nevertheless, the United States learned to make every necessity, and most conveniences, eminently affordable to the residents of its majority culture. Sadly, Native Americans and African Americans did not participate in this bonanza.

Robert Wuthnow, in his landmark study, *God and Mammon in America*, documents in detail how Christians would confess to a love of money but not to greed.[1] His survey results noted that 87

---

1. See Robert Wuthnow, *God and Mammon in America* (New York: Free Press,

percent of weekly churchgoers agreed with the statement that greed is a sin. But only 51 percent agreed that money was the root of all evil. Sixty-seven percent said that "money is one thing; morals and values are something else." Yet they also strongly associated money with the values of feeling good and having freedom. Americans were selective about which values they attached to money. Love of money translated into freedom and good feelings, which were permitted and encouraged in the consumer culture that was being created in the United States.

Wuthnow found that most Americans condemned "materialism" as being wrong because it drove selfishness and individualism, yet also had a great interest in material things. This overlap was seen less in practicing Christians, but it was still considerable. He concluded, "There is enough overlap that most people have to do some negotiating with themselves to explain why their lifestyle isn't really in conflict with their values."[2]

As we know, material affluence does not usually coincide with a parallel spiritual upgrade. In fact, by every measure that counts, US evangelicals began to move down a path away from generosity and giving and toward spending more of their new wealth on lifestyle improvements. Those who went to church began to reduce the percentage of income that they gave in offerings and bequests. Giving as measured in fixed dollar amounts continued to increase, however, because of the greater increases in evangelicals' personal wealth.

That trend reduced giving to 2.5 percent of the average American Christian's income. According to one analysis, evangelical Christians give 4.06 percent of their disposable income (after tax) to their churches.[3] That is down from 6.15 percent in 1968, despite the fact that "disposable" income (in terms of real, inflation-adjusted wealth) has gone up 100 percent since 1968. Confirming that trend is the fact that only 10 percent of "born again" Christians tithe today, compared to about 50 percent in the last century. The pursuit of the good life

---

1994), 128.

2. Wuthnow, 180.

3. See John Ronsvalle and Sylvia Ronsvalle, *Behind the Stained Glass Windows: Money Dynamics in the Church* (Grand Rapids: Baker, 1996) 23.

has affected both the liberal and the conservative, the mainline and the evangelical.

One impact of this was a reduction across the board of the amount of money that the church had available to spend on mission outside its own four walls. Giving to churches went increasingly toward providing spiritual services to members, and while giving for missions was desired, little money went toward it. The percentage of household income that is given to missions has dropped by 1–2 percent since the 1960s.

The rise of the two-wage-earner household, beginning in the 1970s and 80s, enabled Americans to hold on to the economic gains of the post-WWII era and to make leisure and materialism possible on a new scale. However, the need of both spouses to work restricted service and volunteering in the charitable arena. This doubtless impacted many of the women's missionary and charitable organizations that were rooted in the churches. Churches got more money and less volunteer leadership and service.[4]

The one-hundred-year trend of giving by American Christians is thus clearly down. Why? While the cultural outworking of this is complex, the reason, I believe, is clear: it is the pull of what Francis Schaeffer frequently called "selfish personal peace and affluence," combined with a weakening of the church and of people's grip on the gospel itself.

The pursuit of the lifestyle that is possible in the developed world is a powerful force that acts on each of us who are embedded in it. This is perhaps the first time in history that the majority of a culture could have all the essential efficiencies, pleasures, securities, experiences, and lifestyle necessary to create a "good" life. This material good life that people enjoy in the United States is, of course, the American Dream. Pursuing it was thought to have a positive influence on the poor because it gave them hope that with honesty, thrift, and hard work, they could pull themselves out of the poverty their parents had known.

Since the 1980s, we have been in the midst of a second revolution based on a "knowledge economy" and on digital technology. The wave

4. See Ronsvalle and Ronsvalle, 175.

of this revolution is moving much faster than the one that carried the Industrial Revolution and may be creating as much wealth as the first one did—or more. Already the level of wealth enjoyed by industrialized and digitized culture in the last hundred years makes Rome, Egypt, and Babylon look pretty modest, because their wealth was held by so few. These small numbers of people lived in the secure comfort that is now routinely enjoyed by millions in the modern working and middle classes.

Sadly, despite this new explosion of wealth in the United States since the 1960s, the percentage of household income that people give has not changed. It is stuck at around 2.5 percent for American Christians in general. Evangelicals' giving is also stagnant, at about 3.5–4.1 percent. The two exceptions to this rule also still stand: regular church attenders who earn less than $12,499 give away 7 percent of it, and those who earn over $90,000 give 8.8 percent.[5]

Greed Is Good?

However, there is another dynamic at work.

Commenting on people's perception of the American Dream, Denise Delahorne, senior vice president of the marketing firm DDB, proposed that "if you're new to this country, then life seems pretty good here. . . . But for many people who have lived here a long time, they've started to think of the American Dream less as the traditional elements, and more relative to wealth."[6]

The desire for a basic 2,000-square-foot home in Levittown has given way to the vision for a 4,000-square-foot new home in an exclusive suburb, with a vacation home for getaways. The American Dream is now the dream of becoming wealthy. The purpose of this wealth is not to join an elite class of rich but to access all the good things

5. See Christian Smith and Michael O. Emerson with Patricia Snell, *Passing the Plate: Why American Christians Don't Give Away More Money* (New York: Oxford University Press, 2008), 47.

6. "American Dream Lives, but Few People Recognize It," NBC News, July 3, 2014, https://www.nbcnews.com/business/economy/american-dream-lives-few -people-recognize-it-n147446.

that the culture has to offer. For this to actually happen, it turns out, requires an income of $200,000 to $250,000 a year. Advertisers, builders, and banks don't usually mention that, but they offer credit to make at least some of it possible in the short term.

This change in Americans' perspective from wanting a decent life to wanting a wealthy life can be documented in the annual survey of college freshmen that is conducted by the American Council on Education. In 1966, freshmen were asked what objectives they thought were essential or very important for their lives. Eighty percent included developing a meaningful philosophy of life among their objectives. Forty percent included being very well off financially. Thirty years later in 1997, those numbers had reversed: 75 percent of college freshmen said that one of their essential or very important objectives was to be very well off financially, and 40 percent said that one of them was to develop a meaningful philosophy of life.[7]

This question was phased out of later surveys, but it does show a tremendous change in attitudes from baby boomers to their children. Boomers wanted to be better off than their parents and were generally encouraged in that pursuit by their parents. Their American Dream began where their parents' dreams had left off. It is now a pillar of cultural belief that pursuing wealth is something that someone should have the unquestioned right to do. Wealth creators (venture capitalists) are considered celebrities in this pantheon of new gods. In 2016 Donald Trump drew on his status as a wealth producer to offer wealth to those who were missing out, if he was elected president.

This faith has affected giving. Until such wealth were solidly attained, thought the yuppies and "dot-com" millionaires of the 1990s, serious investment in the kingdom of God seemed premature. Generally, it felt to them like poor stewardship to *divert* contributions to a church in view of their long-term goal of attaining wealth first and giving later. That wave passed with the dot-com bust, but today's

7. See Alexander W. Astin, Leticia Oseguera, Linda J. Sax, and William S. Korn, "The American Freshman: Thirty-Five Year Trends," Higher Education Research Institute, University of California, Los Angeles, December 2002, https://www .heri.ucla.edu/PDFs/pubs/TFS/Trends/Monographs/TheAmericanFreshman35Year Trends.pdf, p. 16.

millennials are taking another crack at the wealth goal. Sadly, school loan debt, male immaturity, "useless" college majors, and a wounded economy have consigned many in this generation (and especially young men) to rent communal townhouses in urban centers, work at low-paying service jobs, and hang out at coffeehouses, waiting for a chance to make money using some new technology.

But certain trends remain: 7 percent of income is given by those who earn less than $20,000 and 8.5 percent by those who earn more than $250,000. The former have given up on the American Dream and so give seriously from their current income. The latter have achieved the dream and can enjoy the best of nearly anything in the culture, including giving money away. The current middle class (who earn from $40,000 to $100,000) are the low-percentage givers. They tend to devote every available dollar to the pursuit of a better, more secure life and give only 2.5 percent of it to the Lord's work. Of course, these folks comprise most of the members of our churches.

In the race to the new dream, there is not a lot of money left at the end of the month—especially if people have used debt to attain a certain lifestyle. Advertisers and corporations have beaten the church in creating a vision for people's money, and that vision has claimed most of the money from our middle class. At the same time, most churches have stopped "mission dreaming" and become victims of this dynamic. They don't see that the reason they are starving for money for mission and outreach is because they don't present a vision beyond a 3 percent increase on their previous year's budget—which is built on their members giving only 3–4 percent of their household income. We (and our church and ministry budgets) are now so used to meager support that we consider it normal. Members now see the church as "a place to meet their own needs, not as an agent of change in a hurting world."[8] A gospel-based church that reaps 5 percent of the family income of its members is considered wildly successful in terms of giving.

Thankfully, the church still has its minority of evangelical revolutionaries who provide about 75 percent of the local church and

8. Ronsvalle and Ronsvalle, *Behind the Stained Glass Window*, 211.

mission money. These are the ones who begin by giving 10 percent of their gross income and then look for ways to increase giving. Many, if they could, would give all that they have to the kingdom.

In chapter 14 we will see how middle-class believers can become like these revolutionaries and excel in the grace of giving. But before we do, let's look at the funds that US workers and the subset of American evangelicals actually have available to give from their wallets and accounts.

Show Me the Money?

We have seen that God generally gives his people, in advance, the funds that they need in order to fulfill the commissions he has given them. How much money does that represent in the American church today—and where are those funds hiding?

There is a lot of money within the evangelical Christian community. Mainline, Catholic, and Orthodox believers also control a lot of money, but I thought it best to examine the church community with which I am most familiar and the one that is giving the most per capita.

US Census data seems to be the only source for actual numbers on income and net worth. Otherwise we are dependent on generalizations from survey data by polling firms or from other volunteer sampling techniques. Fortunately, Christian Smith and the Ronsvalles have done the heavy lifting for us on this topic, and we can all benefit by their analysis.

The average income of a household in the United States in 2017 was $60,336.[9] This income varies by state rather dramatically, and there is a large gap between the income of black and white households. For our purposes, we will assume that evangelicals are spread evenly among races, states, and income levels.

There are several approaches to estimating the number of evan-

9. See Gloria G. Guzman, "Household Income: 2017," United States Census Bureau, September 2018, https://www.census.gov/content/dam/Census/library /publications/2018/acs/acsbr17-01.pdf. I am using the term *average income* to refer to what is known as median income. A median income indicates there are an equal number of households who earn more than that figure and less than that figure.

gelicals in the nation. There is the Gallup Survey that identifies those who say they are "born again." Wheaton College Institute for the Study of Evangelicals also uses this approach. Studies such as these try to identify the "experiential evangelicals," who number about 34 percent of the US population, or about 100 million. Then there is the Barna Survey method of asking nine theological questions to identify evangelicals. This type of study identifies the "doctrinal evangelicals," and they are about 8 percent of the US population, or about 26 million.

A third method identifies those who are members of doctrinally evangelical churches. Professor Bradley Wright reports this group as being 23 to 24 percent of the American population.[10] I believe that this is the more realistic number. Gallup's approach does not do justice to evangelical beliefs, but Barna's questions, while accurate, simply describe the beliefs of the *churches* where evangelicals attend. Many of those churches' members would confess Christ adequately but fail the Barna theological examination. For those reasons, I am going to use Bradley's definition for our back-of-the-napkin calculations.

The US population is, as of August 2018, about 328 million, which means that there are about 75 million hard-core evangelicals in the United States—about 23 percent of the population. There are about 29 million evangelical households in the United States and 2.54 people per household. Since average household income in 2018 is $59,000, evangelical households control $1.7 trillion dollars annually. If we assume a 10-percent baseline of giving, in line with what was expected of believers in the Old Testament, then about $170 billion would be available per year from evangelical givers.

About $127 billion is given to churches and other religious agencies in America.[11] We calculate that evangelicals give about $50 billion of that, because they give about 4 percent of their $1.7 trillion

10. See Bradley Wright, "How Many Americans are Evangelical Christians? Born-Again Christians?" Patheos, March 28, 2013, https://www.patheos.com/blogs/black whiteandgray/2013/03/how-many-americans-are-evangelical-christians-born -again-christians/.

11. See "Charitable Giving Statistics," National Philanthropic Trust, accessed July 12, 2019, https://www.nptrust.org/philanthropic-resources/charitable-giving -statistics/.

income. Therefore, this giving *could* increase by $120 billion over current levels if evangelicals simply tithed. But there is more.

While the average net worth of the US is lower than that of seventeen other countries, our total household wealth still makes us the richest country in the world. That is because the wealth held by the top 1 percent of Americans makes up 34 percent of our nation's $81.5 trillion wealth. The 90 to 99th percentiles of households hold another 40 percent of it. Therefore, the top 10 percent of the US population holds 74 percent of its household wealth.[12] These folks will pay most of the estate taxes and make the lion's share of charitable bequests.

Because evangelicals are such a large portion of the American population, there is no reason not to assume that evangelicals also control 23 percent of this $81.5 trillion of accumulated wealth. If that is correct, then evangelicals control $18.6 trillion. If, over the next seventy-five years, that "evangelical wealth" is passed down to the younger generation, then $250 billion will change hands *in an average year*. This assumes that inflation and growth cancel each other out over that seventy-five year period—a very conservative projection.

If evangelicals determined to simply tithe on that inherited $250 billion, then $25 billion would be available each year to finance the kingdom of God, with the other 90 percent passing on to these evangelicals' children and to others. Currently, total bequests in the United States average about $26 billion a year, so if evangelicals are already giving 23 percent of that ($6 billion), then we could increase our charitable bequests by some $19 billion by simply tithing our inherited assets. Most of us, in reality, can give much more than 10 percent of our estates.

So if evangelical Christians tithed both their inherited and earned income, their giving would increase to $195 billion. That represents a potential increase of $139 billion in giving to all causes by evangelicals. This turns out to be close to the $133 billion figure that Christian Smith reports in his much more detailed calculations of potential evangelical giving.

12. See Linda Levine, *An Analysis of the Distribution of Wealth across Households, 1989–2010* (Washington, DC: Congressional Research Service, 2012), 4.

The Empty Tomb, Inc., is a Christian research organization and consultancy that tracks both giving and world needs. They have attained great credibility with denominational leaders over their many years of work. Their calculations from 2016 are in the same ball park as ours but also add giving from non-evangelical sources.

> If Americans who identify with the historically Christian church had chosen to give 10% to their congregations in 2016, rather than the 2.17% given that year, there would have been an additional $172 billion available for work through the church. If those members had specified that 60% of their increased giving were to be given to international missions, there would have been an additional $109.3 billion available for the international work of the church. That would have left an additional $36.4 billion for domestic missions, including poverty conditions in the U.S., and this all on top of our current church activities. [13]

Whether the number is $139 billion or $172 billion, this is a very significant reality for Christians to face. First, it is significant because it is so much. The wealth of Israel's King David, the wealth of his court, and the entire national treasure of Israel amounted to about $250 billion, and most of it—the majority of their net worth—seems to have been handed over to build the temple. If we give only 10 percent of our wealth, we can provide $100+ billion every year! We have been blessed as the richest Christians in world history, and we dare not ignore the profound implications of God's investing so much of his wealth in us to dispense for his kingdom.

These figures are significant because they show us what God has equipped us to do and how far we fall short. Why is it that the richest Christians of all time fall so far short in the grace of giving, compared to the examples we have seen in both the Old and New Testaments? We will wrestle with this question in the next chapter.

13. "The Potential," Empty Tomb, Inc., last updated December 31, 2018, http://www.emptytomb.org/potential.html.

What's the Bill to Do God's Will?

Having looked at the resources that God has provided us, we will now look at the costs of fulfilling the kingdom program to which Jesus called us. Most American Christians have a basic recognition of the reality of poverty, disease, illiteracy, and hunger in the developing world. Evangelicals also have some appreciation of the large numbers of unreached communities and peoples around the world. And yet the resources that are needed to address all this seem, to the average church member, to be far beyond what any one church or mission could do. There is little understanding of how more giving could impact the overall picture.

Most of us evangelicals have had a "save a few" mentality, with no one giving serious thought to how we could address the full need. Bill Bright, the founder and late president of Campus Crusade for Christ (now Cru), did begin a concentrated, multiyear campaign in 1976 to "evangelize the world." His campaign was based on a business model of multilevel marketing for the purpose of evangelism. Other people have raised a vision for world evangelization in our generation, but with few numbers attached to it—except for the cost of the additional missionaries they were seeking to employ for marginal growth in their particular mission.

John and Sylvia Ronsvalle of The Empty Tomb, Inc., have made it their life's work to track the best information available on these difficult-to-quantify amounts. To quote them, "One source estimates that an additional $70 to $80 billion a year could address the basic needs of the poorest people around the world. Additionally, $5 billion a year could end the estimated 5.9 million children under five dying around the globe each year. Basic primary education for all poor children around the globe would cost $7 billion a year."[14]

The Ronsvalles have carefully researched the finances that would be needed to end unnecessary child death around the world. I was shocked to see how little would be needed for the church to fully fund this task. It is hard to imagine the impact that saving 30,000 children

---

14. "The Potential."

a day would have on the families whom this would reach around the world, particularly in the 10/40 window.

In 1984, the Ronsvalles' ministry launched a comprehensive and principled approach to dividing up and quantifying the dollar costs of the world's needs. They broke down the costs for mercy and evangelism, country by country. Their total was a one-time cost of $267 billion to show mercy to and evangelize the world. While that is a lot of money, even giving a portion of that each year would have a huge impact and would not only substantially reduce unnecessary child deaths in the world but also ignite economic well-being and growth that would often become self-sustaining. The Ronsvalles matched those needs with specific states and counties in the United States in what they called "The Yoking Map."[15] A church in any county in the United States can look up the countries with which they were yoked and see the relative severity of those countries' need for mission and mercy resources.

The Yoking Map was recalculated in 2002 and is available online from the Empty Tomb, Inc., website.[16] A new feature that the website contains is the ability to explore the giving potential of any individual county in the United States, which is based on economic and giving stats collected by Empty Tomb, Inc. I quote them on the additional giving potential among historically Christian churches in Montgomery County, Pennsylvania (where I wrote most of this book): "If historically Christian church adherents in Montgomery County chose to increase giving to a congregation-wide average of ten percent, there could have been $1,364,746,000 additional given in 2002 for international outreach and $454,915,333 additional for local outreach to people in need. If church adherents in Montgomery County would choose to contribute their portion of the estimated $5 billion needed to help, in Jesus's name, prevent global child deaths each year, $6,323,575 could be applied to prevent 30,353 child deaths."

15. See John Ronsvalle and Sylvia Ronsvalle, *The Poor Have Faces: Loving Your Neighbor in the 21st Century* (Grand Rapids: Baker, 1992), 55–90. See also John Ronsvalle and Sylvia Ronsvalle, *The Hidden Billions: The Potential of the Church in the U.S.A.* (Champaign, IL: C-4 Resources, 1984).

16. See "Yoking Map," Empty Tomb, Inc., last updated June 21, 2017, http://www.emptytomb.org/yoking.html.

They go on to yoke Montgomery County, Pennsylvania, to Iraq, Yemen, Oman, the United Arab Emirates, Kuwait, Bahrain, and Qatar. The Ronsvalles assume that 40 percent of money that is given should be kept local and 60 percent sent overseas, so they have made allowance for deep local involvement in both word and deed ministry.

Here is an example from the Philadelphia area for what such local giving could do. In Philadelphia, as I have mentioned, I directed an urban mission from 2003–2014 that sought to provide K–12 scholarships to low-income urban families so that their children could attend a network of Christian schools. We had specific confirmation that at least 40,000 low-income Philadelphia children each had a parent who wanted a Christian-based education for their child.[17] They wanted the child to leave the destructive educational environment of low-income neighborhood public schools.

We calculated that our organization would need about $6,000 in order for each child to be educated and discipled in Christ. The bill for that would be $240 million a year. That is a large amount, but it would go a long way toward substantially healing our inner city and creating Christian leadership for the future. If they tithe 10 percent, Philadelphia-area Christians have about $12 billion to give, making the challenge of discipling and educating a huge portion of city kids in Christ an obvious and doable task. It would consume only about 2 percent of our giving. We know that the funds are there by God's providence. What we lack is the giving of those funds— particularly from the circle of 1.5 million Christians who surround urban Philadelphia.

Of course, there are many other highly redemptive relief, development, and outreach initiatives underway, but they also are underfunded. Our organization hopes to fully provide that educational funding someday, as do the other relief and development agencies.

---

17. This number is based on the number of applications received by the Children's Scholarship Fund in 1999, when they published an application in the *Philadelphia Inquirer* offering 1,000 scholarships of $1,000 each for low-income children to go to private schools (almost all of which were Christian or Catholic).

Outside the Developed West

Now let's look at the international scene. On a global scale, there are about 180 million Christians among the 800 million poor. These believers are caught in a destructive, downward economic cycle. Our first responsibility as Christians is to help the household of faith (see Gal. 6:10), though our mandate does not stop there. Obviously, needs are different and conditions are unique among each poor family or people group—there is no one-size-fits-all solution to this need. But for illustrative purposes, consider that if evangelicals tithed, we would have the capacity to make a $750 microloan or school scholarship to each of these poor believers *each year.*

A family of four could receive a loan of $3,000 per year for economic betterment, or strategic grants of the same amount for schooling, health care, and job training. I am not advocating this exact approach—although often such loans or grants are great invest-ments for someone such as a poor but able mother and her family. Muhammad Yunus illustrates how powerful the impact would be if God's people began to give at a baseline of generosity and thereby sponsored loans to the poor.[18]

Evangelicals have, in most ways, done the best job at financing local and foreign missions. Most vital evangelical churches proudly dedicate 20 percent of their budgets to foreign missions and mercy. This is double the national average—but far short of even the baseline of giving in the Old Testament era.

Obviously, a local church that collects 3 to 4 percent of its mem-bers' household income will have the resources to pay its staff and local expenses and then be able to add missions and mercy as con-tributions allow. While we find that conservative churches do attract more funds, their outward missions are still chronically underfunded.

Running a church this way is like putting a small VW Bug engine in a dump truck and finding that we can move it forward at only 5 mph. We don't have the proper engine. We get so used to going slow

---

18. See Muhammad Yunus, *Banker to the Poor: Micro-Lending and the Battle Against World Poverty* (New York: Public Affairs, 2008).

that we forget we could carry ten tons of dirt at 65 mph if we had the right engine. While we putt along slowly, we at least take comfort in the gas money we are saving. The trouble is that we can't haul the dirt needed to finish the job.

I suggest that running churches on 3 to 4 percent of member income is not sufficient for the task God has assigned us. God's purposes cost 10 percent in the Old Testament. Why would things be less expensive today, when the task is now worldwide? We need to address what's wrong and how we can install that larger engine, carry the full load, and fully fund the advancement of Christ's kingdom.

Questions for Review and Reflection

1. Do you think that the American Dream has changed in the last hundred years? If so, how?
2. Has the author convinced you that God has invested enough money in his believing children to both fully fund the Great Commission and fulfill the Great Commandment? Why or why not?
3. Why do you think more of that money is not given to the Lord's work? Identify all the reasons you can think of.

13

Hope for Wealthy Disciples: Lessons from the Church at Laodicea

Behold, I stand at the door and knock. If anyone hears my voice and opens the door, I will come in to him and eat with him, and he with me. The one who conquers, I will grant him to sit with me on my throne, as I also conquered and sat down with my Father on his throne. (Rev. 3:20–21)

For the believer, the Bible defines the purpose of money as being a means for blessing others. We saw how the apostolic church translated this purpose into reality and how it was preserved and expanded through Paul's ministry. We traced some of the ups and downs of the post-apostolic church as it challenged and changed Roman culture with its radical redefinition of life and money, which culminated in the triumph of the faith.

In the Middle Ages, the church fell under state sponsorship during the rise of the Holy Roman Empire. The gospel was rediscovered through the Protestant Reformation, but this did not lead to a radical change in giving patterns, because the old state church structure was retained by Catholic, Orthodox, and Reformation churches. Giving partially rebounded in the United States, since the yoke of state church support was replaced there with a "free church" culture.

Evangelicals have succeeded in leading their churches to give at two to three times the rate of non-Christians, but middle-class American evangelicals still do not give at a 10 percent level, much less at a level that is worthy of the grace of Christ. Churches that are populated by the poor, minorities, and immigrants lead the way in the "grace of giving" at up to an 8 percent rate, and the faithful minority of evangelical revolutionaries give at 10 percent and more—but neither group has been able to lead the evangelical majority to give at their God-given potential.

Given this response they have displayed to his grace, what does Christ think of the churches in the West? Just how serious is this shortfall? Is it merely a budgetary annoyance for our churches, or is the deficiency connected to anything that is central to the gospel and to the progress of the kingdom? And does that deficiency endanger the church itself?

Christ's evaluation of the church in Laodicea in Revelation 3 is very applicable to those of us in Western majority churches. Consider what Christ writes through the apostle John to the churches that were immediately inland from the Isle of Patmos, where John was exiled (about forty miles offshore).

The words of the Amen, the faithful and true witness, the beginning of God's creation.

I know your works: you are neither cold nor hot. Would that you were either cold or hot! So, because you are lukewarm, and neither hot nor cold, I will spit you out of my mouth. For you say, I am rich, I have prospered, and I need nothing, not realizing that you are wretched, pitiable, poor, blind, and naked. I counsel you to buy from me gold refined by fire, so that you may be rich, and white garments so that you may clothe yourself and the shame of your nakedness may not be seen, and salve to anoint your eyes, so that you may see. Those whom I love, I reprove and discipline, so be zealous and repent. Behold, I stand at the door and knock. If anyone hears my voice and opens the door, I will come in to him and eat with him, and he with me. The one who conquers, I will grant him to sit with me on my throne, as I also conquered and sat down with my Father on his throne. He who has an ear, let him hear what the Spirit says to the churches. (Rev. 3:14–22)

Did you notice any parallels between Laodicea and American evangelical churches? Consider some historical facts about Laodicea that will put the church's situation in perspective.

Laodicea was affluent and economically self-sufficient. After much of the town was damaged by an earthquake in AD 60, the town reportedly refused Rome's help and made all the repairs with its own funds.[1] It was a banking and trade center at the intersection of three key roads in the region. It was famous for a well-known medical school, the production of beautiful wool, and a famous salve that promoted healing of the eyes. It was deeply prosperous compared to other places in the Roman Empire, and Laodiceans viewed that prosperity as a reward for their worthiness and excellence. They felt that they had a lot in which they could take pride and satisfaction.

The church had begun to reflect a theological version of this perspective. Its consistent prosperity, comfort, and economic self-sufficiency had tempted the church to say something like this to itself:

We, and the economy we have developed, have produced well for ourselves, our children, and our church. It is helpful to the kingdom that the gospel comes to a prosperous culture like ours. We can support missionaries to more backward places. And here, at home, there will be lots of Christian businesses, civic officials, and major donors. Our industrious culture has been blessed by God. Rather than having an entitlement mentality, we have been rewarded with a good life in this age and with the wisdom to secure the benefits of salvation in the future. God seems to have brought us this blessing, so we should not hesitate to protect and enjoy it. We have rejected the false teaching and immorality that is so prevalent today, and we know that this pleases God and contributes to the success of our churches.

1. See Dennis E. Johnson's note on Rev. 3:14–22 in the *ESV Study Bible*, exec. ed. Lane T. Dennis, gen. ed. Wayne Grudem (Wheaton, IL: Crossway, 2008), 2468.

We own businesses and farms, provide employment, and have literate children who will be future leaders in our culture. We are proof that Christians can be influential and not just slaves, trade workers, day laborers, and poor. In fact, we affirm our status as members of the upper economic class and have no problem living a life that is commensurate with God's blessing on us.

Of course, we hope that others in less productive and more compromised cultures will figure out how to find the prosperity and self-sufficiency that we have. We sometimes wonder why others can't do what we do here in Laodicea and provide for themselves. But we still give back. We send money for missions and mercy as we are able, but we can't unbalance our own budgets or put undue pressure on people to give more. We can provide relief funds if we have any excess.

It seems like other cities either reject the gospel or corrupt it. Their citizens then whine about their troubles, but they are getting what they deserve. If they keep to their old ways, they are asking for trouble. God has enabled us to purchase the things that make for a good life, and we have used our resources to produce a well-functioning church that has excellent staff and programs. Our church's core value is "Please God, and blessings will follow." This has proven true for us.

The result was a well-attended, decent, literate, and doctrinally orthodox church. It was primarily motivated to keep its programs going and to enjoy the spiritual services that made its members' lives more meaningful than their non-Christian neighbors'. They were happy with their lot and avoided much of the debauchery of their culture.

Jesus's Diagnosis

In love, Christ rebukes them, because their priorities had separated them from him and from the gospel. Jesus did not come for the decent and diligent but for sinners who cry, "Lord, be merciful to me, a sinner!" The Laodiceans were on the road to becoming a Greek version of the Jewish Pharisees. They were blinded by their public decency, their moral honor, and their wealth.

As George Ladd points out, "Laodicea was much like Sardis: an example of nominal, self-satisfied Christianity. One major difference is that at Sardis there remained a nucleus who had preserved a vital faith . . . while the entire Laodicean church was permeated by complacency. It is probable that many of the church members were active participants in the affluent society, and that this very economic affluence had exercised a deadly influence on the spiritual life of the church."[2]

Jesus points out that they had become self-centered members of a mutual admiration society. Even the orthodox people at Laodicea could turn their church into a club for mutual benefit. There was doubtless some appreciation for Christ's granting them past forgiveness and future salvation. This freed them up from the bondage of pagan idolatry and made them happier than their pagan neighbors. Without guilt over the past or fear of judgment in the future, they were deep into enjoying the blessings of their current lives in Laodicea, which had been purchased with their own resources, intelligence, and energy. What could be wrong with that?

But Jesus addresses them honestly. He says, in effect, "You are emotionally revolting to me. Repent, or I will spit you out of my mouth." He had been waiting for the works that they were called to do for the kingdom, but there had been nothing but token efforts. Their lukewarm hearts showed through their works. Most of the Laodiceans thought that their good works were not necessary; there weren't many deserving poor in their midst. They were distracted from even thinking about that by their enjoyment of the cultural goodness and happiness they were experiencing.

Paul (reflecting Jesus's teaching) had addressed a similar issue in 1 Timothy 6:17–19.

> As for the rich in this present age, charge them not to be haughty, nor to set their hopes on the uncertainty of riches, but on God, who

---

2. George Eldon Ladd, *A Commentary on the Revelation of John* (Grand Rapids: Eerdmans, 1972), 64.

richly provides us with everything to enjoy. They are to do good, to
be rich in good works, to be generous and ready to share, thus storing up treasure for themselves as a good foundation for the future,
so that they may take hold of that which is truly life.

This remarkable passage warns against the pride that comes from delu-
sions of self-sufficiency among the rich. Paul directs them to do good
as their life goal. This goes beyond generally acting in love in one's
home, church, and community; it involves specifically doing good
works by meeting needs of all kinds. This, Paul says, will include being
generous and sharing readily by means of loans, food, clothing, or
money. For the well-off, this should be a special focus and kingdom
calling. They have been called to pursue good works after the manner
of Christ.

As with anyone, rich people's future relationship with God will be
radically affected by the foundation that they lay. As they love their
neighbors, they will find their fellowship with Christ going deeper and
will experience real life now as well as on the last day. Jesus says in
John 14:23–24, "If anyone loves me, he will keep my word, and my
Father will love him, and we will come to him and make our home
with him. Whoever does not love me does not keep my words."

God had allowed the Laodiceans to be wealthy so that they might
be rich in good works—lending and giving generously to all, both
locally and regionally, and to both friends and enemies. But they
were seduced by the deceitfulness of riches and put their hope in
the possessions they had acquired. The Lord, who did not grasp the
wealth, power, or privilege of the Godhead, came to serve them when
they were doomed sinners. Yet they had no zeal to do good to others.
They professed to have received mercy from God but did not show
it to others.

The Biblical and the Prosperous

I wonder if this does not describe many of our churches today.
We are not theological liberals; our pastors preach the Bible and salvation only through Christ. We have full church programs, due to

some zealous volunteers, and many wonderful friends. There is no pressure on us to give, unless we have a budget shortfall, and yet we still provide 15 percent of our budget for missions.

Could such fully functional Bible-believing churches be as bad as Christ portrays in Revelation 3 or as Paul warns against in 1 Timothy 6? That seems to be the picture that Christ paints. Laodicea (as opposed to the other churches) evokes a visceral, almost spontaneous reaction in him—he will "spit them out of his mouth," as one ejects some nauseating liquid. It is an emotion of revulsion. It is similar to the emotion a parent might feel if he discovered his beloved twelve-year-old son torturing a neighbor's dog or mercilessly bullying a scared six-year-old girl. It is like the revulsion you might feel if you found that your grown son was selling drugs to junior-high kids or assaulting his wife and children. Such evil makes you sick, not just angry.

So Jesus warns them that they have no future in his church and mission unless they repent. They ironically appear to God just like the wretched, blind, malnourished, filthy, homeless man they might have seen downtown. They are like the very people whose fate they thank God that they have avoided.

Is Christ being too hard on this church? After all, they had avoided false teaching, sexual sin, and idolatry in any recognizable form. This was no small accomplishment. They had not entirely lost their first love, though it was on a low flame. Their works were not "dead," though they were sometimes half-hearted.

We might reply to Christ that it is difficult for people in prosperous cultures to free up time, talent, and treasure in order to do good to the needy, the prisoner, the widow, the orphan, the poor, the hungry, and the enemy. These productive Christians work long hours in a competitive world. They feel tapped out, already being responsible stewards of the resources and opportunities that they and their children have.

Jesus, of course, warned all of us that it is harder for a rich man to enter the kingdom of God than for a camel to go through the eye of a needle. Their only hope is God's grace. This same grace leads Christ to profess love for the church and to counsel them to approach God in order to acquire three things (see Rev. 3:18).

"Gold Refined by Fire, So That You May Be Rich"

Jesus addresses their need to repent of laying up treasures on earth instead of in heaven. Instead of acquiring material wealth, Jesus urges them to be rich in good works, generosity, and obedience to the Great Commandment, thereby laying a sure foundation for their everlasting future with God. This would involve their feeling specific sorrow and confessing their sin, asking for God's forgiveness, and showing a new resolve to seek first the kingdom of God and his righteousness.

"White Garments So That You May Clothe Yourselves"

Jesus counsels these Christians to exchange their pursuit of outward clothing for a pursuit of the true raiment of purity, righteousness from God, and good works, by which they may adorn themselves for him. Pagans seek after the things of this age; Christ's disciples are to seek to bring the saving, gracious rule of God into their present lives and circumstances. James 1:27 captures this combination of purity and grace as it defines true religion: "Religion that is pure and undefiled before God the Father is this: to visit orphans and widows in their affliction, and to keep oneself unstained from the world."

"Salve to Anoint Your Eyes, So That You May See"

The Laodiceans could not see the emptiness or the danger of their path toward acquiring earthly wealth, nor could they see the path ahead that would guide them to the wealth of God.

Jesus talked about such blind, professing followers in Matthew 25:31–46, in which the sheep (the saved) are marked out as those who went to the needy, the hungry, and the prisoner and offered them relief. The goats (the unsaved) are condemned, though they complain that they never saw Jesus in need and that, if they had, they would have helped him. Jesus said that to the extent that they did not show mercy to the needy, they did not show it to him. They were blind to the mercy they could have shown. They had no wisdom regarding their opportunities to do God's will.

The Laodiceans' pursuit of the blessings of this age (see Rom. 12:2; Gal. 5:16–25; Eph. 1:15–22; Phil. 1:9–11) left the widow, the prisoner, the hungry, the untaught, the naked, and the sick mired in their affliction. These believers were like the Pharisee and the Levite who walked past their brother who had been beaten and robbed on the roadside, telling themselves they had more important things to do and therefore should not risk their lives for a victim whose value they could not calculate.

The Spirit's illumination is what enables believers to walk in love in the situations that God brings our way. Otherwise, blinded by our own pursuits, we walk by without knowing what is at stake. Jesus counsels the Laodiceans to acquire spiritual sight—to see the world in the light of God's truth and not to stumble and fall through the deceitfulness of riches.

This knowledge is difficult for sinful creatures—particularly those who have been blinded by the deceitfulness of riches. So Jesus speaks graciously, letting the church know that he will fully engage them if they repent and admit him as Lord of their lives. He uses this metaphor:

> Behold, I stand at the door and knock. If anyone hears my voice and opens the door, I will come in to him and eat with him, and he with me. The one who conquers, I will grant him to sit with me on my throne, as I also conquered and sat down with my Father on his throne. (Rev. 3:20–21)

If we hear his voice and open the door, he will not spit us out or extinguish our light. Rather, he will come in to dine with us in deep fellowship and communion. Jesus has been locked out of the church, which has been co-opted and repurposed as a club of comfort for those in pursuit of the blessings of this age. This is not so much a picture of a powerless person pleading for entry into a home but of a father knocking on the locked door of his teenaged son's room—a room in which his son is living in self-induced delusion through head-phones and music videos.

Yes, opening the door will require repentance and submission to Christ's commandments, but it will offer intimate, accepting fellow-ship with the living God. The King will come to us, even though we are in his home. His knock is not the weak tap of a fainting guest but the confident knock of the King coming to his own household.

Christ's willingness to seek reentry into his home is encouraging for those who hear his voice. Christ says, "If *anyone* hears my voice and opens the door, I will come in to him." A believer, even on his own, can respond, repent, accept forgiveness and renewed fellowship with his Savior, and find in that Savior all that he needs in order to joyfully enter his kingdom. Even if others do not come, such a believer is promised that he will be an overcomer and conqueror—one who is qualified to share in the administration of the universe.

Back to the Evangelical Revolutionaries

Surveys and church demographics show that there is a minority within most evangelical churches whose most earnest pursuits are to give, serve, witness, and show mercy. They provide the majority of the funds, the volunteers, the missionaries, the prayer warriors, and the relief workers who are available to do God's work. These revolutionaries are dedicated, passionate, and persistent. They are the ones who are most critical of a complacent church and who often begin new ones in order to meet new needs or correct old failings. They are the point of the spear of God's kingdom, and, according to Revelation 3:20, they are sustained in that work by fellowship with the risen Christ.

What would happen if the majority population of our biblically faithful congregations opened the door to Christ, repented of their self-orientation, and became zealous to bring forth works that were worthy of Christ? We have already seen that, financially, this could result in close to $100 billion annually in new money for the lost and the poor.

What would happen if white evangelicals sought to help end poverty among urban minorities and immigrants in the United States and were willing to work with urban leaders as equals in order to address that? What if we, together, took on the challenge of racial enmity through a practical reconciliation of our churches?

What would happen if evangelicals of all sorts sought the Lord's provision for the prevention of infant deaths around the world, the adoption of all lost children, and the educational development of illiterate children in both American cities and developing nations? We have the expertise and the money—but, so far, the will to give only token amounts to that task.

What would happen if we used our resources to help to establish fair criminal justice systems in our cities and abroad?

What would happen if we assisted Christian attorneys around the world with freeing slaves and sexually trafficked children from their bondage, starving the criminal enterprises that sponsor those crimes, and renewing the lives of those children and their families with a knowledge of the gospel?

What would happen if we provided microloans and small-business loans to enterprising family members around the world, so that they could grow their businesses and hire more of their people?

What if Western businesses that are controlled by Christians planted franchises in Muslim lands to be a place of refuge for Christians of Muslim backgrounds to work, be nurtured, and multiply?

Even secular pagans see the contradiction between Western wealth and the needs of the world and are seeking to address it.[3] How much more should God's people be leading the way!

Thankfully, those who are without Christ can still sense his values and his common grace. Without knowing their hearts, we thank God for those like Warren Buffett and Bill Gates, who are addressing public health and welfare issues with a view toward making a real difference. We commend them and hope that others will follow their example. But there is a limited number of folks who have such surpluses, and giving from Americans who are outside religion will probably continue at about 2 percent. We are thankful for the humanistic sentiment that prompts world relief funds from many nations that distribute their funds through the United Nations, though some of these programs suffer without the guidance of the Christian values and compassion that originally motivated their launch.

3. See Peter Singer, *The Most Good You Can Do: How Effective Altruism Is Changing Ideas About Living Ethically* (New Haven, CT: Yale University Press, 2015). Singer professes to establish an ethical basis for those without God to live for the sake of "doing the most good." He calculates a dollar value for each good work and urges donors to support only those causes that offer the highest dollar value of good being done.

Yet these more humanistic efforts have so far been powerless to mobilize a broad base of sustainable contributions that would provide mercy and justice. There are even serious questions about whether many of these efforts end up hurting, in the long run, the very people whom we seek to help.[4] Yet efforts to offer relief as a global initiative are moving in the right direction. Would that God might move the church to launch and guide such an effort from a biblical perspective of creation, fall, and redemption.

Fortunately, in God's providence, help has been coming from other quarters in the meantime. The growth of market economies and the rule of law in the developing world should continue to reduce material poverty in the next twenty years. As in the past, this will involve the world industrial and service economy expanding to include at least India and Africa. This will increase urbanization and the cultural ailments that affect immigrants in urban areas, but it will also increase spendable income for many, which will move them from a situation of uncertain subsistence to being lower-middle class. This in turn will allow mercy and development agencies to focus on the ills of the urban poor and the remaining communities that live below the $2-per-day income level.

However, the needs of undeveloped countries continue to remain dire. Just as the advocates of the social gospel in the 1920s and of liberation theology in the 1960s failed to engage broader support, we fear that this movement of secular giving will not be sustainable much beyond its present scope of established NGOs and the state-supported United Nations. The Christian church, empowered by the grace of God, is the one entity that has been successful in the past and could be successful in the future.

Since World War II, many such endeavors have been launched by the evangelical revolutionaries, and new ones are starting every day. Some, like The Salvation Army, Compassion International, Bread for the World, and World Vision, have become powerful forces in

---

4. See the documentary *Poverty Inc.*, produced by Michael Miller and the Acton Institute. Another good source for guidance on this issue is Steve Corbett and Brian Fikkert, *When Helping Hurts: How to Alleviate Poverty without Hurting the Poor . . . and Yourself* (Chicago: Moody, 2010).

the world and have demonstrated that aggressive faith like theirs can experience God's blessing as well as dramatic growth in the scale of its outreach. Yet even these endeavors are not largely embraced by our churches, thriving instead off of individual contributions and grants. They are still learning how to scale up their efforts without hurting the long-term prospects for development in the communities that they serve. When this happened in Acts 6, the church learned to strengthen and expand its mercy ministry. In the same way, the Christian church should assign its best and wisest minds to address this issue. Our churches, if they were renewed in the way that Christ had in mind for Laodicea (see Rev. 3:14–22), would indeed start to look a bit like The Salvation Army: a large endeavor of good works with a church attached as its owner.

I pray that Christ's knock will be heard loud and clear—first by the leaders and then by the majorities in our churches. Let's pray that God will move all of us to open the doors of our hearts to Christ, that he might return to his temple and home, thereby bringing back his fellowship with us and, finally, our reward for conquering the plans and temptations that Satan has set for the church.

Questions for Review and Reflection

1. How had wealth affected the Christians at Laodicea?
2. What options did Christ set before them in his message to them?
3. To what extent do you think American Christians suffer from a similar affliction and have similar choices?

14

Teaching Our Churches to Excel in Giving

But as you excel in everything—in faith, in speech, in knowledge, in all earnestness, and in our love for you—see that you excel in this act of grace also. (2 Cor. 8:7)

In chapters 1–10 we surveyed what the Bible teaches about money and its purpose. In chapters 11, 12, and 13, we looked at how that teaching was lived out in the history of the Western church, with an emphasis on the United States today. Now we move beyond describing what should be (theology and ethics) and what is (history) in order to understand how the church can grow to embrace and practice godly giving today.

As we have seen, there is a large and alarming gap between the amounts that Christians are giving and both the provision of God and the needs of the world. We tend to attribute that gap to the high cost of living and the inevitable control of consumerism. We accept giving at 2–5 percent of members' household income and adjust our ministry, mission, and mercy to fit.

But if my thesis is correct that God has given his people the time, treasure, and gifts that are sufficient to carry out all his commissions, then we have a problem. It means that we are holding back a large portion of God's treasure for ourselves. We are bloated with accumulated wealth, which not only cheats God and deceives us but has seriously restricted his mission here and abroad.

That remarkable fact raises the stakes of the next question: how can the church of Christ reverse the downward trend of the last hundred years and grow its giving to make it equal to the tasks to which it is called? How can we see to it that we excel in giving—which Paul calls an "act of grace" (2 Cor. 8:7)?

This is not an easy question to answer. Giving in the United States has been static at 2 percent of GDP for forty years. No amount of fundraising expertise, church growth, or marketing and media efforts have caused it to budge. Giving has been shifting from mainline denominations to evangelical churches and denominations, and there is no sign that this trend will change. This shift does not, however, change the net amounts that are given. Christians' giving has dropped by 20 percent of their income since 1968, while their income itself has increased by 50 percent. The more we make, the less we give as a percentage of our income. Only the growth of the evangelical movement has enabled giving to keep up and increase slightly. In the average evangelical church, between 9 percent and 23 percent of the members tithe. The remainder of members give much less, so that the average evangelical gives about 4 percent of his or her income to worthy causes—mostly to the local church.

Moving from Being a 1 Percent to a 10+ Percent Giver

So how do born-again believers move from giving 1 or 2 percent to giving 10 percent and wanting to do more? How do Christians learn to excel in the grace of giving?

To get started, let's briefly step back to the church in Corinth at the time of the apostles. Tepid giving was a problem for this church as well. Corinth was a wealthy trading center, and some of that wealth was owned by the church members. When the offering for starving Christians in Judea was announced, the elders immediately responded to this offering with an attitude of "no problem." Yet they came up short compared to the Macedonians, who were poor. As a wealthy church, they had a greater responsibility and capacity for giving, yet they gave at levels that were way below what they professed to be able to do (and should have done). Both Paul's letters, culminating in 2 Corinthians 8 and 9, prepared the way for them to make a second try at the offering.

Paul did not make peace with their failure, as we have too often done. He did not thank them for their contribution and fail to challenge them out of fear that he might alienate a rich constituency whom he might need in the future. He saw what was at stake, spiritually and for the health of the communion with all believers that they professed. But neither did he "lay down the law." He masterfully laid out the dynamics of grace that motivate Christian giving. The church rose to the occasion, and the cause of Christ, the Judean church, and Jew-and-Gentile relationships were greatly advanced.

We find ourselves in a similar situation, except that our problem is now more serious, because stingy giving has not been addressed by the church and has become systemic and deeply entrenched. The church and its mission have grown somewhat because of the 10–25 percent who carry the load for the rest of the church. But these revolutionaries cannot make up for the huge numbers of folks who toss in a $20 bill when the offering is passed.

That brings us once again to Paul's words to the Corinthian church: "But as you excel in everything—in faith, in speech, in knowledge, in all earnestness, and in our love for you—see that you excel in this act of grace also" (2 Cor. 8:7).

Paul's challenge is sobering for us as well. He commands this church in a metro area to pursue great generosity. They were well known for their pursuit and cultivation of the more spectacular gifts of the Spirit, and he now teaches them to train that same zeal on generosity.

How can we implement Paul's command to pursue excellence in giving? I would like to suggest nine ways.

1. Strive for Christian Generosity by First Embracing Christian Belief

Paul says that if the dead are not raised, "Let us eat and drink, for tomorrow we die" (1 Cor. 15:32). In other words, if we don't have convictions about Christ's resurrection and our own, the last judgment, and the reality of everlasting life on a renewed earth, we will easily live only for the enjoyments of this age. Many of Jesus's teachings dealt with our need to plan for the age to come by laying up treasures in heaven and becoming rich toward God.

In Randy Alcorn's book *Heaven*, he refers to many surveys that indicate that American Christians view heaven as an undefined, purely spiritual, disembodied existence.[1] He presents the plain biblical teaching that our everlasting life will take place on this renewed earth—one that is embodied and tangible and will include eating, celebrations, cultures, learning, creating, community, care for creation, governance, and relationships. It will be what God created mankind to enjoy before the fall, except that now it will be renewed and redeemed—confirmed in righteousness and in open fellowship with God.

Belief in these realities can be undercut in at least three ways:

- through unbelief in the truth of the Bible, under the influence of materialism, naturalism, or theological liberalism
- through simply ignoring the hard-to-understand parts of Scripture about the future life
- through doubts about whether you will actually be saved to enjoy it all

Since many of us struggle with one or all of these, I encourage you to take God up on his offer to reveal himself to those who seek him (see Heb. 11:6). Since the Holy Spirit exhorted us to "make our calling and election sure" (see 2 Peter 1:10), it must be possible for us to reach strong positive convictions. The assurance of things hoped for (see Heb. 11:1) is certainly one of the greatest blessings of the Christian life, even apart from the impact it has on generosity. But those who are vitally linked to Christ will be progressively transformed into his character, thereby reflecting his generosity. Only if you have known God's lavish giving for you in your own personal poverty can you know the love of God.[2] Only if that love dwells in you will you

---

1. See Randy Alcorn, *Heaven* (Carol Stream, IL: Tyndale, 2004), 301–9.
2. Two excellent introductions to the Christian faith are Timothy Keller's *The*

show it to others. Only God can teach fallen sinners how to love with his compassionate love. (See 1 John for more on this.)

2. Let the Gospel Drive Giving

When Paul wrote to Corinth, he did not "lay down the law" and call for obligations for the members to tithe, as is done in Islamic, Mormon, and Jehovah's Witness circles. Neither did he say that their levels of giving would impact their justification or salvation, as the purists and legalists of his (and our) day would have done. Neither did he promise an upgraded lifestyle or increased net worth to those who gave. Rather, Paul reminded them to walk worthily of God's grace.

> I say this not as a command, but to prove by the earnestness of others that your love also is genuine. For you know the grace of our Lord Jesus Christ, that though he was rich, yet for your sake he became poor, so that you by his poverty might become rich. (2 Cor. 8:8–9)

In Galatians, Paul argues that we cannot enter the Christian life by grace alone and then shift back to works or law in order to complete our salvation or service (see Gal. 3:1–14). As we received Christ, so we should walk in him—by faith (see Col. 2:6). The Christian life must become a lifestyle of repentance, in which we continually turn from sin and toward Christ's grace for forgiveness and our righteousness. This experience of God's love in Christ motivates the love that we show to God and to others. Only then can we obey Christ's law to "love one another as I have loved you" (John 15:12).

Jesus stated it clearly when he responded to the self-righteous of his day. When the "sinful" woman anointed him with perfume and the Pharisees objected, Jesus explained, "Therefore I tell you, her sins, which are many, are forgiven—for she loved much. But he who is forgiven little, loves little" (Luke 7:47).

Prodigal God: Recovering the Heart of the Christian Faith (New York: Dutton, 2008) and John R. W. Stott's *Basic Christianity* (Downers Grove, IL: InterVarsity Press, 1958).

Modern Western churches can easily lose their foundation in the gospel. Conservatives can lose it as the Galatians did—through an unbiblical focus on law-keeping, doctrinal correctness, avoiding "worldly" behaviors, rigorous church attendance, and even a conservative political mindset.

The Reformation under Luther, Calvin, Knox, Zwingli, and Zinzendorf, and the great American revivals in the eighteenth and nineteenth centuries, were all characterized by the rediscovery of God's grace as the means for salvation *as well as* for sanctification and service.

Some churches preach the gospel each week and ask people to make decisions for Christ, but they must go deeper than that and connect the grace of God to everything that the Christian believes and does—be it prayer, marriage, vocation, missions, sanctification, or giving. In each of these areas, the gospel is the motivation. In my view, this is the reason that evangelical churches give 40 percent more than other churches do. They have fostered a love for Christ that can only come as people are forgiven, cleansed, loved, and adopted as sons and daughters.

Another threat to churches' "knowing the grace of our Lord Jesus Christ" was the theological liberalism that flourished from 1900 to 1950. This liberalism disavowed the historic gospel and our need for Christ's substitutionary atonement for sin, urging us instead to simply follow Christ's example of self-sacrifice and address the systemic social ills around us.

While the leaders of theological liberalism were often correct in their analysis of social ills and injustices, their failure to preach the gospel of Christ's death on our behalf and of his power to transform us into his image took the heart out of their message. Without the real gospel, mainline churches began a rapid decline toward impotence. Despite their great wealth, they could not motivate their people to give, volunteer, or minister in support of their vision. This false gospel turned many mainline churches from being vital Christian fellowships into being vestigial congregations that battled to stay afloat. When the gospel dies, outreach and mercy die with it. These churches' seminaries are also dying for lack of people who are motivated to enter pastoral ministry.

Our commission from Christ is to preach the gospel to all humanity and to preach it to ourselves for the challenges that we face daily. The gospel alone is the power of God unto salvation, and it includes within it our motivation for service, generosity, and the good works that God ordains for us.

In order for a church to be generous, its members must know and deal with this generous God. The gospel itself must be guarded, defended, and applied to all races and cultures; it will then bring life, generosity, and service in all cultures and races. We will find our work being done more and more in the Spirit, not in the flesh. The overwhelming love of God will be ever more tangible—redeeming, motivating, and shaping our love and giving.

3. Recognize That Consecration Underlies Stewardship

Consecration means giving oneself—body, soul, mind, and spirit—to God. In 2 Corinthians 8:5 Paul says that consecration is the reason why the Macedonians' giving was so lavish: "They did not do as we expected, but they gave themselves first to the Lord and then to us in keeping with God's will" (NIV). These saints understood that Jesus had left all that he had, taken on human flesh, and given himself as an offering to God for them. Their response was to give themselves for him. He was worthy of all praise, honor, and blessing.

Paul says that the Macedonians gave "as much as they were able, and even beyond their ability" (v. 3 NIV). They "pleaded" with Paul for the privilege of serving the saints in Jerusalem (v. 4). They already saw God as their owner and therefore as the owner of the money that he had entrusted to them. Their job was to dispense as much of that money as possible for the Lord and his saints. Their money was attached to God's purpose for it.

Their attitude reflects the attitude that Paul urges the Roman Christians to adopt in Romans 12:1: "I appeal to you therefore, brothers, by the mercies of God, to present your bodies as a living sacrifice, holy and acceptable to God, which is your spiritual worship." Consecration in response to God's mercy is the essential act of worship for the believer—it must precede any service or giving. No one can be a disciple of Christ without bringing everything that he has and is to Christ. Salvation is free but will cost us everything. In turn, what we give to Christ we can never lose; it will be returned to us many times over on the last day.

Giving 10 percent will generally not occur (and much less will sacrificial giving) without our cheerful, voluntary consecration of ourselves and our money, time, and gifts. When we consecrate it, all our money changes title—from us to God.

So how is consecration pursued in a local church? In order for our churches to participate in biblical giving, pastors and leaders must set the example of consecration and teach it unashamedly but humbly to God's people. This means preaching and teaching the lordship of Christ over every area of our lives. Paul covers some of these areas in Ephesians 4:17–5:33 and in similar passages. Christ's kingdom and the life of the Spirit must come to expression in how we

- relate to members of our churches
- work on the job and relate to bosses and coworkers
- treat our spouses
- view and treat our parents
- rear and teach our children
- relate to civil government, especially regarding taxes
- approach every field of study
- behave with those who are outside the church
- speak to others
- treat our enemies and those who frustrate us
- view and use our money

By actively discipling God's flock to live out the gospel in their daily lives, leaders are helping them to consecrate their lives to Christ. Going forward in a church service to "rededicate" one's life to Christ can be the beginning—but it must only be the start, not the finish. Salvation is by faith alone and by grace alone—but it is never a faith that is alone. It is always accompanied by our following Christ and having visible love for others.

So how can pastors and leaders today urge their people to "offer their bodies as living sacrifices"? By teaching that the faith and repentance that initiate salvation lead to a life of faith and repentance. Pastors and church leaders who testify of their own fresh repentance and acceptance of grace set a powerful example for the flock. The pastor is more of a RIC (repenter-in-chief) than a CEO (chief executive officer).

Church leaders should strongly encourage small groups within their churches, in which adults can find help to live out the gospel in the practical dimensions of life through prayer support, encouragement, and loving accountability.

They should also provide high-quality training, through an adult education program, in how to live out the faith in all areas of life, including marriage, singleness, parenting, peacemaking, the workplace, money management and priorities, overcoming sin, counseling others, addictions, and dealing with loss and grief.

Church leaders must also exercise loving oversight over the faith and lives of their members, entering their lives in order to help them obey and follow their Lord through the hard places. If they fail to do this, it will send a loud message that Christian faith is for church only and that Christ is not Lord over life but only over religion. While exercising spiritual discipline over a wayward member is painful for everyone, unless a church is prepared to do it, it cannot be faithful to Christ's lordship or to the care that it owes its people.

All of these ministries promote a "kingdom mentality" through which members begin to connect Christ's redemption to all areas of life, including to their view of money.

4. Teach and Practice the Communion of the Saints

This phrase "the communion of the saints" appears in the Apostles' Creed, yet this teaching is virtually unknown in Protestant churches.[3]

---

3. For the best doctrinal summary of the communion of the saints, see the Westminster Confession of Faith, chapter 26.

However, this doctrine is not easily accepted in our culture, in which private property not only is protected and legal but has become truly sacred. The idea that love can lead people to use their property to benefit the body is quite radical—and quite biblical.

The doctrine of the communion of the saints is bedrock to understanding the generosity and sharing of the early church. The Macedonian believers lived out this communion with the Judean Christians. Since all believers have an interest in the gifts and graces of all others, each believer is there for the building up of the whole. Each one's gifts, treasure, and abilities have been pre-positioned by Christ so that if all believers do their part, the church grows together into Christ's image. If they do not, all the members suffer.

Christ commands us to remember the poor, visit widows and orphans, minister to the sick and the prisoner, comfort the grieving, and rejoice with those who rejoice. In other words, we have an open-ended responsibility to love one another in tangible ways that minister to the wounds of a fallen world.

In the apostolic church, this sharing of resources was sufficient to end poverty among its members. In order to do that, the church had to function as a community and a fellowship of Christians (see Acts 2:42–47; 4:32–37). This enabled them to deal with poverty and the needs of their widows as people shared their wealth with the apostles and deacons. This enhanced the church's favor with the people of Jerusalem, which in turn produced more growth.

How can we practice this kind of caring within the communion of the saints today? The first practical measure is to ordain deacons who are servant leaders to oversee the mercy ministry of the church. The fact that this office was established by the apostles and therefore by Christ shows its non-negotiable place in the life of the body. Deacons' work goes way beyond caring for the physical building and making arrangements for worship.[4]

The most important thing a church can do to practice the communion of the saints is to begin by addressing suffering within its

---

4. The best textbook on the biblical vision for the diaconate is Timothy Keller, *Ministries of Mercy: The Call of the Jericho Road*, 3rd ed. (Phillipsburg, NJ: P&R

own congregation. This should be carried out by deacons who seek to discover members' basic needs and then marshal resources to meet them.

When I was pastor of a 125-member church, I was tempted to doubt that God would provide for some rather deep needs in the congregation, including those of two attendees who had acute mental disorders and a young man with severe multiple sclerosis. It was hard to see how we could take on their cases without being distracted from the ministry of the Word. Yet God provided faith-filled laypeople who believed that God could meet the needs and who saw him do just that. It resulted in a deepening community within the body that attracted more folks to the church.

Based on my experiences in the northern suburbs of Philadelphia, my sense is that deacons who operate in wealthy suburban communities will usually discover that they can end destructive poverty within their congregations for about 0.5 percent of their members' household income, leaving 9.5 percent of it (the remainder of the tithe) for other causes.

In suburban situations, much of that money will go toward counseling for relational breakdown in marriages and families. Many lower-income middle-class folks will also need financial, personal, or vocational counseling in order to find their way. Other big needs will include health insurance for those who have lost it and rent and mortgage payments for those who are dealing with job loss, poor choices, or divorce.

Larger churches may find it challenging to manage all this without a staff deacon, but in many congregations retired or semi-retired people can be trained to assist in this ministry.

Caring for its internal needs is the prerequisite (and training process) for a church to reach beyond its local congregation in order to care for people in sister or daughter churches or who are not in a church at all. If churches are faithful in sharing their gifts, graces, and treasure in small (local) situations, they will be prepared by God to be a blessing in greater situations.

Publishing, 2015).

Churches in low-income communities will probably find that they do *not* have the resources to address the systemic poverty in their midst. Most of them do not know where to turn for help. They often have the volunteers, wisdom, and leadership necessary to address educational needs, job-training needs, prisoner-reentry issues, and addiction crises in their communities, but lack the funds to deploy those gifts. They often are limited to offering spiritual services, evangelism, and discipleship, while never being able to address the systematic economic needs around them. In Philadelphia I know of five black churches, brimming with teachers and leaders, who started schools for their youth only to have to close them because of a lack of funds.

This is where the communion of the saints can be so powerful. Wealthy Christians often do not know how to give without also wanting control, and urban leaders, having been burned on this issue, are often wary of asking for help. But urban leaders will ultimately need to be willing to accept the help of Christians outside their communities, and wealthier Christians will have to learn to help without hurting. Though sharing between diverse communities of Christians rarely happens today, under the dual oversight of leaders in both giver and receiver churches, it *can* happen and can result in great thanksgiving to God.[5]

5. Teach and Demonstrate Contentment

Contentment will bestow on us the freedom to give not just from true excess (which only the 1 percent have today) but from some of the funds that could be used to upgrade our lifestyles and possessions. Contentment does not increase our income but increases our capacity

---

5. This happened in a dramatic way in Philadelphia with the launching of the Center for Urban Theological Studies in 1978. Leaders from the mostly suburban Westminster Seminary Community and the mostly urban African-American community formed a board made up of equal representation from both communities in order to provide credentialed, college-level ministry training to urban church leaders who did not yet have a college degree. Today, CUTS continues that mission and is owned and managed by Lancaster Bible College.

to give. If we are free from the "I gotta have a . . ." mindset, we will spend less and have more to give.

A key passage on contentment is 1 Timothy 6:8–10.

> But if we have food and clothing, with these we will be content. But those who desire to be rich fall into temptation, into a snare, into many senseless and harmful desires that plunge people into ruin and destruction. For the love of money is a root of all kinds of evils. It is through this craving that some have wandered away from the faith and pierced themselves with many pangs.

Note that Paul does not discourage us from securing the necessities of life. Those who are without food, clothing, or other necessities should seek them in order to live without being a burden on others. Paul is not commending a life of poverty or asceticism. Jesus invites us to trust our Father in heaven for the necessities of life (see Matt. 6:31) and to pray for our daily bread. Being in poverty is destructive and should be resisted by believers and the church, as we will see in chapter 18. Paul is commending contentment, not poverty. He knew how to remain content whether he abounded *or* was in need (see Phil. 4:11).

Paul is stating, however, that once our necessities are secured, we should not seek to acquire more from the motivation of being discontent or of thinking that we are missing out on the good life. Paul knew that those who were married with children would need more than he did—such as stable housing, and so on, in addition to the food and clothing that he needed. Elsewhere he mentions such increased needs as a point against getting married. A married man is divided between how he may please the Lord and how he may please his wife. He implies that if you are married, you *must* be about pleasing your spouse—and this takes time, talent, and treasure (see 1 Cor. 7:33–34). Having children adds another layer of love-motivated provision, anxiety, and worldly stress. Yet Paul recognizes the legitimacy of callings to marriage and childrearing and the necessities that are involved with them. We divide our financial blessings between our dependents and the Lord, right up the income scale.

Today, what it costs to escape poverty and to pay for the necessities of life is high and getting higher. Depending on circumstances and location, this cost for a family of four in the United States could be (in 2017 dollars) anywhere from $50,000 to about $65,000 (which includes the value of any public assistance benefits). In developing world cultures, the cost could be as low as $5 a day. But the principle is clear. Whatever our culture or economy, each believer should strive to reach a point of economic stability that is securely *above* the downward spiral that defines poverty. And once we have reached that stable point, Paul exhorts us to be spiritually content with our lives.

So why would a disciple of Christ ever spend more than what is just enough to escape poverty? If necessities cost $49,000 a year for me and my family of four, why would I, as a Christian, spend any more than $49,000 on our life? Put another way, is it okay to be a part of middle-income culture in the developed world? Is it okay to spend money on piano lessons, a dependable second car, a guest room, a family vacation, fresher and healthier food, a safer neighborhood, or college tuition for a child? Yes—if God has provided the funds for these blessings, they can add substantially to the quality of life that we enjoy and can enhance the service that our lives render to others.

What makes a purchase right or wrong is not the item itself but our motivation. You can obtain such blessings for you and your family and be a contented person when you buy them. There are no biblical rules or laws about levels of expenditure. Few purchases are sinful in themselves.

If an acquisition stems from a motivation to love family members and see them blessed to live with less stress and more security and have greater health and personal development, then it is generosity at work. Such a purchase brings us the joy of providing things that God has granted us to enjoy in this life, and this giving mentality will flow over into greater giving to the church, missions, and mercy. However, if an acquisition is motivated by covetousness, discontent, or the desire to accumulate things, then it is wrong at the heart level. If I buy things in order to gain the "good life" and to be happy in that life, then I simply love the world and the things that are in it (see James 4:3; 1 John 2:15–17). This will whet my appetite for even more, and I will have even less to give.

Complicating the spiritual dimension of our motives is the reality that those motives are often mixed. For example, the blessings that become available to a family of four that makes $75,000 instead of $50,000 are so substantial that the "parental provision instinct" would still drive most of the spending of someone in such a financial situation. Moving to a good school district, providing a second car for a working spouse, providing play space for children, getting medical needs cared for, or building an emergency fund are things that pay large dividends and do not necessarily reflect a "love of money" dynamic. Yet, while the main motivation of someone in this situation might be providing for his family, it may be tainted with the lesser motivation that such upgrades to his family circumstances will demonstrate his adequacy as a person or give him a real life.

So how do you tell if you are "loving the world"? Fortunately, God has provided a simple test. Are you content without your blessings? How do you react when they are denied or lost—are you angry? Depressed? Irritated? Do you fear losing them? Do you find yourself discontent with your place on the middle-income ladder? Are you desirous of your neighbors' economic success or possessions? Do you feel like you will be content only if you get those things? Do you never have enough to be generous with it for the Lord's work? These are signs that your heart is set on the world and what money will buy.

When you find this sin cropping up, the answer to it is to repent, ask forgiveness, and seek your life, hope, and future in Christ and his provision. This may mean saying no to an item that you can't possess in a way that glorifies God. Ask for the Spirit's strength to put off your old mind-set (which convinces you that you need such and such) and put on a new mind-set (one that helps you realize that life does not consist in what you have but in knowing and serving God). I recommend William Barcley's book, *The Secret of Contentment* (Phillipsburg, NJ: P&R, 2010), if this is your struggle.

After Superstorm Sandy, canal-front lots where I fished, in Great Bay, New Jersey, were going for $10,000. These waterfront lots, which now had what remained of flooded homes situated on them, had previously sold for $160,000 for just the lot itself. I thought I was seeing gold. I get a thrill out of a good deal, and I saw this as an opportunity to rack up a win—especially after having lost some money and ego in the great recession. I started researching the costs of cleaning up the lots and contacted a real estate agent. I could feel the excitement of a big win coming my way.

Then God answered my prayers for protection from having a love of money. He put this train of thought in my head: "Hold on, Jim. You are leading an urban mission organization, and you don't have the bandwidth to do more real estate investing while running the mission at the same time. In fact, you took on this ministry because you believed that your past investments had netted enough to enable you to responsibly retire to leading an unpaid ministry. So why do you now want more?" I could have told myself that it is always good to have a greater margin of security, but there is no end to that false train of thought. What were my goals, anyway? I had to decide all over again to be content with what I had and to let the investing opportunity go. I also needed to get back to raising money for urban kids to go to Christian schools. Once I repented for my wasted energy and wayward desire, I felt a noticeable relief—a freedom and peace that surprised me.

6. Teach on the Theology of Money

Giving is an "act of grace" (2 Cor. 8:7). Do our Christian wage earners understand what that means? While most pastors encourage their congregations to give to the Lord's work, most of us shy away from "lifting the hood" on the biblical teaching about giving. We are victims of the cultural taboo against intruding into the "sacred" areas of private property, personal spending, and motivation for giving. We are part of the culture—and the problem.

And the problem is made all the more difficult because so many who do talk about money are in it to make or enjoy money themselves. They are the false teachers and prosperity preachers who "peddle the gospel" for personal gain (see 2 Cor. 2:17; Acts 8:18–24). They are just the excuse that many people need to avoid teaching about money and giving altogether, thereby sending the message that money is sacred, private, and not subject to the lordship of Christ.

Jesus, James, and Paul had no such problem with teaching about money. Christian leaders must be like them in this area. We must seek to grow in faith and wisdom in order to sincerely address the issues of generosity. As mentioned earlier, I have found John Wesley's sermon "The Use of Money" to be the most compelling, personal, positive teaching on this topic in sermon form. He pioneered the way for Christians to connect biblical teaching with their own money. Wesley, however, did not stop with pulpit ministry. He saw that few of us are beyond the need for exhortation, example, and encouragement in this area. His "Holy Club" meetings (small groups) were devoted to applying the gospel to issues in the lives of God's people. In other words, small-group accountability was part of his "method" (hence the term *Methodism*) for helping Christians to pursue holiness in their lives and hearts. Small groups were a setting in which they could talk about earning, saving, and giving money.

7. Provide Knowledge and Tools to Help Families Make, Save, and Give Money

The economic conditions in which American Christians live are, from one perspective, very challenging. Yes, our society has great wealth—especially the upper 5 to 10 percent of it—but the fixed costs of participating in that society have risen dramatically since the 1950s, from 52 percent of each household's income to 74 percent. Fixed costs are bills that must be paid and are thus non-negotiable in the short term—things such as mortgages, taxes, repairs, insurance, and utilities. This means that people's disposable income has been cut in half, creating enormous stress for the lower end of the economic pyramid. There is not nearly as much money left for clothes, vacations, furnishings, entertainment, hobbies, gifts, eating out, and travel.

This means that, in most cases, our parents probably had more disposable income than we do, assuming that the amount they were paid is equal to the amount that we are, when adjusted for inflation. It does not help that most of us remember life with our parents during their peak earning years, not their hard, early years. When we as their children set up our households, have our own children, and find that there is not enough money for anything but surviving, it is often a great shock to us. The economic inequality that has increased so much during the last twenty years shows no signs of slowing down, which means that we will be facing a church composed of executive and professional folks with American-dream salaries of $200,000 and above as well as households that get by on American-stress salaries of under $60,000 and require both spouses to work, if indeed there are two in the home.

The church has a great opportunity to provide help, motivation, and tools for its members to manage their household income and expenses wisely—especially those who are in the lower-earning tier. But there is also a great challenge for such Christians. They must carefully manage each dollar, or they will be swept into debt as they try to finance what the world considers the good life, which they can't really afford. The poor quickly bump up against the real fixed costs of living, which they cannot cover. They will need help with finding ways to increase their family income.

The church should see this as one of its most basic challenges as it considers its adult-education program. Sometimes a gifted church leader can teach wise financial principles and practices out of his or her own experience. More often, a church can use the prepackaged materials of Crown Financial Ministries[6] or Financial Peace University.[7] But simply offering a course will not have much impact unless pastoral leadership promotes it and understands why it is important for all members to take.

I sense that Christians are hungry for a safe place in which to discuss these sensitive, life-controlling issues; but talking about money in our culture is more taboo than talking about sex. The local church, through small groups, Sunday school classes, seminars, and so on, can be a crucial help to households that are struggling through the painful decisions associated with money and giving. All of us have faced issues related to reducing spending, moving, selling possessions, repaying debts, changing careers, or addressing dual earner issues. When the

6. See www.crown.org for more information.
7. See www.daveramsey.com for more information.

church can talk about these issues, it reminds these believers that they are not alone—that they have the guidance and prayers of others who care. This is especially true when those who are more mature in these matters can assist and counsel such believers into the healing light of Christ's values and promises.

8. Pursue Accountability and Results

In 2 Corinthians 8 and 9, Paul documents the fruit that would result from the church's offering, stating that it would produce a biblical equality between the famine-stricken believers in Judea and the rich saints in Corinth. Those who had little would not have too little, and those who had much would not have too much (see 2 Cor. 8:15). In addition, the offering would lead others to "glorify God because of your submission that comes from your confession of the gospel" (2 Cor. 9:13). It would stir people to praise God and would be an example of obedience to Christ.

To document all this, Paul invites other church leaders to accompany him in order to ensure that the gift was administered appropriately (see 2 Cor. 8:16–24). These reps would then report all that they had seen to their churches.

Paul sees it as being important that the donors know what their offering will accomplish and that it will be applied with accountability. This highlights the need for our donors' giving to be used as they designate it and for the donors to be able to see the outcome.

I once knew a church that gave $75 to any missionary who asked for support. They had hundreds of missionaries, but no one knew anything about them, their effectiveness, or how to support them in other ways. The missionaries could not afford to visit the church for a $75 gift. As a church gets closer to meeting its God-given funding potential, it should move toward more substantial involvement with whatever cause it supports. Giving less than $2,000 to support a mission makes little sense if the church expects accountability, reports, and participation in the work.

The same is true for relief and development projects. A gift should be substantial enough to make an impact and to afford hands-on accountability and participation. For more complex relief and development missions, I believe that the lower limit of support should be from $5,000 to $10,000. This should provide a steady flow of reports on ministry accomplishments, prayer support, and accountability for the use of funds and planning for future participation. There is, of course, no upper limit.

Churches will need to engage some of their best minds to meet with mission leaders, review their work and plans, and determine how best to participate in the next year. They will need exactly what the church needed in Acts 6: persons who are full of the Holy Spirit and wisdom (see v. 3).

In one church, the deacons appointed a team to evaluate seven external diaconal ministries each year and to guide the church on how to participate in their support and work. These leaders thoroughly reviewed the work of each ministry to confirm that expectations for the ministry were being carried out, and they documented the ministry's progress toward its goals. Some were dropped for a lack of accountability or clear plans; others were added. This reporting produced not only more knowledgeable prayer support but also more willingness for church members to get personally involved and to give. When this effort was launched, tens of thousands of dollars in new money appeared from "nowhere" without the giving of general funds being diminished.

Reports of God's mighty works should be highlighted for the church as a whole, not restricted to the review of committees. All the saints should be able to hear how God used their gifts. Missions and mercy festivals or conferences are great times for this.

9. Pray for God's Kingdom to Come

Our congregations will not move toward giving a baseline 10 percent of their income, as well as increasing their mission and mercy funding, without the blessing of God. Therefore, this large-scale vision should be a matter of regular prayer in church services, small groups, leadership councils, and ministry teams. Paul's metaphor of a soldier in full armor includes an offensive weapon, the Word of God, which is empowered by prayers in the Spirit (see Eph. 6:17–18). Prayer is needed if we are going to advance Christ's rule in our time.

There are many invitations and commands in Scripture for us to pray for the increase of the kingdom. Jesus commands us to ask the Father to send workers into the harvest (see Matt. 9:38). Our prayers are the means that God uses to provide the workers and their support. These workers do not drop from heaven; the Spirit calls them and moves churches to support them. God invites us to make requests for the advancement of his kingdom (see Ps. 2:8; Luke 11:2; 1 Thess. 3:10). Prayer requires us to have the faith to articulate what we desire God to do for his kingdom. If your church has prayerfully planned for what it believes it should do for that kingdom, you can articulate that to God in prayer, asking him to supply the specific amounts and people needed for the task. God delights in such faith and delights to answer such prayers. Prayer overcomes obstacles and the hindrances of Satan and the flesh (see Eph. 6:18–19; Philem. 22; 2 Thess. 3:1). Paul often appealed for prayer support regarding his ministry and the obstacles that were before him. Many times our plans are not coordinated with God's timing, and the goal-oriented among us may become discouraged. Openly acknowledging our challenges and striving in prayer are what God encourages us to do.

If church leaders determine that their congregations could give more, and if they prayerfully identify how they could advance in ministry with additional funds, God can use prayer to motivate people to increase their giving to the kingdom.

Let's say a church sees that its lower-income suburban neighborhood is experiencing tremendous stress, suffering, and dysfunction because of family relationships, substance abuse, and alienation between the different generations that live there. And this stress, suffering, and dysfunction are also reflected in the people from that community who attend the church. These folks are barely hanging on financially and do not have $100 per hour to get the counseling they need. The church has therefore determined that its next hire should be a director of counseling and discipleship, who could make biblical counseling available to the community on a very low sliding scale or donation basis.

Continuing our hypothetical example, the church estimates that voluntary donations from counselees might bring in $10,000 a year and that they will still need $60,000 in additional funds in order to pay this new counselor. The church has some candidates for the position in mind, but it must wait to hire someone until the giving increases by $60,000 a year. This ministry vision is announced in church and is the focus of much prayer. Giving increases by $30,000 a year—but not yet enough to hire the counselor.

Let's say that I am a member of this church, have received helpful counseling from the pastor, and have prayed with my small group for the additional $30,000 to be given. I have also been thinking about moving to a larger home away from the neighborhood and spending an additional $2,000 a month on a mortgage. But now I see that our church could have a massive impact in my present community through a counseling outreach. I currently give $3,600 a year (or 3 percent of my salary) and suddenly wonder if I should just put an addition on my present home and increase my giving to $1,000 a month (or 10 percent of my gross household income) in order to help pay for the counselor.

Our family prays about it and decides to increase our giving and to put on an addition instead of moving. We let the budget chairman know, and the additional $700 a month ($8,400 a year) is reported to the elders. That leaves $21,400 that is needed to hire the counselor. God uses our pledge to stimulate other officers to give more. The need is then reduced to $4,800, and by the end of the year, the church has its new counselor in place. Counseling ministry takes off, both within the church and in the community. Elders are emboldened to do individual ministry, now that they have this counseling resource on staff. Not long after that, the pastor asks our family to testify as to how God led us to make the decision to give. The church is further challenged by the work of the Spirit in our lives, even as the missions committee asks for prayer for enough funds to begin a safe house for trafficked children in Manila. As the church grows, new donors are moved to give to the safe house through the missions budget of the church. The cycle begins again.

In the urban mission where I worked as executive director, we needed to go from $40,000 a year in donations to $1 million. It was a brand-new mission and was so different from other ministry organizations in our area that we could not easily affiliate with another one that was more established and credible. But in 2004, though we were just a ministry in its start-up phase, we began to publicize our need for prayer that we would receive $1 million. At the time, that amount seemed almost laughable—but since it represented our real need, we prayed. God blessed us with double-digit growth for ten years, and now people are seeing the answer to ten years of prayer, as giving in that range is coming in. God even moved the Commonwealth of Pennsylvania to establish tax credits for businesses that donate to a cause like ours. We could never have foreseen that. God taught us a lot about the power that specific and persevering prayer has to enlist resources for the advancement of the kingdom.

There are other ways to foster excellence in giving among God's people, but I hope that these nine specific suggestions will stimulate us to follow in Paul's footsteps. I hope they will stir us to give in a way that reflects the level of grace God showed to us in Christ.

Questions for Review and Reflection

1. Which of these ways to pursue excellence in giving are best demonstrated by you and/or your congregation?
2. Which of them are least demonstrated by you and/or your congregation?
3. How might you improve and change in one or more of these areas?

15

Leading Our Churches
to Excel in Giving

*And God is able to make all grace abound to you, so
that having all sufficiency in all things at all times, you
may abound in every good work. (2 Cor. 9:8)*

Many churches teach about stewardship, but teaching by itself is inadequate. Since people don't give to budgets but give to visions, church leaders must translate their vision for the expansion of the kingdom into practical plans for mission and ministry.

In 2 Corinthians 8, Paul paints with a big brush in order to cast a vision for the international church to function as the body of Christ, to the benefit of all. He shows how the Corinthians' initial small gift stimulated the Macedonians to supply a big gift and how that in turn challenged the Corinthians to make good on their original goals. He then shows how their offering would be part of God's promise to fully provide for the needs of the saints, just as God had done in the Old Testament with the manna in the wilderness. Paul believes that this can be realized in the church of his own day. He points out that, as the Corinthians' plenty provided for the Judeans' financial needs, the Judeans provided for the Corinthians' spiritual needs.

Such vision casting is needed in the plans that we make for our offerings today. Teaching what the Bible has to say about money can impart a biblical vision for giving in a local church. Often our vision is dictated by last year's budget, plus or minus some percentage that we expect this year. This is work that the budget committee needs to do, but more is needed. What if we actually based our goals on the amount that would result from the households in the church giving 10 percent of their income? The tithe is, after all, the most rudimentary level of giving suggested by the Bible. It should represent the baseline amount that believers in a church give to kingdom causes.

So How Much Could We Give?

So how do church leaders determine the giving capacity of their church? To get a baseline number, I suggest that leaders determine the average income of houses in the zip codes or townships surrounding the church, using the US Census Bureau's online information. Most churches contain a large enough sample of the people in their surrounding area to reflect the average income of that area. Average these zip codes together to obtain a reasonable figure for each household in the church.[1] Then determine the number of giving households or family units in the church and multiply that number by this average amount of income per household. For example, in the seven zip codes around my former home church outside Philadelphia, the average household income is about $90,000. We had 250 giving units in our church, so the total income of the households in the church was about $22.5 million. A tithe on that would be $2.2 million. Since about 90 percent of Christian giving goes through local churches (at least in healthy local churches), a church should expect to reap 90 percent (not 100 percent) of its congregation's tithing. That would put the baseline giving capacity of our church at $1.9 million.

Our church's budget for 2014, which included missions and mercy offerings, was about $1.4 million. Based on average household

1. I suggest using the "mean" (or average) household income. Much of the census data calculates the median income, which does not adequately account for large contributions from wealthy households in a church. Median income is that income level at which there are equal numbers of households both above it and below it. Some churches just obtain both figures and then average them. This gives a more conservative estimate of giving capacity.

income in the seven surrounding zip codes, our people were giving an unusually high 6.2 percent of their income to the church. Adding in their additional giving to other, non-church causes brings the total rate to 6.8 percent. That suggests, according to my calculations, that there may have been about $500,000 that God had given our people that they were not giving back. That said, this church was unusual as American evangelical churches go. Its congregation's level of giving was (and is) the result of a strong, underlying spiritual health in the ministry and body life of the church.

Reclaiming the "Missing" Money

However, what can be done about "missing" money, such as our church's $500,000? Here is where vision and faith can step in.

Rather than only asking what they will do if the offering increases by 3 percent next year, I would suggest that a church have strategic plans for deploying all the funds that would be represented by at least 9 percent of the incomes of its church families. So my former home church could make plans to expand its mission by $500,000 as a long-term goal. Obviously, such planning must be linked to gradual increases in giving. Each new ministry and mission project must be budgeted only as actual congregational giving warrants.

To illustrate, let's assume a scenario like this:

- Elders and/or deacons do strategic ministry planning and present the results to the church. Such a plan answers the question of what God has called a church to be and do for him. It captures the biblical vision and mission of the church and is usually communicated by the pastor in his preaching and teaching. The plan enables the church to participate in the full commission that Christ gave his people—to Jerusalem, Judea, Samaria, and the uttermost parts of the world. That extends beyond the church's internal teaching ministries and includes significant outreach locally, regionally, and internationally—outreach that in turn includes both discipling and mercy ministry.

- The church's leaders then present strategic multiyear goals for each area of ministry, basing them on the vision of the congregation giving 10 percent of their household income. This vision is carefully communicated to the church for as long as it takes them to understand it satisfactorily. This usually includes communicating it at congregational meetings.
- To implement the plan for working toward this vision, three alternate goals can be laid out for each area of the vision, based on the amount of money the congregation gives during each year. So, for illustrative purposes, in the second year of the church's plan for mercy ministry expansion, the goal might be to create either a one-third, two-thirds, or full-time deacon position in the church. The level of giving would determine which of these alternatives was implemented. This would properly tie the church's ministry outreach to the levels of giving it receives, enabling the members to see the difference that their giving makes.
- Because the church's annual goals are related to its long-term vision, each step forward creates a visible connection to its biblical vision and mission. As the ministry goals in different areas are progressively fulfilled, church members see the advancement of Christ's kingdom.

None of this happens through planning alone, but if the spiritual leadership and ministry are there, this process can engage the church to "abound in the work of the Lord" through substantial giving.

The Future of Giving Will Be Focused on Outreach

And there will be another dynamic to watch, besides that of people giving to mission planning. Most of the ministry and mission that is added to the budget will be in the area of outreach. This will show church members that they no longer need to give outside the church budget in order to help the poor or fund missions. Some of what they were giving directly to outside missions and mercy workers can now be given through the church. This happened in my own giving, as I saw the outreach agenda of my church expand.

Many parachurch agencies were first started because the church was not reaching out, but now the church has an opportunity—not to see these agencies shut down but to fund them at much higher levels. For example, a church that wants to sponsor a safe house in Thailand for escaping sex slaves may best do this through an independent mission instead of on its own. I have, however, also seen new indigenous ministries raised up from the church at the local levels.

Does this mean that when the church's giving reaches 10 percent, we should plateau? I hope not—at least in our wealthy Western economy. God made us relatively rich for a reason: that we might give abundantly compared to the 10 percent that poorer saints can safely give. Should I have been satisfied with 10 percent while I attended my church in suburban Philadelphia? Our county was the second richest in the Commonwealth of Pennsylvania. It is also situated in the wealthiest nation in the world—one in which Christians control more money than at any time in previous history.

For those in a Western economy to give only 10 percent seems pretty ungenerous compared to the Old Testament saints. It makes us look rather in need of God's grace in this area—as indeed we are. Once we arrive at that 10 percent level, it is time for us to attempt still greater things for God with the level of wealth he has bestowed on us.

Ron Sider's idea of the progressive tithe[2] embodies the right idea for proportional giving, but I think it is best to use such a scale as a "what if" scenario in order to stimulate the church to think in new ways about outreach. Refraining from suggesting new giving rates that would go beyond those found in the Bible respects the fact that it is the Spirit who leads people to love, serve, and give.

Because God's people are led by God's Spirit, they won't respond well to suggestions such as "From now on, we are raising the tithe to 12 percent, based on the income of our households." Christians give to fulfill the mission that was commissioned by our Lord. When

2. See Ronald J. Sider, *Rich Christians in an Age of Hunger: Moving from Affluence to Generosity*, 4th ed. (Dallas: Word, 1997), 195.

the church engages in that biblical mission through motivation by the grace of the gospel, it will engage the hearts—and wallets—of its members, each according to his or her own ability.

In all this planning, we should have visions that are big enough for wealthier donors to invest larger sums of money into. Generally, local churches provide few opportunities for Christians to pour significant wealth into as a means of doing great things for God. Parachurch ministries like World Vision, Bread for the World, The Salvation Army, and Compassion International have big projects that donors can support with multimillion-dollar gifts. We should thank God for this but, at the same time, ponder why the church itself has had a vision so timid that she has no "billion-dollar projects" of her own. Such large visions would obviously require lots of collaboration between churches, not-for-profit organizations, and mission agencies—which has not been our strength.[3]

As a consequence, wealthy donors do not see the church as being capable of addressing large-scale problems. It is time for us to work through our networks, denominations, co-ops, and agencies to make strategic plans for fulfilling our commission to disciple the world and care for the needy. The church, I believe, has the potential for much greater access to multimillionaires and billionaires than other non-profits do. They identify with their churches more emotionally, spiritually, and personally, but the church has nothing for them to give to—except the occasional building campaign.

I encourage church leaders to reassess the giving potential of their members and then to make prayerful, strategic plans for the church's ministry and outreach that will make use of these funds, if and when they come in.

May we get past the day when we are used to financing God's work on 3–4 percent of our incomes. Our giving is still far from being worthy of the Lord—yet I believe that God has been doing a new thing since the 1950s. He is forcing us to reflect on our giving and

3. Peter Greer and Chris Horst challenge the church in this area in *Rooting for Rivals: How Collaboration and Generosity Increase the Impact of Leaders, Charities, and Churches* (Grand Rapids: Bethany House, 2018).

is bringing our failures to our attention. He is doing this so that we might seek his guidance about how to address it and might see God's people prosper in generosity that is worthy of the Lord.

Stir One Another Up to Love and Good Works

The book of Hebrews exhorts Christians to "consider how to stir up one another to love and good works" (Heb. 10:24). This exhortation comes in the context of urging Christians not to skip church meetings; but, since giving can be one of our greatest expressions of love and service, we also need to consider how to encourage one another in the right kind of Christian generosity.

When we ask how this happens in our churches, the answer is usually that it really does not happen. The pastor encourages giving from the pulpit, but since that is his job and since offerings pay his salary, his appeal is not decisive for many church members. Sometimes having the treasurer explain a dire shortfall in a letter to the congregation will increase offerings for a few weeks. But the best way to encourage generosity is for Christians to testify about why they give and about the joy and privilege they experience when they participate in the Lord's work.

An elder, a deacon, or the treasurer should be looking for stories of giving from inside the church. It is not always good for the pastor to know how much each member gives, in order to avoid the appearance of pressure or financial incentive behind the attention he pays to different members. However, another church officer could know, so that the work of God can be shared for the building up of all.

For example, let's say that an ordinary church member gets a year-end bonus at work and drops a $15,000 check into the offering in order to help retire the building debt. The elder or deacon might ask the person how God led him or her to do that. If it seems appropriate and edifying to share, he could ask the person to share the story two Sundays before the next building-drive offering. It is appropriate to share this in worship, because it is the work of the Spirit's leading and gives glory to God. No humble member will volunteer to share the story; it will become an occasion for encouraging others only if the church invites the person to testify.

We have no problem asking people to testify about how they were saved from alcohol, drugs, illicit sex, and other sins and struggles. We need to add testimonies about salvation from greed and how this results in giving. It is easier for a drug addict to enter the kingdom than for a rich man—but with God, all things are possible (see Matt. 19:24, 26). It is time for us to testify to some of God's greatest works and to do so on a regular basis.

- Let God's people tell what it was like for them to trust God with a tithe for the first time and how God met their needs.
- Let people testify to how God met their needs through the generosity of the church.
- Let people reveal how God led them to realize that they could increase their giving in order to fund a new mission center in Africa.
- Let them glorify God with the joy and sense of privilege they experience when they give to their Lord.
- Let them describe the victory they experienced over temptation when they got a sizable inheritance and gave some of it to the Lord's work.
- Let them testify to God's blessing on their decision not to send their son or daughter to an elite college, thus enabling themselves to maintain a viable budget and avoid debt.
- Honor the work of the Spirit by letting the church know about a family's decision to downsize to one car, live in community with another family, move into a smaller home, or sell a beach property in order to rent a place instead—all to increase their giving to the kingdom of God.

One simple way a pastor can set an example is to enter into a salary reduction agreement with his church, so that his salary is reduced by his giving amount. This saves him from paying Social Security taxes on that part of his salary, but it also reminds the church that the pastor practices what he preaches. Whether he gives 10 percent of his salary or more than that, it will demonstrate his own efforts to walk the walk.

Such testimonies often represent the greatest victories of Christians who live in an age that pursues personal peace and affluence as its most basic value. They can be the greatest help to those who are starting at the bottom of the giving scale and who perhaps did not have Christian parents to set an example of generosity for them. They can help those who are fearful that God may not provide for them if they tithe. And they can challenge those who could give much more but have never been challenged to go beyond the 10 percent mark.

Questions for Review and Reflection

1. In your church, does a smaller portion of the members carry most of the weight of the giving? If so, why?
2. What does this chapter suggest that leaders do to help remedy that common situation?
3. Do you think it is right for those who have learned major lessons of generosity to give public testimony to that fact, even though money is a highly personal affair in our culture? Why or why not?

16

Planning for Generosity
in Retirement

*Make it your ambition to lead a quiet life, to mind your own
business and to work with your hands, just as we told you, so that
your daily life may win the respect of outsiders and so that you
will not be dependent on anybody. (1 Thess. 4:11–12 NIV)*

In these final chapters, we will look at three important issues regarding
our individual financial stewardship that impact our ability to excel in
giving. The first of those issues is retirement. Should Christians save
for their "retirement"? Such savings represent a huge expense—up
to 12 percent of our income for our entire working lives. Should
Christians save for retirement even if it impacts their giving during
their working years? Considering our culture and economy, the Bible's
answer would be a strong yes.

Not to save for the time when you cannot work is to plan to
be dependent on others. This is a direct violation of 1 Thessalonians
4:11–12, in which Paul says, "Aspire to live quietly, and to mind your
own affairs, and to work with your hands, as we instructed you, so that
you may walk properly before outsiders and be dependent on no one."
He is countering the attitude of some in the Thessalonian church
that, in view of Christ's return, we can disengage from self-support
in order to do ministry and church work. Paul is not glorifying work
but is focusing on the issue of dependency. Paul wants Christ's disciples to be financially independent, as soon as possible and as much as

possible. That way they can give themselves to work for the coming of the kingdom of Christ.

For most of us, the point at which we can step back from our commercial work is the point when our Social Security benefits, pensions, or retirement plan benefits become available. Currently that means that most of us could enter into an active retirement in our late sixties while expecting to live an additional ten to twenty years. This is a radical change from the World War II generation, in which most American men died at about sixty-five. For today's Christians, our seventies are not the glory years of self-indulgence and ease; they are the glory years of kingdom engagement as well as of great influence we can have on our children and grandchildren.

In the culture of biblical times, older parents were to be supported by their adult children. I get the impression that much of the parents' capital was passed down to their children at an earlier age in exchange for the promise of life care. The children were not to waste those inherited funds or even give them to the Lord (see Mark 7:11–13) but to use them to bless their parents. In the New Testament era, parents (and especially widows) became a huge part of the church's capacity to minister through outreach and care.

Today, by contrast, people must support themselves from their own funds all the way to the end—including providing for their own funerals. It is considered an embarrassment if we have to ask for money from our kids. In our system, we turn over what we have left after we die to our children, who are often just entering retirement age themselves. This may not be the best system, but it is the one that we work under.

The Bible's teaching on self-support means that most of us today must lay money aside for ourselves so that we do not become dependent on our children or on the state—unless we have no other options. Nevertheless, the Bible makes it clear that children whose parents run out of money should help them and that the church should help to care for those who do not have children to assist them (see 1 Tim. 5:16).

Know Your Magic Number

Therefore, every adult should plan for and seek to provide for his or her financial future. That includes identifying what I call a magic number—the amount of money you should have available when you are no longer working to earn more. Couples can plan this amount together to be enough to sustain both of them to a hundred years of age. Most (though not all) of us will not live that long; yet, in my view, this is the best goal to plan for, if it is possible for you. Each person's situation is different, and so you, your spouse, and perhaps your adult children should be aware of your planning goals. We should all seek advice from trustworthy financial planning professionals who have expertise in this area. For illustration purposes, I will use some common rules of thumb about retirement savings.

So what is that magic number? On the low end, Fidelity Investments says that by age sixty-seven people who are not covered by defined benefit retirement plans[1] should accumulate a minimum of ten times their current annual expenditures—not counting the value of their homes, and assuming that they will receive Social Security benefits.[2] So, if you are currently spending $60,000 a year, you should save $600,000 by age sixty-seven in addition to the value of your debt-free home.

This, of course, is just a rough rule of thumb and must be reviewed and personalized for your situation and age. It does not take into account the costs of long-term nursing care, which would throw someone into Medicaid fairly quickly. I believe that a magic number of only ten times your annual expenditures should be considered a minimum.[3]

1. Defined benefit plans are the older post–World War II retirement approaches in which a company promises to pay workers a certain retirement benefit irrespective of market performance. Those plans are now rare for commercial companies and are only the rule for publicly funded jobs like public schools and city, state, or federal agencies.

2. See "How Much Do I Need to Retire?" Fidelity Investments, August 21, 2018, https://www.fidelity.com/viewpoints/retirement/how-much-do-i-need-to-retire.

3. I am not a certified financial planner and am not offering professional financial advice. I am sharing the observations and knowledge I have accumulated from

With the recent spike in healthcare costs for seniors, there are good reasons for people to save twelve to fifteen times their annual expenditures, if that is financially feasible. In that case, a healthy retiree can often live off of interest and dividends from his accounts without planning to invade their principal amounts (beyond the required minimum distribution set by taxing authorities for tax-deferred retirement accounts).[4]

These higher multiples can be helpful, because they allow for a margin of error, for poor investment return, or for other financial emergencies without immediately reducing the amount of income that a retired person can draw from. Accomplishing this requires planning for a larger amount of savings than the minimum, but since we are pretty much on our own as far as retirement funding in our economy, it is prudent for us to plan on the higher side, if possible. It is also a comfort to know that any leftover funds can be strategically invested in the kingdom of God or in the lives of our children and grandchildren.

So how do we develop retirement savings of ten to fifteen times our current expenditures? This can be challenging for middle-income workers today, as it was for me. But the most important element of successful retirement planning is simply the commitment to begin.

I remember my first year in ministry (1970), when my total retirement savings benefit was $640—8 percent of my income. Yet even these paltry amounts, which were contributed by my small church, compounded and grew until, by the time I was sixty-seven, they amounted to about four times my annual income. My income levels and discretionary income were so low in the 1970s that I could not add to that 8 percent. It is normally recommended that, between company benefits and employee contributions, individuals should save

---

working with donors, counseling with families, and gaining experience with my own financial planners. You should work with your own financial advisors to make your specific plans.

4. In the United States, tax-deferred retirement accounts (except for Roth IRAs) require a specific percentage of the market value to be paid out each year to the retiree so that the government can recoup the tax revenue that was deferred during the person's working life.

about 15 percent of their income for retirement each year, beginning at age twenty-five.

My problem was compounded when, after pastoring for fourteen years, I went to work for a new ministry organization that had no retirement benefits at the time. I realized that part of the challenge of working for a ministry start-up was that I needed to invest in some kind of retirement plan. I got a small (less than $20,000) inheritance when my father died suddenly at age sixty. I was thirty-eight, and I saw this gift as an opportunity to invest for my retirement. My wife and I, along with another couple, bought rental units throughout the next twenty years and managed them in our spare time.

Over those years, our investment appreciated to the point that it contributed significantly to my retirement and enabled me to partially retire at age sixty-one in order to do another ministry start-up. Contributions were made to this retirement account by my church or ministry in only twenty-five of the forty-five years that I worked, yet this provided a critical component of my retirement funding. It would have been tempting for me to spend my small inheritance on something else, but God somehow convinced me that I needed to have a plan for retirement and for the ministry opportunities that might open up to me in later years. Such a vision also motivated me to work a little harder by doing the rental business in my "spare" time.

I can now clearly see God's hand providing for me and my future ministry. We renovated our own homes and drove used cars, and our kids graduated from college with some debt, but God met our real needs. You, too, can have confidence in his care as you strive in faith to provide for your future necessities. I encourage you to envision and work toward adequately funding your future.

In sum, retirement planning is imperative for Christian givers, for four reasons.

1. It helps to insure that you will not become dependent on your children, your church, or Medicaid and that you will be able to keep giving and serving as a senior. Self-support is a biblical mandate and should be pursued by Christ's followers so that they can be positively generous in all occasions.

2. A properly planned retirement provides a cushion for unexpected expenses, nursing costs (for strokes or dementia), and emergency funds for your children or grandchildren.

3. It enables you to be more active in service to Christ and others rather than having to work for self-support into your seventies and eighties. These are often some of our best years, from a ministry perspective.

4. If you plan well, you should be able to make the biggest, most transformative gift of your lifetime to the kingdom of God toward the end of your life. That is when you will have the most wisdom to give strategically. My current plan for "end-of-life giving" will be about 110 percent of what I gave in the previous forty-five years of my work life. That is exciting, if your lifetime financial goals focus on generosity.

The Courage to Track Your Plan

So how do we make this happen? In reality, it is not just one magic number that we need; we need a mini–magic number for each year from age twenty-five to sixty-seven that will help us to gauge our progress or highlight problems each year. These yearly numbers, which will mostly be related to our savings, will enable us to see where we stand each year and to make changes that will bring things back in line with our plan. A periodic review of the plan will also show us if there are things we have previously failed to foresee, ignored, or misunderstood in the planning.

A multiyear plan will often test your faith. It can be scary to look at the numbers and see how far short you might be. This is especially true for couples who are struggling to balance a budget. Fortunately, this process gives you options for addressing shortfalls before you reach the point where there is little you can do about them. It is also a step of faith in the fact that God will honor our efforts, and it can inform our prayers for God's provision. He says, "Ask, and you shall receive." We can bank on the fact that this is true—as long as what we ask for is within his purposes for our redemption.

For married couples, having a plan is important for another

reason. The planning process will force each spouse to learn about savings, investments, financial planning, and charitable giving goals. Such discussions should equip each spouse to manage the finances in the event that the other dies or becomes disabled. They also become an occasion for couples to talk about lifestyle, retirement spending levels, issues like life care, and gifts to their children and to the kingdom. These are things that we should be capable of and comfortable with talking about with our partners.

Most of us will need the help of a financial-planning professional. While insurance agents and security brokers will often offer to do such planning for free, they are not always objective in their recommendations for how the funds should be invested. A "fee for service" planner does not have those conflicts of interest built in and therefore is often a good choice.

Plan for Long-Term Care

For retirement planning purposes, the 800-pound gorilla in the room is long-term-care costs. These potential costs are the real challenge for most middle-income families. With skilled nursing costs running about $250 a day in 2017, such care will eat through a modest retirement account quickly. According to one set of stats, the average stay in a skilled nursing facility is now about fourteen months, while the median[5] is about five months.[6] Owing to the rise

5. The term *median* means that there were an equal number of patients with longer stays and shorter stays at the facility.

6. These are the conclusions of a new study published by the American Geriatrics Society: Anne Kelly, Jessamyn Conell-Price, Kenneth Covinsky, Irena Stijacic Cenzer, Anna Chang, W. John Boscardin, and Alexander K. Smith, "Length of Stay for Older Adults Residing in Nursing Homes at the End of Life," *Journal of the American Geriatrics Society* 58, no. 9 (Sept. 2010): 1710–6. The authors used data from the Health and Retirement Study (HRS) to describe the lengths of stay of older adults in nursing homes at the end of their lives. Out of the 8,433 study participants who died between 1992 and 2006, 27.3 percent of them resided in a nursing home prior to their death. Most of these patients (70 percent) died in the nursing home without being transferred to another setting such as a hospital. The data regarding the length of their stay was striking.

• The median length of stay in a nursing home before death was five months.

of dementia in our population, it seems that planning for closer to fourteen months is advisable. However, the possibility that one could be stricken with a form of dementia in one's early seventies and still live for twenty years is real. That is the reason that median and average stays in nursing homes are so different. The averages are increased by a smaller number of dementia patients who live for years in skilled nursing. With that being the case, it seems prudent for a couple to plan for about $600,000 of long-term care to be available for both of them. Providing twenty years of nursing care for both spouses would require $3.6 million at 2017 rates. The top 1 percent of wage earners can do that without burden, but for most of us it is not feasible.

Obviously, whatever extra money is budgeted for long-term care is an added burden on the retirement planning of most middle-income workers. But we don't face this alone. We know that we are doing our Father's will by seeking to provide for our own care and ensure our usefulness in old age—even in the face of these large numbers. Fortunately, there are a number of alternatives that can help us to address the challenge.

First, long-term care (LTC) insurance can meet this need.[7] This essentially helps you to rent access to a small fortune, in case you need it. This can be a good option for middle-income Christians who are

---

- The average length of stay of fourteen months was due to a small number of study participants who had very long lengths of stay.
- Sixty-five percent of participants died within one year of being admitted to a nursing home.
- Fifty-three percent of them died within six months of being admitted.

Statistics that were relayed to me in conversation with a vice president of Acts Retirement Life Communities, Inc. (the largest not-for-profit CCRC in the United States) found that patients' average stay in assisted living was 1.5 years for females and 0.7 years for males. Stays in skilled nursing facilities added to that and averaged 1.8 years for females and 0.9 years for males. These two sets of statistics confirm the substantial cost to many seniors for their end-of-life care.

7. I have experience as a pastor and a ministry executive and have earned a DMin degree in pastoral counseling. I am not a certified financial planner and am not offering professional financial advice; I am simply sharing observations I have accumulated while working with donors, counseling with families, and gaining experience with my own financial planners. It is important for each of us to have our own financial advisors who can take account of our unique situations.

interested in serving in ministry instead of working into their seventies in order to earn the $600,000 that is needed to cover all those risks. Unfortunately, the insurance companies underpriced these policies when they were first introduced, and many have doubled their premiums in an effort to cover the higher costs. However, they can still be the right option, if they are affordable in your situation. Many of these policies pay for home care, assisted living care, and skilled nursing care up to the amount of the policy—which in extreme cases can easily be in excess of $1 million in total benefits.

Planners often recommend taking out a policy at age fifty-nine. My wife and I followed that advice. Our LTC policy is supposed to cover us for the long-term liability of home health care, assisted living, and skilled nursing care, up to a specific dollar amount. Because of this policy, I was able to begin my "retirement" ministry job at sixty-one, because I did not need to save for that long-term-care contingency. The annual premiums are painful to pay out, but for me it is money well spent, and it has translated into ten years of retirement ministry as I have received only a partial salary.

Another alternative is to plan to enter a Continuing Care Retirement Community (CCRC). For an entrance fee that is roughly equivalent to the value of your middle-class home, a CCRC will accept you into independent living, with the guarantee that it will provide home health, assisted living, and skilled nursing for an affordable monthly rent payment, all the way up to your death. These are great alternatives for Christians, because they provide not just long-term care but (often) Christian community as well. Numerous denominations also sponsor them. Many folks who carry LTC insurance drop those policies when they enter a CCRC community later in their retirement.

A third alternative is to rely on family members for care. Often, if one spouse is in good health, he or she can provide care for the other spouse, up to a certain point. Through heroic efforts (which not everyone can muster), the healthy spouse can provide care that is equivalent to assisted living and early skilled nursing. An unmarried or widowed senior can strike a deal with his child to take him in for a fixed upfront or ongoing payment, and perhaps for some cash to upgrade the child's home. This would be a part-time job for your adult child and would provide a safe place for you to live until you require skilled nursing. This option might not get you all the way "home," but it could get you pretty close. It can be a win-win for a family that does it, but it is not often used, due to the layout of the child's home, job location issues, and relational dysfunction within families.

If we don't plan ahead, we may find later in life that we are not able to get into a CCRC or to qualify for long-term care insurance because we are in such poor physical shape. Federally funded Medicaid homes are places where those who run out of money go. There are plenty of Christians in these homes, and God will be with us if and when we must enter them, but we should not plan to go there because we have failed to plan. As Christians we should work now to address the issue of our future dependency.

In summary, these positive alternatives for financing long-term care will require planning, saving, some deferred gratification, and personal stewardship over our nest-egg savings. So we should trust in the Lord's care as we pursue the amount of savings that we need. Your Father in heaven knows that you need these funds. If you both believe and obey, you will have done what you were commanded to do. Then it is time to trust God's plan for you, knowing that all things work together for good to those who are called to be conformed to the image of Jesus Christ (see Rom. 8:28).

Contribute Excess Capital to God's Work

Planning can also drive your generosity. That, by itself, is a reason for a Christian to plan. If you have a retirement plan in place that has annual milestones noted, you will be in a position to make the best use of any additional wealth that God may bring you. The stock market, the wealth of our parents, and our expenses and circumstances can change each year. If you know where you need to be financially, each year, and you are substantially above that level, then you can begin to give more to others and to the kingdom. If you are behind, you can catch up. Planning enables you to give from God's blessings when they are over and above what you need for your basic needs and responsibilities.

If capital funds come your way (through inheritance, windfall profits, the sale of a business, and so on) and you want to be a giver, it can be much better for you to give the funds away now, when you are alert, clear-headed, and capable of wisely disbursing the funds to the right cause. For example,

> If you are on target for your retirement accumulation and are blessed with a $120,000 gift from your parents' estate, you (and your advisors) can decide to give some or all of it away, since your needs are projected to be covered. If you are behind in your retirement, you can catch up.

> If you are eighty-eight, widowed, and in a CCRC with $500,000 still in your IRA accounts, you should consider (with your financial advisors) the option of gifting all or some of it while you are still living. That way, you have the joy of seeing the difference that a well-targeted gift makes to a Christian mission.

> If you are fifty-five, have been saving for retirement, and are over your target for your retirement milestones, you can (with your advisors) consider beginning to make gifts of capital to the Lord's work. Let's say that you sell the company that you own and then stay on as an officer of the new owner. You receive $1 million. Since you know your magic number for age fifty-five and you are already on target, you have the option to assist others with some or most of that money.
>
> Is it biblically wise or faithful to automatically bank the $1 million in case you don't make any more money? The wisdom of an eternal perspective advises that you should continue to work and trust God to meet your needs through that work, as you have done in the past. We need a reasonable financial cushion and cash-flow fund, but we do not need to hoard out of fear for the future. We have a sound plan and a trustworthy Father in heaven; this frees us up to be generous to our children and to the Lord's work. Those funds have come to you in God's providence and were given to fulfill very specific needs connected to your place in your family, your community, and God's kingdom.

If you receive excess funds such as these, don't change your plan and seek to become wealthy by laying up millions or pursuing the lifestyles of the rich and famous. Rather, make sure that your needs are covered and that you are on target for your retirement, and then come up with a plan to give away profits that are not *needed* by you or your family.

Train for Your Final Career in Ministry

Part of our Christian retirement strategy is to continue to give—not just of money but of our time and life experience in the Lord's work. See what Paul the apostle tells the Corinthian congregation: "Stand firm. Let nothing move you. Always give yourselves fully to the work of the Lord, because you know that your labor in the Lord is not in vain" (1 Cor. 15:58 NIV). One of the clearest ways the early church implemented this principle was by enrolling experienced widows as church workers (see 1 Tim. 5:3–10). As explained earlier, it appears that widows who needed support were essentially hired by the church to do ministry if they qualified spiritually. Thus the New Testament church fielded an army of Christian workers, counselors, deaconesses, and social workers, all of whom brought the gospel and healing to the needy. We saw that they were so effective that they provoked the emperor Julian to start a secular welfare system just to compete with what the Christians were doing.

We are in need of a similar army today, in view of the needs and opportunities for ministry in our cities and regions and around the world. We have a highly educated, healthy, well-taught army of seniors who could augment the work of our pastoral staffs and missionaries to an extent that would be transformative. Here are the sorts of questions that motivated, active seniors could consider addressing for Christ's sake:

- How many crime victims in your township or county have received the comfort of the Lord and the healing, support, and help of the church?
- How many immigrant children are struggling with learning to read in a new language in public or Christian schools?

- How many Christian schools can't open their doors to poor urban children because they lack the funds to provide partial needs-based scholarships?
- How many Christian schools, missions, and food ministries need strong leaders on their boards and committees?
- Most prisoners and parolees, despite their crimes, believe in God and profess some Christian faith. How many are being visited and discipled in your county?
- How many single moms are struggling to find encouragement and help?
- How many couples in the church are in conflict and need mentoring from mature married couples?
- How many ministries in the church need staff executive leadership?
- How many men in your county are enslaved to addictions and need to internalize the good news of the gospel for the addicted?
- How many children are in foster care in your community?

These are all staff-intensive ministries that can't be sustained with a few paid pastors. I believe that the church's supply of seniors is the most revolutionary force in the United States today. Part of our retirement planning should involve preparing ourselves for the day we can more fully give ourselves to the work of the Lord. Seniors can do this by

- discerning their gifts, faith, and spiritual motivations by exercising them in ministry during their working years.
- becoming biblically literate by meditating on Scripture regularly.
- learning to help people make changes in their lives by taking courses and practicums, in person or online.
- leveraging their life experiences to help make themselves knowledgeable about ministering to particular needs such as addictions, grief, trauma, conflict, post-partum depression, job motivation, financial oversight, and so on.

294 Living Out the Purpose of Money

- honing any administrative abilities they have in areas such as accounting, scheduling, secretarial work, economic development, job training.
- learning how regional church and denominational ministries work, so they can upgrade their involvement in them as they retire.
- praying, and asking others to pray, for God's preparation and leading as they move from the paid workforce into volunteer work in the kingdom.
- having the courage to volunteer. Most pastors are hesitant to ask seniors to take staff or worker positions in ministry.

One advantage for ministry volunteers is that they have a ringside seat to what the Lord is doing. They can often target financial gifts so that they solve problems and unleash a ministry's opportunity and potential. I know a small business owner who, in retirement, served on two Christian school boards to enable himself to better direct his gifts to poor young people who could not afford these schools' tuition. Pastors are usually slow to see these opportunities because they are distracted by the burdens of the church and sometimes lack faith in financial provision. They are not out looking for other needs for which they can raise volunteers and money—while many Christian seniors are looking for these exact opportunities.

Once you have a plan for a retirement ministry, you may find it hard to resist jumping in. That is good! Retire as early as financially possible. You might even get excited enough (as I did at age sixty-one) to take some risks with your retirement accounts in order to get started in your retirement work.

Make Your Biggest Gifts

We may bewail the loss of the elder-care system of biblical times, when the oldest son cared for the parents, but there are some wonders associated with our system. Namely, we must all save enough to last us until we are ninety years old or more, even though few of us live that long. Therefore, we often have large amounts of wealth in our accounts when we die. This gives us enormous opportunities to do good works and strategically finance kingdom endeavors, as well as occasions for blessing our children. Some $42 trillion will cross generations in the United States in the next sixty years.

We can tap this capital for our children and the Lord's work through gifts, bequests, and planned gifts. Bequests are gifts that are made through a will and/or a living trust, and planned gifts are tax-saving vehicles that are available to those who survive us to allow them to support charities from the wealth we have accumulated. These are documents that every Christian who aspires to be a faithful steward should have drawn up. Without them, state laws will determine the disposition of your assets. Any attorney, CPA, or financial planner can refer you to someone who can translate your desires and values into a written estate plan.[8]

This chapter has suggested an amount of retirement savings that are on the high side of what is needed, both to help Christians guard against unexpected expenses and downturns and also to enable them to make substantial capital gifts toward the end of their lives. The average net worth of an eighty-year-old who has been married is well over $200,000. That blessing can mean a lot to one's children and grandchildren and to the kingdom of God.

It has been suggested by many gift planners that people with smaller estates (less than $1 million) could make equal gifts to each of their children and then include the Lord's work as another child. So if you had $400,000 in your estate at the time of death and had three children, you could make four bequests of $100,000 to each. If one child has a special and recognized need (such as a disability), that changes things, of course. However, it is often good to assist your children during your life on a confidential basis, based on your discernment about what is healthy and helpful, and then to have the remainder of your money

---

8. In addition to gifts of cash amounts, a donor can usually make gifts through any one of the following avenues: appreciated securities, outright gifts of unencumbered real estate or personal property, gifts from unused IRA or other deferred tax retirement vehicles, charitable remainder trusts, gift annuities, lead trusts, and gifts of paid-up life insurance policies (prior to death). Consult your financial or gift planner for advice.

divided equally after you die. This is not a biblically derived formula, but there is a sense of equity in the way it divides things.

If your final estate will be large or you have few children, this raises the question of how much is good for a child to receive. Getting into that area of planning is beyond the scope of this book, except to say that your primary concern for your children should be their spiritual welfare. Endowing them with wealth is not usually in their best interest. I expect that we all want to pass on capital for our children that will be helpful to them and to their children but not to give them so much that they will be tempted to become dependent on it and to back off from their own vocations and their work for the Lord. If these concerns lead you to limit the amount of money you will leave for your children, it would be wise for you to meet with your family and explain why your money will be divided the way you have planned. This could be a wonderful opportunity for you to witness to the role that generosity and commitment to the kingdom of God have had in your life. Unmarried or childless couples are (in this respect) in the enviable position of being able to leave their entire legacy as a strategic investment in the kingdom of God.

It is sad to note that bequests have gone down significantly in the last one hundred years. I hope that as we learn to give again, God will move many seniors to become warriors at the frontiers of ministry by wielding the mighty power of their checkbooks in the service of the kingdom—a kingdom in which the gospel will not return void but will accomplish every good purpose of God's will.

Questions for Review and Reflection

1. What does the author mean by knowing your "magic number"?
2. Should a Christian save for the goal of financial self-sufficiency in retirement even if it impacts his current giving? Why or why not?
3. What advantages and opportunities in the area of Christian ministry are available for seniors who have sufficient retirement savings? Can you describe a senior who has utilized some of them in his or her life?

17

Help for the Financially Stressed

Therefore do not be anxious about tomorrow, for tomorrow will be anxious for itself. Sufficient for the day is its own trouble. (Matt. 6:34)

Shannon and Jeff have three children and own their own home. Jeff is a sales manager, and Shannon works part-time as a nurse. Six months ago their adjustable mortgage payments went up, and now they are having trouble paying their bills. At the end of each month, they wonder where all the money went. They are afraid they will end up losing their home.

Richard worked for thirty years as an engineer for a computer company. His company survived many economic crises, but it didn't survive the most recent one. He was laid off and is now on unemployment. He lies awake at night worrying about unpaid bills, what he should do next, and how his family will cope with their sudden decrease in income.

Tamara and Andy just got married and are both still in college. They are working part-time and borrowing money to pay their tuition. They have just enough to live on, so if they have an unexpected expense, they put it on their credit card. Now Tamara is expecting a baby. They are happy but anxious. How will they make ends meet now?

Fear . . . worry . . . anxiety—these are some of the ways we typically respond to financial stress. There are many reasons why people struggle financially, but, whatever the reason, money troubles are serious, painful, and stressful. If you are experiencing financial difficulties, you might be feeling anger, discouragement, fear, or even panic.

But take heart: as a Christian, your financial troubles take place in the larger story of God's sovereign plan to redeem you in and through your unique trials. You are joined to Christ in such a way that your suffering is tied to the outcome of Christ's suffering, which is new life. Your financial trials are opportunities for God to change you in ways that, eventually, you will not want to trade for all the money in the world. Let's consider the redemptive opportunities that financial troubles provide for you to change, to grow in contentment, to gain an eternal perspective, and to use wisdom in your financial management.

Opportunity for God to Bring about Change in Our Lives

When we are financially stressed, it is easy for us to be dominated by worries and to forget what is truly valuable. Jesus knows this, so he reminds his followers not to

> set your heart on what you will eat or drink; do not worry about it. For the pagan world runs after all such things, and your Father knows that you need them. But seek his kingdom, and these things will be given to you as well.
>
> Do not be afraid, little flock, for your Father has been pleased to give you the kingdom. (Luke 12:29–32 NIV)

If we have trusted God for our provision, then we are free to pray for it. Jesus himself taught us to pray for our daily bread. There is a reason why he wants us to ask the Father for what we and our dependents need. He already knows our needs—but we need to ask for them for our spiritual benefit. God has ordained faith, exercised through prayer, as his means of delivering his blessings. As we saw in 2 Corinthians 9:8–15, we can pray fervently for God's physical provision in the knowledge that he hears us and is able to answer us and do what we ask. We should not be ashamed to ask for more income when we need it to provide for our dependents. Fasting and prayer are appropriate, both publicly and privately, when we ask God for our daily bread. Enlisting the prayers of other believers is a step of faith that is encouraged throughout Scripture.

Prayer is important because it supports our hope. Hope is what keeps us working and looking for how God will answer us. It builds our faith so that we are able to step out into new territory as we search for jobs, gain new skills, and assess our gifts and the job prospects in our current location. When our prayers stop, our hope falls back onto our own weak flesh. We settle into an empty confidence in ourselves or cave into the resignation of drifting instead of working to better our circumstances. Eventually we settle into an ungodly dependence on others. So begin by praying to your Father about your job search and your efforts to provide for your family.

Don't, however, fall into the traps of false prosperity teachers. They ask you to exercise "faith" by sending *them* money in order to "release" the prosperity that Christ is holding for you until you believe him enough to get him to release it. That means you must believe that God will make you prosperous with just as much faith as you believe that he will forgive your sins. If you doubt, it will be taken away. This, of course, is the reason these teachers say that you are poor now. The more money you send them, as an expression of your faith in the wealth and health they guarantee, the more you will receive back. This is nothing more than paganism in the guise of Christian faith.

While we can't make trials and stress go away through pagan offerings to shamans, the trials that God allows in our lives are for the redemptive purpose of giving us his kingdom. Jesus (see John 15:1–3), Paul (see Rom. 5:3), and Peter (see 1 Peter 1:6–8) all teach that we have solid grounds to rejoice in the middle of our trials— which includes your trials now. God has so redeemed our lives that he works in everything to transform us into his character and image. If that goal of being transformed is your highest desire, know that God is sovereignly and comprehensively at work to move you toward that goal. Even God's discipline is not for the purpose of punishment; in the words of Hebrews 12:10–11, "[God] disciplines us for our good, that we may share his holiness. For the moment all discipline seems painful rather than pleasant, but later it yields the peaceful fruit of righteousness to those who have been trained by it."

You will look back and see the hand of your heavenly Father in your circumstances. You will be able to rejoice not just in how he sustained you through the trial but in how he changed your life to enable you to know and reflect him. You can know that Jesus will be with you in your financial storms—not just as a kind, therapeutic presence but as your mighty deliverer and the King of your life. We, like Jesus's disciples when they were caught in a storm, need to open our eyes to see who is with us in the boat during our raging financial storms (see Luke 8:24–25).

An Opportunity to Gain the True Wealth of Contentment

The apostle Paul explains it like this:

> I have learned in whatever situation I am to be content. I know how to be brought low, and I know how to abound. In any and every circumstance, I have learned the secret of facing plenty and hunger, abundance and need. I can do all things through him who strengthens me. (Phil. 4:11–13)

True contentment is usually learned when we are on the down cycle—in loss, deprivation, and financial need. If you are in such a down cycle, you have a great opportunity. As your dreams of long-term financial security and well-being evaporate, you can turn from placing your hope in them. You are free to reconnect to the God who is life and to live as he directs.

Paul is saying that true contentment doesn't come from our circumstances; it comes from "him who strengthens me." Because Paul trusted Jesus, he was at peace and content in different material circumstances. He knew that even in times of financial stress, he was not missing out on anything that was essential to life. His identity, hope, and well-being did not come from what he owned or what he achieved. Rather, they rested on his relationship with the Father who loved him and gave his Son's life so that Paul could be reconciled to him.

Before your financial crisis hit, you might not have realized how much of your hope, contentment, and sense of well-being was attached to your job, your possessions, and your bank balance. So don't be discouraged as you struggle with these common issues. Instead, do three things:

1. Ask yourself whether you really want a God-centered contentment, given your circumstances and frustrations. Many times we want contentment, but only on our terms. Turning to God in times of loss, and learning to let go of our requirements or goals, can be deeply challenging.
2. Identify what you fear losing or what you demand in order to be happy. Give these things over to God, trusting him to supply all of your needs in Christ Jesus. Begin a lifestyle of repentance for discontent.
3. Cultivate an awareness of your phenomenal wealth in God the Father. He is your God, your refuge, your treasure, your true inheritance, and your portion forever. Meditate on this wealth using Ephesians 1:3–23 or any number of the Psalms (like 62, 63, 65, or 73).

When our real treasure is in our relationship with Christ, then we, like Paul, can be freed from seeking life in the things that we possess and freed to live in the fallen world while remaining in the living Branch that bears fruit for eternity (see John 15:16).

Godly contentment enables us to react without despair if our lifestyle shifts downward (or without pride if God grants us economic success). It guards us from becoming prisoners of what we own or the lifestyle that we enjoy. It protects us from regret over what we don't have or haven't achieved. Lastly, it guards us from being pierced by the "many pangs" that come from the pursuit of riches (1 Tim. 6:10). Godliness with contentment is truly great gain (see 1 Tim. 6:6).

An Opportunity to Examine the Value of Money in Our Lives

Much of the value that we place on money is tied to things we want it to do for us. Some of the more common ones are

- providing safety and security
- providing validation in the competition of life
- providing power to enable us to control people and circumstances
- giving us enjoyment and pleasure
- enabling us to impress others (with what we own, how we look, and so on)
- enabling us to please those whom we care about (our children, spouses, parents, friends)
- enabling us to identify with a particular group

This list does not include what God values about money—its potential as a means for us to bless and give to others. His perspective on money never emerges from the natural human heart—our values emerge from our particular personalities, life experiences, and family backgrounds. But no matter what money means to you, if you're relying on it for your security, identity, comfort, and purpose, then you are trusting in it to give you a life apart from God.

Money (or the lack of it) easily becomes the secret "mistress" of our soul. We can go through the motions of church activity and Christian talk while our hearts are elsewhere. Whenever our hearts' loyalty is directed toward something other than God, we become what the Bible calls a spiritual adulterer (see James 4:4–5)—a friend of the world and, sadly, a functional enemy of God. As Jesus said, "No one can serve two masters, for either he will hate the one and love the other, or he will be devoted to the one and despise the other. You cannot serve God and money" (Matt. 6:24).

Most likely, each of us will be tempted at some point to make money (and what we think it will provide us) into the functional source of our lives. This alluring temptation will poison our relationship with Christ.

Apart from going to Jesus in repentance and faith, all our efforts to reform ourselves will fail. But when we know God's love for us in Christ and turn to him for life, we will be freed from captivity to our fears and our desires for what money can provide. We will be able to budget, spend, and give with an open hand, as those who find security, meaning, validation, and pleasure in God himself. As Hebrews 13:5–6 teaches,

> Keep your life free from love of money, and be content with what you have, for he has said, "I will never leave you nor forsake you." So we can confidently say,
>
> > "The Lord is my helper;
> > I will not fear;
> > what can man do to me?"

Make this passage your everyday prayer, and God will give you a new contentment and the power to change the way you view money and your purposes for spending it.

Gain a New Perspective on the Purpose of Money

Learning godly contentment will free you to take on another opportunity: gaining a new perspective on God's purpose for money—the central theme of this book. Paul shares this perspective in his first letter to Timothy. He begins by warning him not to make the pursuit of wealth a personal goal, but to be content with God. Paul, like Jesus, acknowledges our need for the necessities of life (see 1 Tim. 6:6–10). In 1 Thessalonians 4:11–12, he adds to this thought, saying that, as followers of Christ, we should have the ambition to lead a quiet life—to pursue our calling and accomplish real work—so that we may win the respect of outsiders and not be dependent on anybody.

So, while the pursuit of riches is sin, it is God's will that we work hard to provide our families with the necessities of life. But Paul does not stop here. He says that the fundamental goal of our work is to give us something to share with others, as we saw in his farewell to the Ephesian elders in Acts 20:34–35 (see also Eph. 4:28 and 2 Thess. 3:10).

God's will for us in the financial realm is both profound and simple. The money God grants us as a fruit of our labor is for us to love our neighbors as we love ourselves. We provide for ourselves so that we will not be a burden on others and will have something that can help the weak, the lost, and the needy. Work is truly a "labor of love."

Very few Christians who give 10 percent or more of their income to God have a problem with overspending or excessive debt. Right giving seems to be a means of adjusting our choices about money so that we move toward controlled spending that is rooted in contentment.

Practical Strategies for Seeking Wisdom in Our Spending

I remember, as a young pastor, being irritated with my wife when our bank account hit zero. Since my wife paid the bills, I expected her to control our household spending. But when we sat down together to determine where all the money had gone, I was shocked to discover that, in one year, I (not my wife) had spent 20 percent more than I earned.

Suddenly I was confronted with the challenge of living within my means on a modest salary with a wife and three children. I was supposed to be an example to my church of mostly young Christians, and yet my desires to possess were running ahead of what God had provided me. I remember being embarrassed and fearful. I was used to getting what I wanted, from my upper-middle-class upbringing—how was I to learn how to downsize my expectations and my spending?

My wife and I started by praying that God would free us from our desire to have a certain lifestyle and get what we wanted. We asked him to teach us how to live within the financial boundaries he had given us and to be content.

God answered those prayers by helping us to develop a disciplined system of spending for not-so-organized folks like me. This plan helped us to make the spending changes that we needed and to grow in contentment. Within a few months, we were living within our means, and with a slight surplus.

Not all of our attempts to economize went smoothly. Our children still remember our homemade root beer blowing up in the basement and our VW van breaking down on three consecutive trips (thanks to Dad's amateur engine-repair efforts). But even they were eventually glad for a family culture that was not based on spending. And, in a deeper sense, economizing helped us to learn to be satisfied with the basics that God had supplied us. Even our kids began to learn that saying no to something does not result in a loss of anything that is essential to life.

If you are behind on your bills but willing to take a faith-filled look at what it would mean for you to live within God's provision, I encourage you to do the exercise that follows. It will give you an honest picture of your financial situation and will show you what you need to do in order to bring your expenses in line with your income. It doesn't guarantee contentment, but it can be an occasion to learn it (as it was for us) and to flow into a life of financial realism, wisdom, and obedience.

Step One: Assess Your Financial Situation

Paul advised the Ephesians to "be very careful, then, how you live" in light of the opportunities they had been given (Eph. 5:15 NIV). Living within the means that God has provided reflects wisdom and submission to him. In order to do so, you must first determine which of two causes your problems stem from. First, they can be caused by not having enough money to support the necessities of life; or, second, they can be caused by overspending. While the stress of both causes can feel similar, they each require a different solution. If you do not have enough money for your necessities, you need to earn more or to make major changes in your cost of living, if that is possible. Some people make a sustainable wage but still fall behind on their bills every month because they spend too much. This exercise will help you decide which category you fit into.

A financial assessment is the first step in helping you to see why your money has run out. You may find that the cost of even a low level of participation in our economy is a rude awakening—particularly in the suburbs. You may be further surprised at the price of the "extra enhancements" that are considered necessities in our culture. Whatever your preconceived thoughts, you need the facts that will reveal your true financial position and allow you to respond to reality—not to hunches, emotions, or premonitions.

Start by gathering your financial information. The twelve bank statements from the previous year are usually the most important documents. Go through them and add up the total deposits you have received from all sources of income. Subtract from this total any deposits that weren't income (such as transfers into your account from savings, home equity loans, or other loans). This is your net income for the year. Add up your total expenditures, including checks, ATM withdrawals, and electronic deductions that flowed through your bank account(s). Subtract these total expenses from the total income to get your net gain or loss for the year.

If you are having problems paying your bills, then your expenses most likely exceed your income. This exercise will give you an estimate of how large your shortfall is. As difficult as it may be to face this number, doing so is the precondition for reaching a solution. So take this step in faith, remembering that you are God's child. Your identity does not lie in how much money you make or don't make, and God has promised to provide all that you need (see Matt. 6:31–34). Facing your deficit without denial or terror is an act of faith—the equivalent of depending on God and praying, "Give us this day our daily bread."

Step Two: Plan Your Spending

After you face your deficit, it's time for you to create a spending plan for the next twelve months. If you are married, it is essential that your spouse fully participate in this. Without his or her cooperation, perspective, and accountability, this plan will be greatly weakened.

Project your income. For employees, this is fairly simple. You and your spouse's net paychecks (minus taxes and retirement contributions) can be added up for a year. If you are self-employed, use last year's income as your guide and project next year's income based on your past experience and the current market conditions. Make sure that you include interest, dividends, gifts, royalties, rental income, income from retirement accounts (if you are retired), debt repayments, settlement payments, and tax refunds. Once this figure is complete, you should have a good estimate of the total income you have available for the next year.

Project your expenses. Look at your expenses from the previous year. Gather as many of the checks, receipts, credit card statements, monthly invoices, and bills from that year as you can find, and list the various categories of these expenses. Some tips that will help you to do this are to break down your credit card billings into the actual items that were bought (food, clothing, gas, entertainment) and then look at each line of each credit card bill and assign it to a category. If you use Quicken or a similar electronic checkbook, this will be much easier if you have used its split transactions feature. ATM cash withdrawals may be difficult to break down, but do your best. You may end up with a category called "Cash." Once you have this list of categories, put them under one of two general headings.

The first heading is *Fixed Expenses*. Here, list all of the expenses that are fixed by someone else (such as mortgage, utility bills, car payment, insurance, and so on) or by you (such as tithes to your church, a savings plan, and so on).

The second heading is *Variable Expenses*. Here, list expenses that you have some control over (such as food, eating out, gifts, vacations, clothes, and so on). Between these two headings, you should have a complete list of the twenty or thirty categories of expenses that you incur in life.

After you have listed your expense categories under these two headings, begin to plan your spending and project numbers for each expense category. Using your expenses from last year as a guide, project your spending for the next twelve months. Remember to use a twelve-month figure for planned spending, because this will cover bills that are paid annually or quarterly.

Once you have a dollar amount for each spending category, add these amounts up and compare this total cost with your total expected income for the next twelve months. It will probably result in a loss—perhaps one that is similar to your actual loss from the previous twelve months. Don't be discouraged if your first projections are in the red. (When my wife and I use this system, we often begin with a spending total that is about 10 to 20 percent more than our income. We have to work in order to pare it down to size.)

Follow this up by praying for God to guide you toward living within his financial will and provision. God is sovereign over the situation he has assigned for you and loving in his intentions for you, so there is a way for you to move forward. As you seek God's will, he promises to work wisdom into your life (see James 1:5–6). You can enlist the prayers of others as you embark on this challenge of faith and stewardship.

Reconcile your income and expenses. To begin this step, assume that all your fixed expenses will be paid in full every month. That leaves a fairly small amount of money to be used for variable expenses. Use your creativity to identify items you can eliminate or reduce, such as cable television, club memberships, or magazine and newspaper subscriptions. Consider eating at home instead of dining out, taking bag lunches, and shopping at thrift and discount stores.

Once you have estimated how much you can reduce your expenses "on paper," add them up again to see how much of the deficit you have eliminated. Cutting these costs is often not enough to balance your income and expenses. It is very common for some fixed expenses to have to be cut as well. Since 1970, the fixed costs faced by the average American family have risen from 54 percent to 75 percent of their average household income, leaving a smaller and smaller piece of the pie that is variable and discretionary.

If you cannot balance your budget by cutting variable expenses, look back through each category in the fixed-expense list for ways you can reduce your structurally fixed expenses. Most of our large spending mistakes occur in the expenses that we box ourselves into—primarily our housing, auto, and debt payments. Consider relocating to a more affordable home or apartment, getting rid of your second car (or both cars) and using public transportation, getting rid of your landline (if you have a cell phone), and doing your own home repairs. You can save money if you are willing to let go of your vision of the "good life" and to commit yourself to living within the boundaries of God's will and provision.

Get outside help if you need it. If, after cutting your variable and fixed expenses, you are still not on a positive cash flow basis, you need some help. Go to your pastor, your elders, or your deacons and ask them to give you (or point you to) financial direction. If you are overwhelmed with debt payments to the point that you have no choice but to stop paying them, get credit counseling to help you seek principal debt reductions or, failing that, see an attorney about filing for bankruptcy. Our modern bankruptcy laws were inspired by the Bible's provision for canceling debts every seven years so that the indebted and poor could have a fresh start (see Lev. 25).

You may conclude that you are simply not earning enough to provide for your family. In that case, you are called by God to seek to earn more income. This may mean starting the sometimes scary process of changing your vocation and perhaps retraining. As you face this reality, remember that you have a heavenly Father who cares for you and hears your prayers. When your life is built on God and his love for you, change doesn't have to be a threat—it can be an opportunity for you to see how God will lead and provide. Don't give up until your income and expenses balance on your worksheet.

Step Three: Put Yourself on an Allowance from the Bank

Once you are balanced on paper (and only then), you can move to the next step of putting things into practice. While the key to controlling your spending is a willingness to change your lifestyle so that it honors God, that willingness must be matched by a practical plan to carry this out. People often try to control their spending with complicated budgeting systems, but these are hard to maintain. The following approach is for people like me, who need limits on their spending but are not disciplined enough to budget or to keep detailed records of where all their money goes. The heart of this system involves putting yourself on an allowance that is controlled by your bank account. The system will help you to control your variable expenses, pay your bills on time, develop habits of saving and giving, and build up a reserve for unpredictable expenses.

Here's what you need to do:

1. Open a second checking account that has no overdraft protection and no built-in credit line.
2. Continue to deposit all your income into your original checking account, but pay only fixed expenses from that original account. Do not pay any bills from your list of variable expenses.
3. Twice a month, deposit (or transfer) the equivalent of half a month's worth of variable spending from your original checking account into the new variable account.
4. Use only this second account to pay for items that fall under your variable expenses. When the money in this account is used up, you will be forced to stop spending. You will have to wait to spend on any variable purchases until you make your next bimonthly deposit from the fixed account.
5. If you have a long history of rigidly paying off credit card charges each month, then you can keep using them. But if you are in credit card debt, cut up your cards and get a bank debit card for each checking account.
6. Resist the temptation to pay variable bills with fixed account money.
7. Be accountable. Ask a deacon, elder, friend, spouse, or counselor to look at your bank statement each month, give you advice, and pray with you.
8. After a year on this plan, if you have built up a surplus in your fixed account, transfer it to a savings account.

Once your finances are stabilized and your debt is being paid off, you can begin to set more thoughtful long-term goals or adjust those goals to the longer-term expenses that you envision in the future, such as savings for your children's college, more adequate insurance, retirement investing, and increased giving.

Whether you live in plenty or in want, I trust that God will use this process to help you to live out Ephesians 5:15–17 (NIV):

> Be very careful, then, how you live—not as unwise but as wise, making the most of every opportunity, because the days are evil. Therefore do not be foolish, but understand what the Lord's will is.

I trust that, having embraced God's will for your finances, you will gain a new contentment and joy from finding your true life in God.

Questions for Review and Reflection

1. What are some of the spiritual opportunities that financial stresses can provide?
2. Do you agree with the author that some kind of trackable spending plan is an important part of Christian stewardship? Why or why not?
3. According to the author, what are some of the advantages of having a two-checking-account system for getting spending under control?

18

How to Give More

Look carefully then how you walk, not as unwise but as wise, making the best use of the time, because the days are evil. Therefore do not be foolish, but understand what the will of the Lord is. (Eph. 5:15–17)

If the ultimate purpose of a Christian's labor and wealth is to enable him to give, to love, and to serve others, then our financial planning should reflect that goal. God does not measure our financial success by our level of self-support but by how much we give beyond that level. The amount that we give is a result of both our motivation and our capacity to give. So far we have focused primarily on the component of motivation, which will always be the most important component of our giving, both spiritually and monetarily. However, this chapter will look at our *capacity* to give and ways in which people who are motivated to increase it can do so. Wise financial habits often yield the fruit of an increased capacity for giving.

Obviously, having more money will not increase our giving unless we also make a decision to be generous. But, if we have the motivation to be generous, there are many lawful, wise financial practices that may help us to garner more household wealth and be able to give more. This reflects the counsel of John Wesley in his three simple mandates for the Christian: "Earn all you can, save all you can, and give all you can." These mandates translate into three virtues that the Christian should pursue simultaneously: diligence in work, wisdom in finances, and generosity in giving. In this chapter I hope to suggest ways that we can better accomplish the first two of these.

1. Seek Work That Utilizes Your God-given Design

Jesus's disciples are commanded to work diligently from their hearts—not unto man but unto God (see Eph. 6:6–8). Christians should be known as honest, focused workers no matter where they work or what they do. But that is not the end of the matter. Jesus introduces a radical new element into our perspective on our effectiveness in our work, and Paul goes on to articulate it most clearly.

For most of human history, people's labor was largely determined by their class, their slave masters, or their parents' occupation. When Paul introduced the idea that each person in the body of Christ is gifted differently and that their gifts all work together for the building up of the whole, it was revolutionary. The self-examination that is necessary for us to discern how we are gifted to serve in the church is clearly commanded in Romans 12:3–8, which follows Paul's discussion of how we are to consecrate ourselves to God and have our minds transformed in order that we might know the will of God. He says,

> For by the grace given to me I say to everyone among you not to think of himself more highly than he ought to think, but to think with sober judgment, each according to the measure of faith that God has assigned. For as in one body we have many members, and the members do not all have the same function, so we, though many, are one body in Christ, and individually members one of another. Having gifts that differ according to the grace given to us, let us use them. (vv. 3–6)

The church mirrors and redeems the diversity of gifts and motivations that are found throughout mankind. The church became the first place where even poor people could assess their giftedness and serve accordingly. This helped to produce a powerful organizational movement that tapped the motivation of both lay folks and clergy. Today, all large organizations at least try to assess this aspect of how God created us, but only about 20 percent of our workers are deployed on the basis of their giftedness and motivation.[1] The effectiveness of our workforce suffers tragically from these low numbers.

Today, the diversity and wealth available in Western culture gives us the option of asking, "What do I want to do when I grow up?" We have a huge labor market—13,000 job titles are listed in the Dictionary of Occupational Titles. This requires much more discernment from us about setting a vocational direction. We begin to do this by choosing after-school jobs and making decisions about whether to pursue vocational training or secondary education, college majors, and grad school.

As Christians, we have a great advantage in knowing the nature of our Creator, the image he has placed in mankind, and the purpose he has for his world. This is brilliantly expounded by Arthur Miller and Ralph Mattson in their groundbreaking book.[2] Miller's system rejects the rigid typological approach used by most other vocational-giftedness assessments as being simplistic and impersonal. He holds that such testing cannot account for the diversity of God's creation that we see in man and woman and the diversity of the roles available to such a rich creation. Anyone can take typological assessments such as the Self-Directed Search, Meyers-Briggs, and Interest Inventory systems easily over the internet, but do not rely too heavily on the limited set of types that such systems present. They are like painting a landscape using only primary colors.

Miller believes that we have an internal sense for the way we were designed to work and that, by asking the right questions, we can become more aware of the work-related DNA we have each been given by the hand of our Creator. God designed each of us to have different roles and to serve our neighbors through our work in different ways. When we are blessed to find work that taps into our own unique design, motivations, and abilities, we will usually be happier and more successful and will end up earning more.

There is a particular temptation for us to seek to become wealthy

1. See Ralph T. Mattson and Arthur F. Miller, Jr., *Finding a Job You Can Love* (Phillipsburg, NJ: P&R, 1999), 55.

2. See Mattson and Miller, *Finding a Job You Can Love*. See also Miller's work *Why You Can't Be Anything You Want to Be* (Grand Rapids: Zondervan, 1999).

as our primary career goal. Such motivation is forbidden to Christians. Wealth may come as a by-product if we are placed in a job with high earning potential and are really good at what we do. But riches should never be the goal of the Christian's vocational decisions.

Yet, even if we don't take this approach to determining what kind of job we should have, most of us have felt the pressure of other external factors as we weigh our options, such as these:

- parental, spousal, or societal expectations
- level of job security
- respect and recognition from society
- potential for power and authority
- availability of a job—any job

None of these pressures draws on our giftedness or the design we were created with; we discover these things as we see ourselves expressing them in unconstrained work environments (through childhood play or in a church, club, or volunteer organization). That is why, according to Miller, our experiences in our elementary, high school, and college years can be very significant and are worth careful attention.

Christians who are stranded in job roles far from their giftedness and internal motivation can take comfort that God knows their situation and will give them the strength to serve in those roles until he provides a way out. Our need to provide for our families takes clear precedence over finding a job that we love. Moses and Paul both served in roles that were outside their comfort zones and areas of giftedness, but God had a specific purpose for them: that they might always remember that their weakness was their strength because of what God was doing through them.

The message of all this for young adults and "midlife-correction" workers is to seek wisdom and discernment as they consider their God-given design, capacities, and internal motivations. A good career fit will bring joy to your service and reap the rewards of better health, greater job satisfaction, good workmanship, and job security—not to mention a better chance for you to be successful at what you do and end up earning more money.

I struggled with this in my career path. I made a transition at age thirty-five from the pastorate to counseling and ministry administration. Within God's providential plan, I got into the pastorate somewhat unwisely, from a human perspective. My four co–church planters all left our church for other ministries, and I was providentially left holding the ministry "bag." I remained at the church and pastored there for twelve years. Eventually, I discerned that at that time I lacked the leadership experience and communication gifts that would enable a church to grow much larger than 125 people, and since we were situated in a university community that had a high degree of turnover, we needed the church body to be larger than this.

It was not totally clear where God would lead me, but he opened a door for me to move into fundraising and ministry management in 1984. I realized that I was a starter more than a developer, which helped me to begin initiating new things in ministry. I took a sizable salary reduction, but it was truly worth it. A huge weight was lifted off my back, and I flourished—beginning three new initiatives. God was also preparing me to begin a totally new organization, the Children's Jubilee Fund, in 2004. Even my salary cut in 1984 was used by God to motivate me to invest in real estate, which enabled me twenty years later to partially retire early in order to do urban mission work. I could not have devised a better preparation.

So consider carefully how you serve the Lord in your vocation. Working is not for wealth, recognition, status, or power. We work in order to faithfully use the gifts and design we have received from God as we serve our neighbors. Many who do so will earn significant wealth, but this is a by-product that brings us greater responsibility to do financial good works. Others will serve in fields that lead to a much more modest paycheck. Those of us who are in this category can still be as content as those who are wealthy, since life does not consist in the abundance of what we possess.

2. Start Giving Early, and at 10 Percent

A second way for you to increase your giving is to start the habit early (or at least start it *now*). Immediately begin giving 10 percent of your income to Christ's kingdom. Even if your income is small and you are in your twenties, it is financially safe[3] for Christians to give 10 percent of their income to God's mission. Don't put off beginning, because the total amount of your giving will be dramatically increased by the number of years you contribute and the proportion of your funds that you give.

If you begin by giving ten percent of your income to God's kingdom, your giving will be double that of the average American evangelical, who gives between 3 and 5 percent. Here is a place where all of us (poor, middle class, and rich) can begin—with the discipline of giving 10 percent of our income. God promised Old Testament believers that if they would give, through faith, the required tithe of the increase of their harvests and flocks, he would bless them so much that they would not be able to contain the blessing (see Mal. 3:10).

Paul reflects this Old Testament promise when he tells the Corinthians, in 2 Corinthians 9:1–11, that if they give to help the Judean Christians they will be "enriched in every way to be generous in every way" (see v. 11). These are not predictions that our future on earth will involve wealth, but the result of our giving will be an increase in the things that make us rich as disciples of God. This is something that believers can discern only by looking back on our lives and thanking God for how he has worked in them.

As we saw in 1 Corinthians 16:1–2, God still asks us to give proportionally to our prosperity. He does not require tithing in the New Testament era, but he commands that our giving reflect the degree to which we prosper and that it be worthy of the grace we have received in Christ. It is hard to conceive of proportional giving that would arise from a sincere love for God but begin at less than 10 percent.[4]

We all try to invent alternate giving plans that cap our giving, instead of making it proportional, and that don't arise from our response to the gospel. Let's have some fun at our own expense and

---

3. See the next footnote, about tithing and indebtedness.

4. A person with debts that are past due or with family obligations should pay those off before offering funds to God.

sample some of the other schemes that contrast with the Bible's approach and can easily take over our giving plans.

The "Buddy, Can You Spare a Dime?" Approach

We take this approach when we give God our spare money—as we might give to a beggar on the street. The rich who give from their excess fall into this category. They deny themselves nothing of the blessings of life before they decide to give. Such gifts can be huge and helpful to ministry, but they do not represent biblical generosity. Middle-income Christians often struggle to give anything, in view of the cost of middle-class living. The most basic financial commitment of those of us who are in this category is to seek all the things that our lifestyle makes possible. Any giving happens only after this commitment is met, whether we admit it or not. We simply toss stray bills into the offering plate. We don't want to consider what we will give, so we give randomly from our excess.

The Tipping Approach

In this approach, we recognize that it is standard to give a gratuity for services that are rendered, so we provide a token of appreciation for the minister and the church by dropping some money in the plate. But this never reaches the level of a 17-percent restaurant gratuity; it is usually calculated from the perceived value to the household of what the church offered through its services that day, and it rarely gets much above 1 percent of the household's income. People who give like this have no idea of the true value of the love that has been offered to them in Christ's incarnation, death, and resurrection.

The Pew-Rental Approach

People who take this approach don't want to think of themselves as being a mooch, so they give to defray the cost of their seats in church. This might be $10 for each member of the household each week. In colonial days, churches did rent out pews in order to provide supplemental revenue, in addition to the support that they received from the state. And, just as in colonial times, such revenue cannot come close to underwriting a church member's part in Christ's mission. Such "renters" leave the real support of the church's service and mission to others.

The "Membership" Approach

This is an improvement over the pew-rental approach. A quick calculation of the church's annual budget divided by the number of its members yields an amount—say $2,900 per household, or $56 each week. That becomes your membership fee. This "fair share" that members pay is how country clubs and homeowners associations are financed. Under this approach, the church becomes a co-op to deliver spiritual goods and services to its members, and "responsible members" pay their full fair share. There is no proportionality. This deprives poorer members of help from wealthier members, and the church ministry suffers.

The Social Transaction Approach

Donors who take this approach wait for opportunities to receive public recognition or personal benefit from their gifts. Outside the church, they might sponsor a piece of a public project or donate to a cause that will list them as a donor for the sake of their reputation with a needed constituency. Inside it, they might support the new church playground if their grandchildren will be using it. Many of us give in situations that might involve some recognition or indirect benefit, but hopefully this is not our motivation.

Pagan philanthropy was based on this approach. Donors gave to honor those from whom they expected reciprocal recognition, which created a closed circle of benefit for the honorable among the populace. The apostles worked hard to dispel this mentality and to tie giving to the grace that we have received and the command we've been given to love others as we have been loved.

The Tax Approach

This is the approach of the legalist. It is proportional, but it operates by law, not love (see 1 Cor. 13; 2 Cor. 9:7). Even if someone gives all that he has and has not love, it profits him nothing (see 1 Cor. 13:3). Christians who take this approach see 10 percent of their money as being owed to God but the remaining 90 percent as being outside his claim. This is tempting to those who seek a straightforward, measurable way to establish their rightness with God.

Yet because they are not giving in love, such legalists usually find ways to whittle down what they owe—such as basing their tithe on their net pay rather than their gross pay or deducting Christian-school or medical expenses before calculating the tithe. While Jesus does not condemn the giving of 10 percent if it is done out of love, this is a dangerous substitute for faith that expresses itself through love.

The "Quick Return Investment" Approach

This is known today as the prosperity gospel. This distortion of the true gospel qualifies as a heresy. It preys particularly on the financially stressed, who are promised that they will become well off if they turn over money to the particular minister or church who is teaching this wealth principle. This heresy goes beyond the Bible's promise that God will meet our needs within his redemptive purposes (see Phil. 4:19). Its proponents claim that God will give you what you want in this life—and that if he doesn't, it is because you lacked the faith to trigger the wealth response from God. This approach is the essence of pagan worship. In order to foist it on gullible or desperate Christians, seasoned practitioners of this deception usually start with a call for listeners to "get saved." Such an altar call can result in real salvation, but then it leads gullible believers toward the spiritual slaughterhouse of prosperity, success, and earthly health being the essence of Christ's work.

None of these approaches reflect the basic dynamic of biblical giving. Each seriously twists the biblical picture of giving in order to bring it into the service of our own desires for our selfish personal peace, self-esteem, freedom from guilt, pursuit of self-righteousness, and desire for riches.

For those who know that they are forgiven and loved based on Christ's work alone, the discipline and guideline of the Old Testament's 10-percent tithe is a healthy place to begin. It is love in action. Looking at the tithe as a guideline of giving for beginners has saved many—like me—from falling into destructive patterns, and it has helped me to instill good ones instead, such as these:

- developing a sense of control and discipline over money
- finding freedom from the urge to consume all the affluence of our society
- helping my family to consider giving instead of spending, as a normal part of our prayerful planning
- giving thanks to God when he would meet our financial needs even though we did not feel like giving in a particular month
- teaching our children effective ways to develop into givers
- becoming more faithful in giving, through my habit and lifestyle
- finding joy in knowing that I was giving at a level that was equal to some of the saints who went before me
- experiencing a joy from giving that motivated me to find ways to give even more

While many blessings are attached to it, this practice is not a requirement. There may be times when it is wrong for us to give 10 percent. For example, money should not be given to the Lord if it is owed to someone else and the payment is overdue; the debt should be repaid first. If we owe money to our children or parents that will provide them with the necessities of life, the money should be given not to the Lord but to them (see chapter 17 of this book). Despite these exceptions, however, tithing is the baseline God requires of us that will launch us into a life of generosity in response to the gospel.

3. Plan to Enable Greater Generosity

Can we increase our capacity for giving if we plan financially? The answer is a strong yes! Because God promises to meet our needs, refusing to plan would be "testing" God, which is forbidden in Scripture (see Matt. 4:7). Faith does not transfer our responsibilities to God. True faith motivates us to action because of God's promises and his calling for our future.

In a subsistence-based fishing, hunting, or farming community, there is a yearly cycle of storing up food for the winter, which requires both short-term and longer-term planning. If planning and steward-ship are required in subsistence cultures, how much more are they required in a more complex economy? Prayerful, informed planning is necessary for us to protect and steward our funds in order to reach the priorities we have established. Such planning usually requires at least the following:

- knowing how much we earned and spent the previous year, in all categories
- deciding how much we plan to earn and spend in each category during the coming year
- making sure that we contribute to an emergency fund for unforeseen expenses
- deciding how much we will allocate to the paying down of debt, to savings, to retirement, and to giving, in view of these constraints

These are difficult decisions—particularly for those with five-figure incomes. Many people are intimidated by even basic budgeting, so we feel tempted to misuse God's promised care as a reason for us to avoid planning our finances and spending. Facing these realities causes many of us stress, so we ignore them, worry, and use God's promise to cover our fear.

But we are called to be stewards of what we have while looking ahead to the service and fruit we seek to provide for his kingdom. In the area of finances, loving God and our neighbors means working to provide for our dependents and contributing to the needs and oppor-tunities of God's kingdom. As Christians, we work to sustain ourselves, meet our families' needs, and reach out to love others—our brothers and sisters in Christ, our neighbors, and even our enemies. We need a plan for how we will produce fruit for these kingdom purposes.

Instead of falling prey to laziness, fear, or hiding because we are averse to taking risks in our responsibilities and relationships, we need to be aware of the shortness of time and our need to act now in order to provide for future needs. Wisdom thinks through the chain of events that allow us to do this.

The two things we are not to do regarding the future are to worry about it (see Matt. 6:34) or boast about what we will do in it (see James 3:14; 4:13–16). Jesus reminds us that the evil of each day is sufficient for that day. Conversely, his grace is also given each day for that day. Using the language of Matthew 6, it is okay for us to worry about today (i.e., to think and act so that we address challenges today), but our nervous system was not constructed to carry the worries of the future at the same time.

We should spend the energy, grace, and motivation from fear that we have each day on the challenges of that day, not on the specter of what might happen in the future. We are to plan for the future but not worry about it. We make our future plans with the powerful caveat "If God wills, I will do such and such" (see James 4:15).

We see many examples of planning in Scripture: Noah's plans for the ark, David's plans for the temple, Jesus's strategy to reach all the cities of Israel, Paul's detailed plans for his missionary journeys and for the empire-wide offerings for the Jerusalem saints. Planning is a biblical way for us to carry out our calling. It is also a necessity for us to avoid massive wastes of time, energy, and money. Failing to make major spending decisions will just make you a servant of someone else's agenda. Everyone else has a plan for your life and your money—so why shouldn't you?[5]

A lot of us are tempted to avoid this kind of planning and calculation because we do not really want to know the results. We are afraid that we are in the red or close to it, which makes us fear. This is a lack of faith in our heavenly Father and his provision. As his children, we can be bold as we face the challenges and realities he has assigned us and can know that he will lead us along the paths of life for his sake, if we will but follow.

Some couples may draw back from planning their spending because they cannot discuss money without causing conflict, feeling

---

5. See the resources published by Crown Ministries, Inc. at www.crown.org, as well as the information on Financial Peace University at www.daveramsey.com.

intimidated, blindly delegating, or feeling that "forgiveness is easier than permission." None of these reactions are healthy for a couple or represent biblically motivated efforts for them to be of one mind and flesh. This can be a matter of prayer for the couple as they seek to learn to be constructive by looking at their past expenditures and projecting those for the upcoming year.

Don't give up on this, because a purposeful spending plan becomes the template and venue for prayerful discussion, wisdom, listening, and expressing deeply held values about money. The plan is part of the solution. It also calls us to pray together—particularly for good discussion and discernment regarding what we want to spend in each of our categories during the coming year.

God delights when we approach him for wisdom in these matters, and he commands us to do so (see James 1:5). Believe this, and step out in faith in his promised guidance as you look for direction to resolve your financial shortfalls.

I have been in the position of taking this step of faith three or four times in my life, and God used these steps to move my family into gaining a new discipline in our spending, restructuring our fixed expenses, and finding new avenues of income. All of these turned out to be blessings later in our lives.

4. Save Money by "Renting a Life"

Christians have a secret financial weapon: contentment. It protects us from the drive to upgrade our way into debt and from foolishly using our capital until we have little left to give. Instead, it enables us to reduce our expenses and save large amounts—which is possible even in our economy.

We have seen that John Wesley said that Christians should "save all they can." A major opportunity for us to do this is by sharing and by substituting rentals for purchases. I believe that Christians ought to default to rentals and shared ownership as much as possible—particularly on depreciating assets. Of course, we can own possessions outright—especially when other options are not available, wise, or feasible. And we should rent and share not because we are tightwads or hoarders but because this saves money that we can spend on higher purposes. These funds can be used where they might be more strategic—for our children's future, business expansion, or kingdom causes.

Christians have as a basic value the communion of the saints, which provides a framework in which cooperation and sharing can take place in a way that is financially and spiritually profitable.

First John 2:15–17 reminds us that the love of the world and of the things of the world are incompatible with love for God.

> Do not love the world or the things in the world. If anyone loves the world, the love of the Father is not in him. For all that is in the world—the desires of the flesh and the desires of the eyes and the pride of life—is not from the Father but is from the world. And the world is passing away along with its desires, but whoever does the will of God abides forever.

The phrase "pride of life" can also be translated "pride of possessions." It warns of the danger of a possession-centered spending strategy. Our choice possessions will never satisfy our inner thirst for beauty or significance, yet all of us have the pursuit of possessions as our default setting due to our fallen nature. While ownership can be financially beneficial to a family, it has no redemptive power against our fears, inner thirst, or need for meaning. In addition, each thing that we own comes with built-in responsibilities for us to properly care for, use, and dispose of it.

Here are some examples of how we can limit our ownership.

Share a Vacation Home

I know of ten couples in a church who bought a condo together at a beach location. Each of them gets it for five weeks a year, which are spread across the four seasons in order to leave a reasonable amount of time for each couple's vacation. The condo provides some capital appreciation, and while someone has to manage it, their joint ownership of it greatly reduces the expenses for each of them. This is a great model for Christians who don't seek pride in owning things.

Rent a Property

Christians can enjoy retreats and vacations by renting a home or unit for the exact time that they need it. My family sold a beach property in 1986 that we weren't using regularly. Instead, we began renting a beach property for the specific times that we needed it. We have maintained this approach to our vacation time, which has now turned into a family reunion and involves renting four properties for thirty-six people. This could never have happened if we had been set on owning one, and the reunions have been a powerful benefit to our family. This approach has also saved us mountains of money and maintenance time.

Another good reason to take this approach is that it's not a foregone conclusion that real estate is the best investment. My parents bought a North Carolina canal-front property for $50,000 in 1980 and put another $25,000 into it, only to sell it a few years later because of lack of use. It is worth about $400,000 today. The Dow Jones industrial average in 1980 was about 800. As I write, it is 25,000. If my parents had invested that money in the DJI, it would have given them $2.3 million, plus thirty-five years of dividends. Even if keeping the property would have saved us $3,000 a year in rentals for those thirty-five years, this would not be close to the amount the stock market would have given us if we had invested the money there. It might make us feel good to own vacation property, but it is usually not good stewardship—especially for middle-income families.

Rent a Boat

I love being on the water, especially if I can fish, and have owned and built numerous small skiffs. However, as boat owners know, "Boats are a hole in the water into which one pours money." I really "need" to be on the water at least every two or three months, just to flush my emotions and stress. I am tempted to think that boats are redemptive, but I know as a Christian that they are not. I can give thanks for the fish, the wind, the beauty, and the mystery of the sea, but I dare not look to them for my sense of well-being, vindication, or purpose in life.

I overstepped the bounds of wisdom a few years ago by commissioning a custom fishing skiff I had designed. My love for this design fogged my financial eyesight and made me not want to ask the hard questions about cost and stewardship. While I enjoyed the boat, it set me back financially. My next boat was a ten-year-old fiberglass boat that cost only 25 percent of what the custom boat had cost, and I found a way to share that cost with another family member. Rather than being a drag on my finances, it has enhanced my ability to make friends by allowing me to take other men out fishing, and I have used it with just as much joy as I got from the boat that was much more expensive.

As we see in this and the previous examples, we should approach larger-ticket items carefully because they can become a financial liability that is disproportionate to the amount of rest and refreshment they provide.

Share a Ride

Sharing cars and using public transportation is a natural for Christians who live in more compact communities. When we lived in urban Philadelphia, we were able to get by with one car because of public transportation. We could walk or take public transportation to the mechanic, the grocery store, church, school, and even work. Our kids did not need drivers' licenses or insurance until age eighteen, yet they went everywhere they wanted to from the time they were about twelve. We also lived close to others with whom we could share car ownership. And this was before Uber and Lyft! This option is a good reason for lower-income Christians to live in urban or row house communities. And, if you need a car for a longer, one-time trip, renting one for the individual trip is a more economical option than buying one.

Share a House

Our family has done this from day one. We initially shared a home fifty-fifty with another couple. As our families grew, we separated, but for almost thirty years we always had a renter/friend living with us. While not everyone has the constitution for this, it has been a huge blessing to our family—not just because it provided financial help but because it provided a ministry to singles, a richer context for our children's lives, and a long train of dear friends we feel close to even today. Today we share ownership of a home with another family member, though we no longer rent out a room.

Keep or Downsize Your Home

Keeping your home instead of buying a larger one, or even downsizing it, is a prime means of freeing up assets for a higher use. I have been blessed in that two of the three homes we have lived in have cost less than the selling price of the home we were moving from. One was a fixer-upper, which required extra money beyond the buying price, but we stayed there for twenty years, so it was not a major issue.

There are many other ways in which people can "rent a life"— through renting gowns, jewelry, furniture, garden plots, RVs, and so on. Even if it's best to live in a suburban neighborhood for the sake of its schools, renting a home can be a good investment if the monthly cost of renting it is less than mortgage payments would be. Save the difference, and you will be ahead. Each household should at least consider these alternatives as they contemplate how to best use the funds God has granted them. This is especially relevant to middle-income families, because such items can eat up a larger percentage of their household income than they would of families who earn $200,000 or more.

5. Don't Spend Too Much on Your First House

The late Dr. Richard Chewning, economics professor at the University of Richmond and a noted Christian economist, alerted me to this advice in an article he published in the 1980s. He proposed that Christians should buy starter homes that are worth only half of what their household can afford. He advised this because of the dramatic increase in wealth it would afford the person who is willing to wait seven years for a "proper" home. Of course, no bank or real estate agent would try to sell you such a "cheap" home, but the rewards of choosing one are dramatic. Let me illustrate.

Mr. Big and Mr. Little both had salaries of $70,000 per year, and both had $70,000 to put down on a home purchase. Mr. Big bought a home for $350,000, and Mr. Little bought one for $150,000. They both put down $70,000. Each paid about $1,500 per month toward his mortgage. Mr. Little got a better interest rate because he had a seven-year ARM (adjustable-rate mortgage), and he paid it off in seven years and was mortgage-free. Mr. Big paid for thirty years at a higher interest rate.

During those seven years, homes appreciated by 2 percent per year. Mr. Little went out and bought a larger home like Mr. Big's, which now cost him $402,000. He sold his small home for $212,000 and put that money down on the new, larger house. Mr. Little could now afford a fifteen-year mortgage of $191,000, which he paid off at $1,500 per month over fifteen years at 4 percent interest. So, after twenty-two years, he owned his home free and clear and began putting his $1,500 monthly payment into his IRA. If the IRA earned 5 percent for eight years, this would leave him with over $145,000 by the time Mr. Big paid off his mortgage. Mr. Big got his home first, but it cost him $145,000 for that privilege, which is the cost of a college education.

While each of our family and financial situations is unique, the principle remains that a starter home can yield huge dividends for a middle-income family by helping them to meet their financial goals more quickly, freeing up money for college, retirement, and giving above a 10 percent tithe.

6. Beware of Wasting Money If You Become Affluent

Once the income of our household surpasses about $100,000 per year, the world and much of its bounty begins to open up to us. Most of the raises we receive after reaching this level go straight toward our discretionary income. Everything can now begin to be bigger and better, including our cars, furniture, location, homes, decor, vacations, schools, clothing, food, and retirement accounts. Now we can begin to get the "good stuff." Stress and deferred gratification can give way to the better life we have envisioned.

As this happens, most middle-income people reduce the percentage that they give to the kingdom. If you find yourself there, you are wise to take notice of this. You are being tempted to believe that a person's life consists in the things that he possesses. This will dramatically reduce your giving and impoverish your riches toward God.

If you have learned to be content at your current income level and will stay at a similar lifestyle, such an increase in your income will allow you a wonderful freedom to decide what upgrades will add the most to your life and how much of that increase can now be given to the Lord's work, which will increase your joy in the Lord and advance his kingdom.

Because many of us are relatively rich by biblical (and world) standards, we have a dangerous journey. We will need to follow Christ closely through the temptations and traps that are set for the affluent by our Enemy.

Jesus said, "It is easier for a camel to go through the eye of a needle than for a rich person to enter the kingdom of God" (Matt. 19:24). We in the developed world live in the richest tier of people who have ever lived. All our basic needs are met, and only some of our wants are outstanding. Therefore, we need to heed Jesus's warning and ask what it means for us to follow him. Ask him. He will not fail to guide you. Christ, by his Spirit, can expose when our riches are being deceitful and choking out the seed of God's Word. He can usher you into the positive generosity that reflects his purposes for giving you the wealth in the first place. But when he does lead you—as he led the rich young ruler—don't turn away. In a real sense, our lives and futures are at stake.

In order for us to better define what enhanced giving means for the wealthy, it is helpful for us to understand that donors fall into three economic groups. The dynamics of giving are different for each group. These are very general guidelines that do not try to account for exceptions.

The Wealthy

The wealthy are those in the top 5 percent of households who usually earn $250,000 or more per year. Normally they are able to afford all the truly, substantially good things our culture can provide. Spending above $250,000 per year on themselves does not seem to significantly improve their quality of life. Three cars can be helpful, but six will not add a lot to our lifestyle. The wealthy tend to give from their excess funds, not the funds that they use to buy all the good things our economy offers. In that sense, their giving costs them nothing, but this is hidden by the large dollar amounts they can offer. The challenge for wealthy believers is to give all their excess plus something from the funds that buy them the goods that are available in our economy. Giving that costs them nothing, while helpful to the recipient, does not represent much biblical generosity. Real giving costs the giver something of the good things that our economy offers. Most of us know wealthy Christians who live at much less than $250,000 because they are content in Christ and would rather give than spend. They are the happiest wealthy people I have ever met.

The Middle Class

Middle-income households earn in the $50,000 to $250,000 range. This group has stabilized itself from a downward spiral of poverty and has the means to purchase *some, but not all*, of the good things that our culture offers. Within this group are the "affluent," which I define as those who earn $100,000 or more. However, both lower- and upper-middle-income people can give only if they free up funds by *not* spending everything on themselves. Middle-income givers give at real cost to their households. They have fewer of the good things of this life than they would have if they did not give. Those who have ambitions to be affluent or rich give the least of people who are in this group.

The Poor

The poor are those who are below the poverty line, which varies from place to place based on the local economy. A family with two children that earns about $28,000 (not counting the value of public assistance) meets this standard. Their giving involves the greatest sacrifice, because it comes from their necessities, not from optional things. Their giving is like that of the widow from the Bible, who gave just two pennies—all she had for that day. Jesus said that she gave more than all the rich, because they gave from their excess (see Mark 12:41–44).

As noted earlier, the percentage that low-income Christians give is much higher than the percentage that middle-income Christians give. I can't wait for our poor brothers and sisters to be revealed as the greatest givers in history, exceeding Andrew Carnegie, John D. Rockefeller, and Bill Gates in their giving because they have excelled in their love for Christ and their neighbor. They gave at the greatest cost to themselves.

No matter what group you find yourself in, ask Christ to disciple you to more closely reflect his image and to lead your heart to love him. We need to read his Word daily and pray that God's will would be done in us and in our world. Submit to taking part in his fellowship in a local church and in its work of worship, edification, and witness. It is easy for people who are economically independent to be tempted to also be independent of God and other believers, but we all need a forum where we can talk about what it means for us to follow Christ and about the blindness that affluence induces.

I am a middle-income Christian, but my life has been so blessed that I feel rich, comfortable, and often cut off from the needs and suffering of others. I have asked Christ to save me from myself and from the many ways in which I could fool myself. I profess my desire to love him—but has it really taken hold of my heart? I am unable to navigate this by myself.

There is good news for the rich, affluent, and comfortable: with God, salvation is possible even in these very difficult cases, if they are walking in a healthy fear of Christ. To be sure, it is a dangerous journey, but it is one that he calls quite a few of us to walk. He will guide and prompt us into such generosity that, on the last day, God will vindicate our justification through Christ's work and will silence the mouth of our Accuser (see Matt. 25:31–45).

It is challenging and encouraging to read the stories of those who were rich but were found by God and called to be servants of his kingdom. There are many such stories in the Bible and many more in the history of the church. God saves and uses the rich despite how impossible this may seem from our human perspective.

As affluent Christians, we will find that following Christ results in large increases in our giving. Evangelical Christians already give twice as much as others in our culture do, but such giving represents only about 50 percent of our capacity for basic tithing. From a dollar perspective, we have a huge potential to be generous and to help to advance God's mission on earth. Once we believe that God grants us our money so that we can be givers, it changes our perspective on spending and saving and motivates us to find more funds to invest in for eternity. As this perspective and attitude spreads, it will double the giving of many evangelicals, who will join the ranks of the evangelical revolutionaries. This level of generosity will enable future kingdom advancement in ways that we can only pray for today.

Questions for Review and Reflection

1. Do you consider yourself to be in a job that taps into your God-given design and motivations? If yes, explain how that is the case. If not, what stands in the way of that happening?
2. Which of the wrong approaches to giving that were listed in this chapter are you prone to take, if your attitude toward giving is left unchecked by what the Bible says?
3. Which ways of reducing expenses that you read in this chapter would work the best for you and would enable you to use your funds for more important purposes?

Summary and Conclusion

For we are his workmanship, created in Christ Jesus
for good works, which God prepared beforehand,
that we should walk in them. (Eph. 2:10)

We have argued that for those who are in God's kingdom, the purpose of money is to bless others. This involves giving in one form or another. This is also the purpose of the time and talents God has granted us. Time is created for us, and our talents are inborn and/or bestowed, but God grants money to us mostly through our work. Biblically, our earnings have a distinct purpose. They are given to us as the means and capacity for us to love and bless others and, thereby, to advance the mission and commandments of God on earth. That, in a nutshell, is the Christian theology of money. It answers the questions "What is money" and "What is it for" from God's perspective.

We have seen how this purpose was illustrated by characters from the Bible. Like Abraham, we are blessed in order to be a blessing to all the nations of Earth. Like David, we devote our wealth to making the Lord known to the nations and to bringing them to his light as we support the kingdom mission. Like Paul, we work with our hands so that we might help the needy. Paul instructs thieves and frauds to do the same. Paraphrased, he says, "Don't steal (or plan to be dependent), but fulfill the law by becoming generous with the fruit of your labor."

Paul teaches that we are created in Christ Jesus *for* good works, which God prepared for us beforehand (see Eph. 2:10). We will certainly do individual good works (acts of mercy, evangelism, edification, and worship) using our own time, talent, and treasure. Yet most of these good works are carried out and funded with contributions that are offered through the church and carried out by its members, usually when they are organized as a body or mission agency. This allows these enterprises to reach a scale that enables them to potentially meet large needs and opportunities—locally, regionally, and internationally.

Thankfully, churches and Christian agencies are now, in God's providence, positioned in almost every nation and accessible to every people group. While this is something to rejoice in, there is also the irony that Christians in the West have the money to make large-scale good works happen but give only enough to get these works started, not to complete them. The Christian mission boards and relief and development agencies have the vision, connections, and expertise to complete these works but don't have the money to do anything but begin them. Each of us should ask how we can be part of fixing what is wrong with this picture.

Though progress has been made toward funding God's mission, we have seen that most of our funds still go to local staff and buildings, not toward reaching the lost and needy. This creates the shortfall of over $100 billion in our giving to evangelism, discipleship, and mercy ministries.

We argued that God does supply all that we need in order to complete his mission, as he did at every point in the biblical record. He still does this if we will trust him to do it, plan for it to happen, and ask him to supply us with the resources of time, talent, and treasure. These are resources that he has already put within the church but that are not currently being given. In the twenty-first century, we need the same faith and provision that empowered the care of the poor and widows in the first century, the care of plague victims in the second and third centuries, and the evangelism of the English slums and the powerful evangelical missions to the great continents of the newly discovered world in the eighteenth and nineteenth centuries.

My prayer and hope is that God will use this book to help us raise our financial goals beyond the level of necessary self-sufficiency. I pray that we would embody Christ's love for us in our love for others and would demonstrate it by reaching the lost and showing mercy to the needy.

We have good grounds to pray for this. God is still teaching his church today, using the Holy Spirit who speaks through his Word. As he taught the church about the nature of Christ and the Trinity in the early church councils, about the substitutionary atonement through Anselm in the eleventh century, and about justification by faith alone through Luther and the doctrines of grace through Calvin in the sixteenth century, so I believe he can teach us to "excel in giving" in our time.

Our entry into a post-Christian West could actually help the church to start to recover the giving patterns of the apostles. Giving is only beginning to recover from its 1,600-year famine that was caused by the state church mentality. We have seen how evangelical and African-American Christians have led the way in giving so far. Real progress was made in the nineteenth and early twentieth centuries, but since the 1950s we have been standing in danger of losing those gains to the demands of the new American dream and to habitual low expectations for outreach of all sorts. Alarms are being sounded on many fronts, as illustrated in the selected bibliography that follows.

So let's raise our prayers that the Lord of the harvest will send forth a new army of workers who are equipped with the full resources of money and the gifts of service with which God has endowed his people. Substantial battles have been won against the state church mentality, theological liberalism, the false social gospel, pagan religions in Asia and Africa, and ignorance of the kingdom of God—but not since the fourth century has the world seen the full force of the church's generosity and outreach in Christ's name. I pray that the twenty-first century will be the season when we as God's people learn again to "excel in this act of grace also," just as we excel in faith, speech, and knowledge.

How well are you doing as a Christian with fulfilling God's purpose for the money he has granted you? Can you joyfully give 10 percent yet? No matter what you give, do you do it with a giver mentality—asking, "How much can I give to God's mission?" If not, this can change if you want it to and if you seek it from Christ.

One easy way to start is to get to know some other believers who are givers. I expect that you already know some of them. Ask them to share the story of how they changed into givers. How might their story apply to you? Then take some baby steps of love: Become involved in missions or mercy situations in your community or church. Modestly increase how much you give to God's mission, and do it on a regular, planned schedule. Look for other giving opportunities in your personal life—for instance, start sharing the gospel and/or resources with people who are in need of either. And follow up with them! Be a friend! Get them connected to God's people. Let it grow from there. Most of all, make it your goal to grow as a Christian. As you grow in Christ, you will also grow a giver's heart—like his. Also, take advantage of the means God has provided for us to grow in grace by associating yourself with a gospel-based congregation of believers. Get to know some of them, and begin giving to them and loving them as the opportunity arises. Let them love you, too, as needed. You will be influenced by seeing God grow them as givers.

Remember, your interest in and pursuit of a life of giving indicate that the Holy Spirit is already working in you. As you and your fellow Christians enter into this life, that beginning will itself be blessed by the Spirit. A beneficent cycle will begin that will feed upon itself and keep increasing your joy in and knowledge of Christ. This, in turn, will increase your pursuit of love and giving.

This is the dynamic that we encountered in Isaiah 58 in chapter 4 of this book. I would like to close by suggesting that you and I prayerfully read and meditate on the exalted promises that God makes to those who pursue his commandment to love him and our neighbors— right where he has put us.

> Will you call this a fast,
>   and a day acceptable to the LORD?
>
> Is not this the fast that I choose:
>   to loose the bonds of wickedness,
>   to undo the straps of the yoke,
>   to let the oppressed go free,
>   and to break every yoke?

Is it not to share your bread with the hungry
>and bring the homeless poor into your house;
when you see the naked, to cover him,
>and not to hide yourself from your own flesh?
Then shall your light break forth like the dawn,
>and your healing shall spring up speedily;
your righteousness shall go before you;
>the glory of the LORD shall be your rear guard.
Then you shall call, and the LORD will answer;
>you shall cry, and he will say, "Here I am."
If you take away the yoke from your midst,
>the pointing of the finger, and speaking wickedness,
if you pour yourself out for the hungry
>and satisfy the desire of the afflicted,
then shall your light rise in the darkness
>and your gloom be as the noonday.
And the LORD will guide you continually
>and satisfy your desire in scorched places
>and make your bones strong;
and you shall be like a watered garden,
>like a spring of water,
>whose waters do not fail. (Isa. 58:5–11)

Amen!

Questions for Review and Reflection

1. How would you describe the primary role or purpose that money currently has in your life?
2. Would you say that you think about how to excel in generosity more than about how to have more money?
3. What particular steps can you take to excel in your giving at this stage of your life?

Recommendations for Further Reading

Alcorn, Randy. *Money, Possessions, and Eternity.* Rev. and updated ed. Carol Stream, IL: Tyndale House, 2003.

————. *The Law of Rewards: Giving What You Can't Keep to Gain What You Can't Lose.* Carol Stream, IL: Tyndale House, 2003.

Bloomberg, Craig L. *Neither Poverty or Riches: A Biblical Theology of Possessions.* Downers Grove IL: InterVarsity Press, 1999.

Eskridge, Larry, and Mark A. Noll, eds. *More Money, More Ministry: Money and Evangelicals in Recent North American History.* Grand Rapids: Eerdmans, 2000.

Hardy, Lee. *The Fabric of This World: Inquiries into Calling, Career Choice, and the Design of Human Work.* Grand Rapids: Eerdmans, 1990.

Hewitt, Brad, and James Moline. *Your New Money Mindset: Create a Healthy Relationship with Money.* Carol Stream, IL: Tyndale, 2015.

Jeavons, Thomas H., and Rebekah Burch Basinger. *Growing Givers' Hearts: Treating Fundraising as Ministry.* San Francisco: Jossey-Bass, 2000.

Kapic, Kelly M, with Justin Borger. *God So Loved, He Gave: Entering the Movement of Divine Generosity.* Grand Rapids: Zondervan, 2010.

Keller, Timothy. *Ministries of Mercy: The Call of the Jericho Road.* 3rd ed. Phillipsburg, NJ: P&R Publishing, 2015.

Noll, Mark A, ed. *God and Mammon: Protestants, Money, and the Market, 1790–1860.* New York: Oxford University Press, 2001.

Petty, James C. *When the Money Runs Out: Hope and Help for the Financially Stressed.* Greensboro, NC: New Growth Press, 2009.

Rodin, R. Scott. *Stewards in the Kingdom: A Theology of Life in All Its Fullness.* Downers Grove, IL: InterVarsity Press, 2000.

Ronsvalle, John, and Sylvia Ronsvalle. *The State of Church Giving Through 1999.* Champaign, IL: Empty Tomb, Inc., 2001.

———. *The Poor Have Faces. Loving Your Neighbor in the 21st Century.* Grand Rapids: Baker, 1992.

Sider, Ronald J. *Just Generosity: A New Vision for Overcoming Poverty in America.* Grand Rapids: Baker, 1999.

Smith, Christian, and Michael O. Emerson, with Patricia Snell. *Passing the Plate: Why American Christians Don't Give Away More Money.* New York: Oxford University Press, 2008.

Tripp, Paul David. *Redeeming Money: How God Reveals and Reorients our Hearts.* Wheaton, IL: Crossway, 2018.

Willard, Chris, and Jim Sheppard. *Contagious Generosity: Creating a Culture of Giving in Your Church.* Grand Rapids: Zondervan, 2012.

Willmer, Wesley K, ed. *Revolution in Generosity: Transforming Stewards to Be Rich toward God.* Chicago, IL: Moody, 2008.

Wuthnow, Robert. *God and Mammon in America.* New York: Free Press, 1994.

Volf, Miroslav. *Free of Charge: Giving and Forgiving in a Culture Stripped of Grace.* Grand Rapids: Zondervan, 2005.